JOHN HENRY
NEWMAN

MODERN SPIRITUAL MASTERS SERIES

John Henry Newman

Spiritual Writings

Selected with an Introduction by

JOHN T. FORD, C.S.C.

ORBIS BOOKS
Maryknoll, New York 10545

Founded in 1970, Orbis Books endeavors to publish works that enlighten the mind, nourish the spirit, and challenge the conscience. The publishing arm of the Maryknoll Fathers and Brothers, Orbis seeks to explore the global dimensions of the Christian faith and mission, to invite dialogue with diverse cultures and religious traditions, and to serve the cause of reconciliation and peace. The books published reflect the views of their authors and do not represent the official position of the Maryknoll Society. To learn more about Maryknoll and Orbis Books, please visit our website at www.maryknollsociety.org.

Library of Congress Cataloging-in-Publication Data

Newman, John Henry, 1801–1890.
   Spiritual writings / John Henry Newman ; selected with an introduction by John T. Ford.
      p.   cm. – (Modern spiritual masters)
   ISBN 978-1-57075-954-3 (pbk.)
   1. Newman, John Henry, 1801–1890. 2. Catholic Church–Doctrines. I. Ford, John T. II. Title.
BX4705.N5A3 2012
282.092–dc23
   [B]   2011039713

Contents

Introduction

On a winter Friday afternoon decades ago, when I was a theology student in Washington, D.C., snow was beginning to fall. Then as now, a snowfall in the nation's capital is headline news: at the first snowflake, many people panic, abandon work, and rush for the safety of home. In Washington a couple of inches of snow often causes chaos, and half a dozen inches become a veritable disaster. The window of my room looked out on a main street: snow was falling furiously; cars were careening downhill; drivers struggling uphill were abandoning their cars. The forecast was for a dozen inches or so; it was immediately evident that I was going to be snowbound for the weekend.

For me, that prospect was not a problem: spending a warm comfortable weekend reading and relaxing was decidedly appealing. What was a problem: there wasn't much in my room to read other than theology textbooks: no novels, no mysteries, no short stories. As I looked through my bookcase, I found an as-yet-unread paperback of John Henry Newman's *Apologia pro Vita Sua*; for want of anything better, I decided to sample it. That weekend I became fascinated by John Henry Newman (1801–1890).

As I soon discovered, my fascination with Newman was not unique. His *Apologia* has been considered a classic example of Victorian autobiography from the time of its original publication (1864), and, a century and a half later, it is readily available in paperback for use in courses in English literature; few personal memoirs have a comparable track record. More important, Newman's autobiographical account of his personal search for religious truth still inspires followers; one of my students, a former naval officer, told me that he had decided to follow Newman's example and become a Roman Catholic, after reading his *Apologia* during night watch, while the ship was on autopilot.

If people who are interested in literature are attracted to Newman because of his masterful command of language and engaging style, many educators consider Newman an outstanding educational theorist. *The Idea of a University*, which is a collection of presentations and essays that he wrote in his capacity as rector of the Catholic University in Dublin, continues to attract attention: first, for its emphasis on the importance of a liberal education as a preparation for life; second, for its claim that theology should be part of a university's curriculum; and third, for its conviction that a university education should be not only a process of technical training and acquiring information, but also a time of personal formation and moral development.

If Newman's educational ideas still merit consideration, the same must be said for his philosophical view about the relationship of reason and faith. In *An Essay in Aid of a Grammar of Assent* (1870)—which is his most systematic, as well as his most challenging, work—Newman showed how faith is an eminently reasonable decision, even though no one can ever rationally demonstrate the existence of God, much less understand the mysteries of Christianity. Similarly, in theological circles, Newman is credited for the then innovative proposal in *An Essay on the Development of Christian Doctrine* (1845) that Christian doctrines have really developed over the course of centuries. Many of Newman's creative proposals and seminal insights in philosophy and theology that were sometimes suspect in his own day have since become commonly accepted.

Yet if Newman was variously litterateur and educator, philosopher and theologian, he was also a spiritual guide—in his sermons and conferences, in his pastoral counseling both in person and in his correspondence. As an Anglican, while he was vicar (1828–1843) of St. Mary's, the university church at Oxford, he regularly preached at evensong (vespers); so popular were his sermons that many visitors to Oxford felt that a visit was incomplete unless they heard Newman preach. In fact, his Anglican sermons were so popular that 191 were published in the eight volumes of his *Parochial and Plain Sermons* (1834–1843), another 15 in his *Oxford University Sermons* (1843), and an additional 26 in *Sermons on Subjects of the Day* (1843).

Newman's beatification by Pope Benedict XVI on September 19, 2010, highlighted the fact that Newman was not only a spiritual writer, but a saintly person, who practiced what he preached. In contrast to those biographies of the saints whose lives are portrayed as spiritual success stories—some saints have been depicted as examples of perfection from cradle to grave—Newman's life was one of spiritual development in the face of continual challenges. His spirituality developed as part and parcel of his pastoral ministry—both as an Anglican and as a Roman Catholic. His spirituality was both scripturally based and theologically insightful; his spirituality was the product of his own spiritual journey, which was linked to the events of his life and especially to the people who influenced him and whom he influenced. In sum, Newman's spirituality was both biblical and theological, both contextual and personalistic.

Hopefully the following pages will provide readers with a sense of Newman's spirituality as it developed during his life. Although there are numerous biographies of Newman—a few are listed in the bibliography—the introductory biography in this book attempts to highlight the key events and the key persons in his spiritual journey. Newman's spiritual journey is illustrated by thematic selections from his writings; correspondingly, the selections from his writings are linked to events of his life. As Pope Benedict XVI remarked at Newman's mass of beatification: "In Blessed John Henry, that tradition of gentle scholarship, deep human wisdom, and profound love for the Lord has borne rich fruit, as a sign of the abiding presence of the Holy Spirit deep within the heart of God's people, bringing forth abundant gifts of holiness." Hopefully readers of this selection of Newman's spiritual writings will find Newman a spiritual mentor, as did many of his contemporaries.

Biography:
JOHN HENRY NEWMAN
(1801–1890)

1. FAMILY, EALING SCHOOL,
"FIRST CONVERSION"

John Henry Newman was born in London on February 21, 1801, and was baptized in the Anglican church of St. Benet Fink on April 9, 1801. His father, also named John (1767–1824), was a banker and businessman, whose family came from Cambridgeshire. His mother, Jemima Fourdrinier (1772–1836), came from a French Protestant family, which had emigrated to England after the revocation (1685) of the Edict of Nantes (1598), which accorded religious liberty to Protestants. John Henry was the oldest of six children: he had two brothers, Charles (1802–1884) and Francis (1805–1897), and three sisters, Harriet (1803–1852), Jemima (1808–1879) and Mary (1809–1828). Their religious upbringing was typical of a middle-class English family in the early nineteenth century: regular attendance at church and reading the Bible at home.

In 1808, at the age of seven, John Henry was sent to a boarding school at Ealing, a town west of London, whose headmaster was Rev. Dr. George Nicholas of Wadham College, Oxford. Dr. Nicholas would later say that no boy had run through the school, from the bottom to the top, as rapidly as John Henry Newman. During his last year at Ealing, Newman came under the influence of a teacher of classics, Rev. Walter Mayers (1790–1828), whose Calvinistic spirituality made a deep impression on Newman. During his final months at Ealing, Newman experienced a "conversion," which convinced him that he was "predestined to salvation" and so would persevere in his Christian faith. This conversion experience also produced in Newman a "mistrust" of "material phenomena" and a sense of the invisible world—which he later described as "the thought of two and two only absolute and luminously self-evident beings, myself and my Creator" (Readings 1.1, 1.2, 1.3, 1.4).

2. STUDENT AT TRINITY COLLEGE

After finishing Ealing School, Newman was enrolled in Trinity College, Oxford, on December 14, 1816—two months short of his sixteenth birthday; due to the lack of rooms, however, he was unable to begin residing at Trinity until the following June. During the waning days of the school year, he had the good fortune to meet another freshman, three years his senior, John William Bowden (1798–1844), who became his inseparable companion as well as his partner in several joint literary endeavors and a life-long friend (Reading 2.3).

Newman's tutor, Thomas Short (1789–1879), who had recently arrived at Trinity from Rugby, was initially suspicious of the youthful Newman's abilities, but was soon convinced of his talents and encouraged him to be a candidate for one of the competitive Trinity scholarships. Newman later described the rigorous exam for the scholarship: "They made me first do some verses; then Latin translation; then Latin theme; then chorus of Euripides; then an English theme; then some Plato; then some Lucretius; then some Xenophon; then some Livy"—a formidable challenge for a teenager. After waiting in suspense, on May 18, 1818, Newman recalled: "At last I was called to the place where they had been voting; the vice-chancellor [the president] said some Latin over me; then made a speech. The electors then shook hands with me, and I immediately assumed the scholar's gown."

Newman had won a scholarship with a stipend sufficient to pay his college expenses; moreover, the scholarship was good for nine years, along with the possibility of a fellowship for an additional five years. At the age of seventeen, Newman's future looked bright. The Monday following Trinity Sunday, however, was not only the day when Trinity College announced the selection of its new scholars and fellows, it was also the date of the annual college "Gaudy"—a term derived from the Latin *gaudium* (joy)—which undergraduates celebrated with "a drinking bout"—a custom that Newman felt contradicted the name and nature of Trinity College (Reading 2.2).

Encouraged by his success in achieving the Trinity scholarship, Newman began studying in earnest for honors in his baccalaureate examination. As he later recalled, from the summer vacation of 1819 to "my examination in November 1820 it was almost a continuous mass of reading. I stayed in Oxford during the vacations, got up in winter and summer at five or six, hardly allowed myself time for my meals, and then ate, indeed, the bread of carefulness." During the twenty-four weeks immediately preceding his examination, he read for an average of twelve hours a day. Newman's family and friends not only wished him well on the examination; they expected him to win honors in both classics and mathematics. Unfortunately, he had over-exerted himself, and when he was called by the examiners a day sooner than he expected, "he lost his head, utterly broke down, and, after vain attempts for several days, had to retire, only first making sure of his B.A. degree."

When the list of graduates was posted, Newman's name "did not appear at all on the mathematical side of the paper, and in classics it was found in the lower division of the second class of honours, which at that time went by the contemptuous title of the 'Under-the-line.'" Newman was not only disappointed; he found it painful to inform his family of his poor showing (Reading 2.3). Newman's parents replied that they were more than satisfied with his efforts and advised him to be patient and cheerful. His poor performance on the examinations was also an occasion for personal reassessment: instead of a career as a lawyer, he decided, with his father's approval, to become a clergyman in the Church of England. This seemed a reasonable decision: he had the support of the Trinity scholarship for another half-dozen years; he could privately tutor students to earn additional income; and he could support his brother, Francis, as a student at Oxford—a necessity in light of the failure of his father's bank and, as a result, the straightened circumstances of his family. It would have been a modest yet unspectacular life had not another opportunity presented itself.

3. FELLOW OF ORIEL COLLEGE

In spite of his poor performance on his baccalaureate examination, Newman decided to become a candidate for a fellowship at Oriel College—much to the concern of his friends, who felt that he was only setting himself up for another failure (Readings 3.1). An Oriel fellowship—at the time the most prestigious in Oxford—was unlikely to be awarded to a person who had not graduated with honors. Although his Trinity tutor, Thomas Short, did not expect Newman to be successful in the examinations for an Oriel fellowship, Short felt that Newman would make a credible showing. Accordingly, Newman began studying the topics that would be covered on the week-long Oriel examinations, but, mindful of how he had over-exerted himself in preparing for his baccalaureate examinations, he also attended a series of lectures on geology and wrote his first musical composition (Reading 3.2).

On April 12, 1822, the butler of the provost of Oriel—who by custom was responsible for informing the successful candidates—made his way to Newman's lodgings on Broad Street and found him playing the violin. This surprised the butler, who did not associate "fiddling" with a candidate for an Oriel fellowship. The butler's perplexity increased when, after delivering the usual message on such occasions—that "he had, he feared, disagreeable news to announce, viz. that Mr. Newman was elected fellow of Oriel and that his immediate presence was required there"— Newman, thinking that such language was impertinent, merely answered—"Very well"—and went on playing his violin. The butler then asked whether he had come to the wrong person, and Newman replied that he was the right person. As soon as the butler left, Newman put his violin aside and dashed downstairs with all speed to Oriel College.

Newman's election as a fellow of Oriel College not only restored his reputation that had been tarnished by his poor performance on his baccalaureate examinations, it also opened a promising future, either to pursue a career in law and government or to seek ordination in the Church of England. Newman considered his selection as an Oriel fellow nothing less than providential (Reading 3.3).

4. ANGLICAN DEACON AND PRIEST

In preparation for ordination in the Church of England, Newman attended theological lectures and studied Scripture—he even memorized entire books of the Bible (Reading 4.1). Before being ordained an Anglican deacon on Trinity Sunday, June 13, 1824, Newman confided to his father that he was "convinced it is necessary to get used to parochial duty early, and that a fellow of a college, after ten years' residence in Oxford, feels very awkward among poor and ignorant people." Ten days after his ordination as deacon in Christ Church Cathedral, Oxford, Newman preached his first sermon at Over Worton, the parish of his Ealing School mentor, Rev. Walter Mayers.

The opportunity for pastoral experience soon became available. The elderly rector of St. Clement's Church, Rev. John Gutch (1746–1831), was no longer equal to the task of parish ministry without assistance. St. Clement's, which was then located just across Magdalen Bridge from Oxford, was a populous but poor parish. Newman, then age twenty-three, began the task of house-to-house visitation, "asking the names, numbers, trades, where they [the people] went to church," etc. His parishioners responded by calling Newman "a proper minister" and "a nice young gentleman" (Reading 4.2). More importantly—from both a theological and pastoral perspective, Newman soon discovered that "real" people didn't fit neatly into his Calvinistic categories of the "predestined" and the "reprobate." Most people were in between: his parish visitation resulted in a re-evaluation of his Calvinist theology (Reading 4.3).

The people in St. Clement's Parish flocked to hear Newman preach and had to be turned away at the doors since the old church could hold only some two hundred people. Accordingly, Newman began collecting funds for a new church; in addition, he established a Sunday school for the youngsters of the parish. Newman's ministry of preaching and teaching prompted him to write a personal memorandum: "Those who make comfort the great subject of their preaching seem to mistake the end of their ministry. *Holiness* is the great end. There must be a struggle and a toil here. Comfort is a cordial, but no one drinks cordials from morning to night." Newman had been at St. Clement's only a few months when he was unexpectedly called home for what proved to be his father's last illness. Newman had the consolation of helping his father prepare for death—which came on Wednesday, September 29, 1824 (Reading 4.4).

After his father's funeral, Newman returned to Oxford and quickly resumed his various parochial duties—ranging from fund-raising to visiting the sick, from teaching Sunday School to preaching (Readings 4.5, 4.6). In addition, he was invited to write a couple of articles for the *Encyclopædia Metropolitana*. Nonetheless, his principal concern was preparation for his ordination as an Anglican priest, which occurred on May 29, 1825 (Reading 4.7). Newman continued his curacy at St. Clement's until February 1826, when he was appointed vice-principal of Alban Hall and a tutor of Oriel College.

5. TUTOR OF ORIEL COLLEGE

At the time of Newman's appointment as Tutor of Oriel College, tutorships were generally considered an instructional responsibility for preparing students for the Oxford university baccalaureate examinations in mathematics and the classics. Although college tutors were usually Anglican clergymen, religious instruction was not ordinarily considered part of their tutorial responsibility. Newman, in contrast, considered a tutor responsible not only for academic instruction, but also for the spiritual formation of his students (Reading 5.1). Indeed he felt that it would be wrong for him to accept a teaching position if it were a purely secular position (Reading 5.2). In addition, Newman was quite aware that some Oriel College students had little interest in either academic studies or spiritual development and so, like a "new broom," he tried to sweep out non-productive students, while simultaneously devoting special attention to the best and the brightest (Reading 5.3).

Newman's efforts to promote academic achievement and moral integrity eventually brought him into conflict with the new Oriel provost, Edward Hawkins (1789–1882), who considered Newman's tutorial approach a form of favoritism. When Newman refused to change his methods, Hawkins refused to assign Newman and two other tutors any more students, thereby effectively removing them from their positions: within a couple of years—as their students graduated—Newman and the other two tutors had no one to teach. Hawkins's decision was particularly ironic insofar as Newman had campaigned for Hawkins's election as provost in 1828; in addition, when Hawkins became provost and resigned his position as vicar of St. Mary's, the University Church, Newman was his replacement (1828–1843) (Reading 5.4).

Newman's removal from the tutorship had long-lasting consequences. The replacements for Newman and the two other tutors devoted less attention to instructing students capable of gaining "first-class" degrees; as time went on, fewer students gained "firsts," and Oriel began to lose prestige (Reading 5.5). Although obviously an embarrassment, Newman's dismissal proved to be a blessing in disguise: without tutorial responsibilities, he had time for other pursuits: he was able to finish his first book: *The Arians of the Fourth Century*; then he was able to go on a Mediterranean voyage (1832–1833) with Richard Hurrell Froude and his father; and most significantly, Newman had time to become involved in the Oxford Movement—which might never have happened the way that it did—had Newman remained in a labor-intensive tutorship.

6. VICAR OF SAINT MARY'S

The provost and fellows of Oriel College had the responsibility for appointing the vicar of Saint Mary's, the university church of Oxford. When Edward Hawkins was elected provost, he resigned his position as vicar, and in his place, on March 14, 1828, Newman was "instituted" as Vicar of St. Mary's—a position he held for the following fifteen years. At the age of twenty-seven, Newman was entrusted with the most prestigious pulpit in Oxford as well as an influential position in the Church of England.

Newman preached regularly at the Sunday afternoon service—evensong (vespers). His sermons quickly attracted both students and visitors; indeed, visitors considered a visit to Oxford incomplete unless they heard Newman preach. As an Anglican, Newman wrote out his sermons and then read them from the pulpit. He initially shared his written sermons with his mother and his friends. Other people, however, wanted copies of his sermons, and eventually ten volumes of his Anglican sermons were published: eight volumes of *Parochial and Plain Sermons*, a volume of *Oxford University Sermons,* and a volume of *Sermons on Subjects of the Day.* In an age when "keeping holy the Sabbath" was customary, many people read sermons at home on Sunday and Newman's sermons became popular spiritual reading.

Although Newman's sermons usually took between thirty and forty-five minutes to deliver, according to W. J. Copeland (1804–1885), Newman's former curate at Littlemore and later the editor of his *Parochial and Plain Sermons*, Newman's sermons "found a response in the hearts and minds and consciences of those to whom they were addressed, in marvellous proportion to the affectionate and stirring earnestness with which their Author appealed to the conscious or dormant sense of their needs, and his zealous and energetic endeavours, under God's blessing, to show, in every variety of light, how the grand central Verities of the Christian Dispensation, entrusted as the good 'Deposit,' to the Church, were revealed and adapted to supply them."

Copeland's description highlights three important aspects of Newman's preaching: first of all, his "earnestness"—his audience had no doubts about the sincerity of his convictions; he preached what he believed. Second, Newman was able to show in a convincing way how a particular scriptural passage or spiritual topic was applicable to the lives of his listeners. Finally, people in the audience felt that he was speaking directly to them: his sermons were not merely addressed to their minds, but also to their hearts; listeners felt that Newman was personally challenging them to live better lives as Christians. To recapture some of the original force and spiritual depth of Newman's sermons, readers today might well read his sermons aloud (Reading 6.1).

Newman's appointment as vicar of St. Mary's was the capstone of a half-dozen years of achievements—from his election as a fellow of Oriel, through his ordination as a deacon and a priest of the Church of England, to his appointment as an Oriel tutor. These evident changes in his public life were accompanied by a series of gradual changes in his personal theological views. Newman had arrived at Oxford an Evangelical of a decidedly Calvinistic complexion; by the end of the 1820s, his Calvinism had waned as a result of his pastoral experience, while his Evangelical devotion to Scripture would serve him life-long.

Simultaneously, Newman came under the influence of the "Noetic" views of Edward Hawkins, provost of Oriel, and Richard Whately (1787–1863), a fellow of Oriel and principal of St. Alban Hall, where Newman served for a year as vice principal. In his *Apologia*, Newman credited Whately "to the effect that he had not only taught me to think, but to think for myself." Similarly, Newman credited Hawkins as being "the first who taught me to weigh my words, and to be cautious in my statements. He led me to that mode of limiting and clearing my sense in discussions and in controversy, and of distinguishing between cognate ideas, and of obviating mistakes by anticipation."

Although the Noetic method helped Newman become an effective thinker and writer, it was not without its dangers. As Newman later acknowledged in his *Apologia*: "The truth is, I was beginning to prefer intellectual excellence to moral; I was drifting in the direction of the Liberalism of the day." What rescued Newman from the rationalistic tendencies of the Noetics was not intellectual argumentation, but "two great blows—illness and bereavement." In November 1827, Newman experienced a physical/nervous breakdown that temporarily paralyzed his ability to function as an instructor and examiner; he had to request a leave from his academic responsibilities. The following January, the unexpected illness and then sudden death of his youngest sister, Mary (1809–1828), left him heart-broken (Reading 6.2). A second bereavement came the following month with the unexpected death of his mentor, Walter Mayers, who had been Newman's instructor at Ealing School and the curate of Holy Trinity Church, Over Worton, where Newman preached his first Anglican sermon—"Waiting on God"—on June 23, 1824; Newman preached Mayers's funeral sermon—"On the Death of a Very Dear Friend"—on April 2, 1828.

7. DISCOVERY OF THE PATRISTIC CHURCH

During his first years as a fellow of Oriel College (1822–1826), Newman was influenced by the Noetic approach of Hawkins and Whately—from whom he garnered two important doctrinal positions: Hawkins taught him the importance of Tradition as a necessary companion to interpreting Scripture, and Whately taught him the importance of the visible Church. Gradually, however, Newman found more congenial the theological positions of three other fellows of Oriel: John Keble (1792–1866), Edward Bouverie Pusey (1800–1882) and Richard Hurrell Froude (1803–1836).

Keble, who published anonymously a book of poems entitled *The Christian Year* in 1827 and four years later was later elected the professor of poetry at Oxford, gave the Assize Sermon on July 14, 1833, which Newman considered the beginning of the

Oxford Movement. Pusey, who had convinced Newman that Baptism was not merely an external sign, but an interior spiritual regeneration, was appointed Regius Professor of Hebrew and a canon of Christ Church in 1828. Froude, the most outspoken in his views, was one of the leaders of the Oxford Movement until his premature death in the midst of the Tractarian Movement.

In addition to theological discussions with his three Oriel colleagues, Newman began a systematic reading of the Fathers of the Church in 1828 (Reading 7.1). Gradually his reading of the Fathers brought Newman to an increasing dissatisfaction with the then conventional views of religion along with a more "orthodox" understanding of Christianity in general and of the Church in particular (Reading 7.2). Two events marked the gradual shift of his theological views from Evangelical and Noetic to Anglo-Catholic. First in 1829, Robert Peel (1788–1850), then the Member of Parliament for Oxford, announced that he had decided to support the Emancipation Bill, which would extend many civil rights to people who were not members of the Church of England. Newman felt that such a reversal was a betrayal of the Church of England and joined in what proved to be a successful campaign to defeat Peel's bid for reelection; Newman's opposition to Peel, however, strained his relationship with both Hawkins and Whately. Also in 1829, Newman was elected joint secretary of the Church Missionary Society—an organization that was Evangelical in orientation; however, just a year later, he was replaced in that position—an indication that some Evangelicals no longer felt that his views were congenial with theirs.

In 1831 Newman was invited to write a history of the councils of the Church—a task that he undertook with energy and enthusiasm in light of his patristic studies. However, he became so fascinated with the Arian controversy in general and the role of St. Athanasius in suppressing Arianism in particular that his book turned into a work focused not on the councils—as the editors of the "Theological Library" wanted—but on Arianism and Athanasius. Although Newman's *The Arians of the Fourth Century* (1833) was "plucked" from the series because of its failure to treat all the councils, it was eventually published by another firm.

8. MEDITERRANEAN PILGRIM

Since his responsibilities as an Oriel tutor had been terminated and since his book on the Arians was en route to publication, Newman accepted an invitation from Richard Hurrell Froude and his father to join them on a Mediterranean voyage that had been recommended for Froude's health. Newman initially had qualms about accepting the invitation, since he did not feel that a "Grand Tour" was appropriate for a clergyman. However, he persuaded himself that the proposed Mediterranean voyage would be beneficial both for his teaching and his preaching by providing first-hand knowledge of the sites of classical antiquity as well as an opportunity to retrace the paths of the apostles through the Mediterranean to Rome.

On December 8, 1832, Newman and the Froudes sailed from the port of Falmouth on the *Hermes*. At sea, Newman passed the time by writing poems—many of which were later published in his *Verses on Various Occasions* (1867) (Readings 8.1). After sailing through the Bay of Biscay, the *Hermes* passed Cape Ortegal, Lisbon, St. Vincent and Cape Trafalgar; in mid-December, Newman arrived at Gibraltar, "the first foreign soil I have come near." The *Hermes* then departed Gibraltar for Malta, where Newman and the Froudes spent Christmas. Next the *Hermes* sailed along the coast of western Greece before returning to Malta, where Newman spent almost a month, including a dozen days quarantined in the Lazaret, since the port authorities were afraid that Newman and his shipboard companions might be carrying a fever.

In February, Newman and the Froudes traveled from Malta to Sicily, where they spent several days before going on to Naples with side trips to such well-known sites as Herculaneum, Pompeii, Salerno, Paestum, and Amalfi (Reading 8.2). In early March, Newman and the Froudes arrived in Rome, where they spent over a month, visiting churches and historic sites, attending ceremonies, and meeting people—including Nicholas Wiseman (1802–1865), then the rector of the English College and later cardinal-archbishop of Westminster.

In early April 1833, the Froudes decided to return to England, but Newman opted to go back alone to Sicily, where he became "very weak and ill." After ten days of convalescence at Castro Giovanni, Newman was sufficiently recovered to sail on the *Conte Ruggiero* from Palermo for Marseilles. While at sea off the coast of Corsica en route to France, he wrote what would become his most famous poem: "Lead Kindly Light" (Readings 8.3, 8.4). From Marseilles, he traveled across France, crossed the Channel and arrived back at Oxford on July 9, 1833.

Although Newman began his Mediterranean voyage with the anticipation that he would become familiar with the monuments of classical and Christian antiquity, while serving as a companion for his close colleague, Hurrell Froude, in fact, he also gained first-hand knowledge of Roman Catholicism through his visits to Malta, Sicily, and Italy. In addition, as a survivor of a life-threatening illness, he returned from his trip with a heightened sense of mission: "I have a work to do in England."

9. EARLY YEARS OF THE OXFORD MOVEMENT: 1833–1839

On returning to England after his Mediterranean voyage, Newman found Oxford in an uproar over the Whig government's proposal to suppress many dioceses and parishes of the Anglican Church in Ireland. For the Whigs, the Irish Church Reform Bill was basically a practical measure: since the overwhelming majority of the people in Ireland were Roman Catholics, there was little need for Anglican parishes and dioceses in places where there were few Anglican parishioners; the money that was being expended in maintaining little-attended churches and supporting clerical sinecures could be better spent for educational and social projects.

To many at Oxford, the Whig proposal was a case of the unjustifiable interference of the government in the very life of the Church. Many Anglican clergymen at Oxford, including

Newman, decided to campaign against the Whig proposal. Among their protest strategies was the publication of a series titled *Tracts for the Times*, calling upon the clergy to defend the prerogatives of the Anglican Church. The idea of publishing tracts was not original; in the eighteenth century, for example, John Wesley (1703–1791) had used pamphlets as a way of furthering an Evangelical renewal within the Church of England. In contrast to these "Methodist" pamphlets, which were directed to Christian laity at a popular level, the *Tracts for the Times* were intended to rally the Anglican clergy and educated public in support of reform within the Church of England.

The *Tracts*, which were originally published anonymously, called for a renewal of the Church of England through a retrieval of its apostolic heritage as manifested in the teachings of the early Church. Each author was personally responsible for the contents of his *Tract*. The result was a multi-pronged approach to Church reform and so more of a program in progress than a definite agenda guided by a single vision. Newman, along with John Keble, Edward Bouverie Pusey, and Richard Hurrell Froude, was at the center of this reform initiative, which became known both as the Tractarian movement after the series of *Tracts* and also as the Oxford movement after its place of origin.

Newman considered Sunday, July 14, when "Keble preached the Assize Sermon in the University Pulpit"—a sermon later "published under the title of 'National Apostasy,'" as "the start of the religious movement of 1833." Following Keble's call for "remonstrance" against the Whig government's interference in Church affairs, Newman, on September 9, anonymously published *Tract One*, which called upon people to come to the defense of the Church of England and its "Apostolical descent" (Reading 9.1). Over the next eight years, a total of ninety *Tracts* appeared—a third of them written by Newman.

The first half-dozen years of the Oxford Movement were a time of intense activity for Newman, who preached sermons, delivered lectures, wrote letters, and published a couple of books and a truly amazing number of articles, poems, essays, and tracts advocating the return of the Church of England to its Apostolic origins (Reading 9.2). Some of his publications involved him in controversy—particularly with people whose "Liberalism" in doctrine he strenuously opposed (Reading 9.3). Simultaneously, Newman continued his parochial ministry at St. Mary's and supervised the building of a church at Littlemore, a small village about three miles from Oxford whose pastoral care was part of his responsibility as vicar of St. Mary's. The year 1836 brought happiness at seeing the dedication of the new church at Littlemore and the weddings of his two sisters to two brothers: Jemima to John Mozley and Harriet to Thomas Mozley. Unfortunately, 1836 also saw the death of his good friend and colleague Hurrell Froude in February at the age of thirty-three and the death of his mother in May at the age of sixty-three.

Newman's efforts to revitalize the Church of England by reclaiming its Apostolic heritage required him to elaborate his understanding of Anglicanism in relation to other Christian churches. Newman responded by depicting the Church of England as occupying a *via media*—"middle road"—between the doctrinal diminutions of continental Protestantism and the devotional exaggerations of Roman Catholicism. Newman claimed that the Church of England had not succumbed to the temptation either to water down Christianity as had continental Protestantism or to over-state Christian beliefs as had Roman Catholicism. Indeed, Newman's *via media* seemed to be a cogent justification for the position of the Church of England until he read an article by Nicholas Wiseman about St. Augustine and the Donatists in 1839.

10. CRISIS YEARS OF THE OXFORD MOVEMENT: 1839–1845

For a movement that was attempting to find its way while on its journey, the first half-dozen years (1833–1839) of the Oxford Movement went remarkably well. The attempt to reinstill a sense of "apostolicity" both in theology and in worship within the Church of England became the focus of national, even international, attention though not always of acceptance. On the one side was opposition from "liberals" who considered the Tractarians not only conservative but also antiquarian. On the other side was suspicion on the part of evangelicals who felt that the Tractarians were becoming excessively Catholic in their views. On balance, while there were differences and difficulties, the Oxford Movement seemed reasonably on course; as Newman remarked in his *Apologia*: "In the spring of 1839 my position in the Anglican Church was at its height. I had supreme confidence in my controversial *status*, and I had a great and still growing success in recommending it to others" (Reading 10.1).

In September 1838, Newman published *Tract 85*, Part One, which alleged that the rationalistic tendencies of continental Protestantism had led to a basic diminution of Christianity; his readers awaited the second part in which Newman presumably would show how the devotional and doctrinal excesses of Roman Catholicism had led to an exaggerated distortion of Christianity. The second part of the tract never appeared; Newman's theoretical *via media* was about to collapse.

The first "hit" against the *via media* came in the summer of 1839, when Newman read an article by Nicholas Wiseman about St. Augustine and the Donatists. Newman was struck by Augustine's phrase *securus judicat orbis terrarium*—"the Universal Church is secure in its judgment"—which Newman understood to mean: "the deliberate judgment, in which the whole Church at length rests and acquiesces, is an infallible prescription and a final sentence against such portions of it as protest and secede." Gradually Newman came to the conclusion that the Church of England was in the position of the Donatists and the Roman Church was what it had always been: "the Church of the Apostles."

Newman was not the type of person to come to a quick decision; he wondered whether the doctrines of the Church of England were compatible with the Roman Church. Since the *Thirty-Nine Articles of Religion* of the Church of England, which had been approved under Queen Elizabeth I in 1571, had been designed to be interpreted in a broad fashion, Newman proposed in *Tract XC* (1841) that the Articles could be interpreted in a Catholic sense (Reading 10.2). Whatever the theoretical merits to Newman's argument, it quickly became clear that his Catholic interpretation of the *Articles* was unacceptable to most Anglicans: bishops, clergy, and laity. In fact, the opposition to *Tract XC* was so strenuous that Newman agreed to terminate the publication of further *Tracts* and decided to move to Littlemore, where he had purchased a former stable, which he converted into a retreat house for himself and a few of his closest followers.

During the next two years, Newman pondered his future in the Church of England. He eventually came to the conclusion that he could no longer minister as an Anglican cleric and in September 1843, he resigned his position as vicar of St. Mary's and preached his farewell sermon as an Anglican—"The Parting of Friends"—at Littlemore on the seventh anniversary of the church's dedication (Reading 10.3). Newman decided to continue as a lay communicant in the Church of England, while praying and working on various projects, including a translation of *Select Treatises of St. Athanasius*.

However, the question that continued to haunt Newman and many of his contemporaries was "where is the Church of the Apostles today?" Some felt that the Church had been essentially corrupted; for some, this meant that the Church must be reformed; for others, it meant that Christians must restore the early Church. For others, the Church was a community that is always in the process of remaking itself: while one can point to historical continuity, the doctrines and structures of the Church are subject to change, always in flux. In contrast to such opinions, for Newman, the Church must embody both continuity and change; on the one hand, the basic type of the Church must always be preserved; on the other hand, the Church must have an assimilative power that enables it to self-adapt to the different and ever-changing worlds in which it preaches and lives the Gospel.

When Newman was puzzled by a question, he often resolved it by writing a solution. In answer to the question of where is the Church of the Apostles, he proposed what in the mid-nine-teenth century was a very innovative hypothesis: the Church and its doctrines have developed over the centuries; accordingly, in order to recognize the Apostolic Church, one must discard both fraudulent diminutions of the faith and unwarranted accretions to the faith (Reading 10.4). Newman's *An Essay on the Development of Christian Doctrine* was his attempt to show that the Roman Catholic Church was the present embodiment of the Apostolic Church (Reading 10.5). Convinced that the Roman Catholic Church was where his favorite patristic writers—Athanasius, Ambrose, Augustine—would worship were they alive today, Newman was received into the Roman Catholic Church by an Italian Passionist missionary, Dominic Barberi, on October 9, 1845, at Littlemore.

11. ORATORIAN

After being "admitted into the Catholic Church," Newman visited Oscott College, Birmingham, where he was confirmed as a Roman Catholic by Bishop Nicholas Wiseman on November 1, 1845. On February 22, 1846, Newman left Littlemore and, after spending the night at Oxford, went to Maryvale, Birmingham, which was his temporary home until he left for Rome at the beginning of September (Reading 11.1). Arriving in Rome in late October, Newman and Ambrose St. John (1815–1875) began their theological studies at the College of Propaganda Fide at the beginning of November.

While preparing for ordination to the priesthood, Newman and Ambrose St. John considered both the diocesan priesthood and various religious communities; eventually, with the approval of Pope Pius IX (1846–1878), Newman and St. John decided to enter the Oratory of St. Philip Neri (1515–1595). An Oratory is a house of diocesan priests who live together in community and undertake various types of pastoral ministry such as staffing parishes, conducting schools, giving conferences, etc. Newman felt that the Oratorian vocation was both suited to his personality and adaptable to the needs of pastoral ministry in England

(Reading 11.2). After his ordination as a Roman Catholic priest on May 30, 1847, Newman and St. John made their Oratorian novitiate and then returned to England to establish the English Oratory.

The first Oratorians included Newman's followers at Maryvale and those of Frederick Faber (1814–1863), who had established a community known as the Brothers of the Will of God (Reading 11.3). Since the members of the combined group were too numerous for a single Oratory, Newman divided the group in two to form a Birmingham Oratory, where he became rector, and a London Oratory, whose superior was Faber. During the next few years, Newman was occupied with the myriad practical details connected with establishing a new religious community, along with the regular parochial work of preaching and celebrating the sacraments, counseling, and responding to the needs of parishioners, as well as lecturing and writing. In 1850 Newman presented and then published a series of lectures, *Certain Difficulties Felt by Anglicans in Catholic Teaching*, which provided an answer to prospective converts about their "perplexities in the proof of Catholicity, which keep the intellect from being touched by its cogency, and give the heart an excuse for trifling with it."

On September 29, 1850, Pope Pius IX issued *Universalis Ecclesiae*, which officially restored the Roman Catholic hierarchy in England and Wales. Nicholas Wiseman was named a cardinal and the first archbishop of Westminster; simultaneously a dozen suffragan dioceses were established. These papal appointments reflected the notable change in the situation of Roman Catholics in England since the time of the Reformation: they were a small group of perhaps fifty thousand at the beginning of the nineteenth century, but the influx of Irish immigrants had increased the Roman Catholic population tenfold by midcentury. The first Provincial Synod of Westminster met at St. Mary's, Oscott, and Newman was invited to preach on July 13, 1852 (Reading 11.4).

12. EDUCATOR

The restoration of the Roman Catholic hierarchy in England was greeted with vocal and sometimes violent protests by English Protestants against what they called "papal aggression." Taking advantage of this public outburst of "no popery," the Evangelical Alliance invited Giacinto Achilli, an excommunicated Dominican priest, to deliver anti-Catholic lectures in various cities in England. In response, Cardinal Wiseman publicly criticized Achilli for moral turpitude and Newman castigated Achilli in his *Lectures on the Present Positions of Catholics in England* (1851). Achilli then sued Newman for libel and the jury found Newman guilty for not legally proving all his allegations. After an unsuccessful appeal, Newman was fined the then significant amount of £100 and also had to pay huge legal expenses—which were met by donations from Newman's friends in England, Europe, and America. Once the truth of Achilli's flagrant immorality became public, he abruptly left England; simultaneously, many people, both Anglican and Catholic, came to feel that Newman's trial had been exceedingly unfair; as a result, Newman gained popular vindication.

Just as the Achilli trial was getting underway in November 1851, Newman was named the first rector of the newly established Catholic University of Ireland. Among his numerous tasks as rector were recruiting faculty, designing the curriculum, fostering public relations, and fund-raising. In order to gain support for the new university, Newman gave a series of public lectures, which, along with various articles and addresses to the faculty and students, were later collected and published as *The Idea of a University.*

Since Newman felt that religious practice was an essential part of a university education, he arranged for the building of a university church, where he regularly preached (Reading 12.1). He wanted university students to have not merely a superficial knowledge and conventional observance of Christianity, but a deep personal faith (Reading 12.2). In effect, his vision of a university included many of the ideas that he had tried to implement as a tutor of Oriel College, especially a close relationship between students and their tutors. The tutors were to be responsible for the academic achievement of their students, but they also were to be good examples and thus mentors of moral integrity (Reading 12.3).

During his years in Ireland, Newman faced a number of problems. First, as university rector and simultaneously superior of the Birmingham Oratory, he had to make frequent and time-consuming trips from Dublin to Birmingham and back. In addition, the recruitment of students was a continual problem and fund-raising required considerable effort. But most of all, he often found that his administrative proposals went unheeded by Archbishop Paul Cullen (1803–1878) and the Irish hierarchy. Frustrated and exhausted, he tendered his official resignation on November 12, 1858.

However, Newman's resignation as rector of the Catholic University in Dublin was not the end of his educational endeavors. In 1859 he established the Birmingham Oratory School to provide an education for boys whose parents did not want to send them either to Anglican private schools in England or to Roman Catholic schools abroad. Newman not only designed the curriculum and supervised the administration of the boys' school, he also was regularly involved in the students' activities: coaching them in their studies, directing them in their theatrical productions, chatting with them during recess, and walking to the school's playing fields to watch their sporting events.

13. ADVOCATE FOR THE LAITY

The half-dozen years following Newman's resignation as rector of the Catholic University were plagued by difficulties with ecclesiastical authorities. In 1857, Newman was invited by Cardinal Wiseman to supervise a new translation of the Bible into English; only after expending a great deal of time and money recruiting prospective translators and beginning work on the translation was Newman informed that the project had been cancelled. In 1859, Newman was asked by Bishop William

Bernard Ullathorne (1806–1889) of Birmingham to assume the editorship of *The Rambler*—a journal sponsored by a group of laymen to discuss the arts, history, politics, science, and topics of the day from a Catholic perspective. Although reluctant to accept Ullathorne's invitation, Newman did so because he was a firm believer in the important role of the laity in the Church (Reading 13.1).

Unfortunately, the tenor of some of the articles in *The Rambler* had upset the English hierarchy. When *The Rambler* began discussing government support of Catholic education, the bishops felt that *The Rambler* was intruding into matters that were the bishops' prerogative to decide. Newman, in contrast, believed that the bishops should "consult" the laity in such matters, just as Pope Pius IX had consulted the bishops of the world about the belief of the faithful prior to the proclamation of the dogma of the Immaculate Conception in 1854. For Newman, the fact of such a consultation was a recognition of the *sensus fidelium*—the instinctive understanding of believers about what is truly a matter of Christian faith and what is not.

Newman's essay "On Consulting the Faithful in Matters of Doctrine" in *The Rambler* emphasized that while the bishops are the official teachers in the Church, the laity have an important role as witnesses of doctrine; indeed, Newman cited many instances in the early Church where the bishops had betrayed the Christian faith, while the laity had resolutely defended it (Reading 13.2). Newman's views were not well received by the English hierarchy; Bishop Thomas Brown of Newport formally denounced Newman to Rome. The Vatican subsequently forwarded a list of objections to Newman's essay to Cardinal Wiseman, who neglected to inform Newman of the charges against him.

When Newman did not respond, Vatican officials interpreted his silence as a refusal to answer these charges. As a consequence Newman unintentionally found himself "under a cloud"; indeed, one curial official described Newman as "the most dangerous man in England." It was only in 1867, after Wiseman's death, that Newman was finally able to respond to the charges against him. Fortunately, however, a chance event allowed Newman to regain his reputation in the eyes of the English public, both Anglican and Catholic.

14. DEFENDER OF BELIEF

In December 1863 Newman received in the mail a copy of the January (1864) issue of *Macmillan's Magazine*, which had a book review of two volumes of James Anthony Froude's *History of England*. The reviewer, identified by the initials "C.K.," commented in passing: "Truth, for its own sake, had never been a virtue with the Roman clergy. Father Newman informs us that it need not, and on the whole ought not to be; that cunning is the weapon which Heaven has given to the saints wherewith to withstand the brute male force of the wicked world which marries and is given in marriage. Whether his notion be doctrinally correct or not, it is at least historically so."

Such an aspersion on both his personal integrity and the truthfulness of the Roman Catholic clergy prompted Newman to demand an apology. The editors of *Macmillan's* forwarded his request to the review author, Charles Kingsley (1819–1875), an Anglican clergyman and Regius Professor of Modern History at Cambridge (1860–1869).

When Newman denied that he had ever made such a comment and demanded a retraction, Kingsley published a condescending reply but refused to apologize. Newman then published their exchange of correspondence, to which Kingsley replied in a pamphlet: "What, Then, Does Dr. Newman Mean?" Newman replied with two additional pamphlets, but was aware that pamphleteering was at best a half-measure (Reading 14.1).

Newman realized that he needed to provide the public with a detailed response in order to refute Kingsley's allegation that as a leader of the Tractarian Movement (1833–1845), Newman had been guilty of dishonesty. Indeed, there were some who insinuated that Newman had really been a papist in disguise, sent by Rome to promote Catholicism under the pretext of reforming the Church of England. In response to Kingsley's attack against both the integrity of his own conversion to Roman Catholicism and the honesty of those who had followed him into the Roman Catholic Church, Newman wrote his autobiographical *Apologia pro Vita Sua*, which traced the history of his "religious opinions" from his adolescent Evangelicalism, through his flirtation with Liberalism to his endeavor to recapture the Apostolicity of the Early Church during the Oxford Movement to his decision to become a Roman Catholic.

In an engaging yet candid way, Newman showed how his decision emerged only gradually from a series of theological discussions, historical reflections, and church-related events. His *Apologia* not only became a best seller that is still regarded as a classic example of Victorian autobiography, it also convinced the British public of his integrity. As a "self-defense," Newman's *Apologia* succeeded in re-establishing his stature among both Anglicans and Catholics. On the one hand, the *Apologia* enabled Newman to reconnect with many of his Anglican friends; on the other hand, his *Apologia* provided not only a biographical argument for his decision to become a Roman Catholic, but a rationale for other Anglicans who had followed his example. As Newman eventually came to realize, Kingsley had inadvertently done him a great favor (Reading 14.2).

Just as Newman's *Apologia* presented an autobiographical account of his search for the true Church, his *Essay in Aid of a Grammar of Assent*, published a half-dozen years later, described the search for faith as a *via media*—a middle path—between Evangelicalism (where a believer's faith is seen as depending on love) and "Evidentialism" (where the degree of a person's assent purportedly depends on scientifically verifiable evidence). Dissatisfied with both these alternatives, Newman used a realistic approach to show that if ordinary people must trust in order to live their everyday lives, it is reasonable to assume that they must be guided by faith in religious matters (Reading 14.3).

Newman's analysis of the process of faith began with the fact that everyone asks questions, considers evidence, and comes to conclusions. In some cases, such as logic or mathematics, when the data and the process of reasoning are identical, everyone comes to the same conclusion. However, in those cases where the data are variable and can be understood in different ways, then it is not surprising that people come to different conclusions. If this is true in daily life, it is not surprising that it is also the case in religious matters. Newman gave the example of three brothers who grew up in the same family and so presumably had the same religious background. Because of their different personalities and different experiences, the brothers came to different conclusions about Christianity: one brother became an agnostic, another a Unitarian and the third a Roman Catholic. Such was the case with the three Newman brothers: Charles, Francis, and John Henry (Reading 14.4).

By explaining how different people come to different conclusions about the same evidence, Newman's *Grammar* provided an explanation of why some Tractarians, like Keble and Pusey, remained within the Church of England, while others followed Newman's example and became Roman Catholics. Faith decisions, like decisions in everyday life, depend on the way that each person interprets the evidence in light of their conscience.

15. CHAMPION OF CONSCIENCE

Even as an Anglican, Newman believed that Christ had endowed the Church with the gift of infallibility so that its dogmatic teachings were free from error. For Newman, both as an Anglican and as a Catholic, the core question was the way in which this gift of infallibility could and should be exercised in the Church. During the nineteenth century, some Roman Catholics insisted that the pope was the one person empowered by Christ to exercise infallibility; other Catholics, however, felt that for an exercise of infallibility, dogmatic declarations needed to be approved by a general council or accepted by the bishops throughout the world.

These discussions about the papal exercise of infallibility were complicated by the fact that in the nineteenth century the pope was not only the spiritual leader of the Church but also the temporal ruler of the Papal States in central Italy. Due to a series of wars and revolutions, by 1864 the Papal States, had been reduced to a small area around the city of Rome. On the one hand, many Catholics rallied to help the pope preserve the remainder of his political power with the conviction that the pope could not really be a spiritual leader unless he was politically independent. On the other hand, some Catholics felt that the Papal States were an anachronism: the pope did not need to be a political ruler in order to be a spiritual leader.

On June 29, 1867, Pope Pius IX announced the convocation of a general council of the Roman Catholic Church. Immediately, the new archbishop of Westminster, Henry Edward Manning (1808–1892), like Newman a convert from Anglicanism, made a private vow to work at the Council for a declaration of "papal infallibility." Although Newman acknowledged both the infallibility of the Church and the authority of the pope in doctrinal matters, he did not see any need for such a definition: he felt that it would be difficult to express such a definition in appropriate theological terminology; in addition, he feared that such a definition could place Roman Catholics at a disadvantage in England and elsewhere due to prejudice against Roman Catholicism in general and the papacy in particular; nonetheless, he stated that he would accept a definition if the Council promulgated one.

After prolonged debate about "the infallible magisterium of the Roman Pontiff," the First Vatican Council (1869–1870) on July 18, 1870, declared that when the pope, as pastor and teacher of all Christians, solemnly defines a doctrine of faith or morals, he exercises the infallibility bestowed by Christ on the Church (Reading 15.1). After carefully examining the new definition, Newman came to the conclusion that it stated what he had long believed. Nonetheless, he was upset at the exaggerated interpretation of Manning, W. G. Ward, and others, who insisted that practically every papal statement should be considered an exercise of infallibility. For Newman, the Vatican definition implied a rare and restricted use by the pope of this Christ-given gift. Although Newman expressed this moderate interpretation of infallibility privately, he did not publish his views in order to avoid public disagreement with Archbishop Manning.

In 1874, the British prime minister, William Gladstone (1809–1898), published a small book, *The Vatican Decrees in Their Bearing on Civil Allegiance*, which asserted that Catholics could not be considered loyal citizens if they acknowledged the infallibility of the pope. Newman seized the opportunity to reply in *A Letter Addressed to His Grace the Duke of Norfolk* (1875), which simultaneously corrected Gladstone's misunderstanding of the council's teaching and rejected the exaggerated misinterpretations of people like Manning. Newman's *Letter* effectively showed that a good Catholic could and should be a good citizen.

In addition to discussing papal authority in the ancient and modern Church, Newman devoted a section of his *Letter* to the pivotal question of the obligation of Catholics to follow their conscience in accepting the definition; he gave a memorable summation of his position: "Certainly, if I am obliged to bring religion into after-dinner toasts (which indeed does not seem quite the thing) I shall drink—to the Pope, if you please,—still, to Conscience first, and to the Pope afterwards" (Readings 15.2, 15.3, 15.4). In addition to giving an effective response to Gladstone, Newman's *Letter* provided a moderate interpretation of the papal exercise of infallibility that countered many popular misconceptions of infallibility.

Gladstone's pamphlet had inadvertently provided Newman with an opportunity to explain Roman Catholic ecclesiology, just as Kingsley's aspersion had given him the chance of explaining his journey to Roman Catholicism a decade earlier. Following the favorable reception of his *Apologia* (1864), Newman decided to republish many of his Anglican writings. He republished his *Parochial and Plain Sermons* in 1869 and his *Oxford University Sermons* two years later. In 1877, on the fortieth anniversary of its original publication, he republished *On the Prophetical Office of the Church* with a new preface. That same year, he was pleasantly surprised to receive an invitation from his undergraduate alma mater, Trinity College, to become its first honorary fellow. He was delighted at the honor as well as

the opportunity to revisit Oxford for the first time since he had
left it a third of a century ago (Reading 15.5). As a token of his
esteem, he dedicated the revised edition (1878) of his *Essay on
the Development of Christian Doctrine* (1845) to the president
of Trinity College.

16. CARDINAL

In January 1879, Newman was informed that the new pope,
Leo XIII (1878–1903), wanted to name him a cardinal. On the
one hand, Newman was deeply grateful because such an honor
would forever lift "the cloud" that had plagued his life for three
decades: many Roman Catholics, including some members of
the English hierarchy, had viewed his doctrinal positions with
suspicion. On the other hand, at that time cardinals who were
not diocesan bishops were expected to live in Rome, but Newman wanted to continue to live at the Birmingham Oratory. His
request was initially misunderstood—perhaps deliberately mis-
construed by some people who did not want him to receive the
cardinalate—but the pope granted his request to remain at the
Birmingham Oratory, and Newman gladly accepted the offer of
a red hat. Once the news became public, Newman was inun-
dated with congratulations from both Catholics and Protestants
(Reading 16.1).

Named cardinal deacon of the Church of San Giorgio in Vela-
bro, Newman selected as his cardinalatial motto, *Cor ad cor
loquitur* ("Heart speaks to heart"). While in Rome for the ceremonies, Newman took the occasion of the official announcement (*biglietto*) on May 12, 1879, to give a speech about his
lifelong campaign against the "spirit of liberalism in religion"
(Reading 16.2). Two days later, a congratulatory reception was
sponsored by English-speaking Catholics in Rome, who presented him with vestments embroidered with his cardinalatial
coat-of-arms (Reading 16.3).

Yet even in the midst of the customary ceremonies, Newman was still concerned about pastoral ministry. For decades,
he had been corresponding with William Froude (1810–1879),

a brother of his friend Richard Hurrell Froude, who had died in the midst of the Oxford Movement. William Froude, a distinguished naval architect, was an agnostic who held that there was no scientific basis for belief. Froude's correspondence with Newman on the relationship of faith and reason was reflected in his *Grammar of Assent* (1870). After the publication of his *Grammar*, Newman, hoping to convince Froude of the reasonableness of belief, continued his corresponding and was working on another letter while in Rome, when he received word of Froude's death.

Newman also hoped to take advantage of his return trip to England to visit Johann Joseph Ignaz von Döllinger (1799–1890), a German priest and professor at Munich, who had been excommunicated in 1871 for not accepting the teaching of Vatican I on the infallible magisterium of the pope. In addition, Newman hoped to visit the sister-in-law of Walter Mayers, Maria Rosina Giberne (1802–1885), who became a Roman Catholic in 1845 and entered the Visitation convent in Autun, France, in 1863. Unfortunately, due to illness and infirmity, Newman was unable to make either of these visits, because he was ordered by his physician to return to England as directly as possible. Newman finally arrived at the Birmingham Oratory on July 1, 1879, where during the formal ceremony of welcome, he expressed his joy at his "homecoming" (Reading 16.4).

After this and many other celebrations, Newman spent the remaining years of his life as rector of the Birmingham Oratory, continuing his priestly ministry, participating in activities at the Oratory boys' school, editing some of his Anglican works for publication, writing articles and memoirs, receiving visitors and carrying on an extensive correspondence. During the last years of his life, his eyesight weakened so that he could no longer read, and he was debilitated by several falls. He celebrated Mass for the last time on Christmas 1889; but surprisingly, he was well enough to preside at the concluding ceremonies of the school term on July 23, 1890.

A couple of weeks later, Newman contracted pneumonia. After receiving the last rites on August 10, 1890, he died the following day. At his request, he was buried next to his friend and fellow Oratorian Ambrose St. John, in the Oratorian cemetery at Rednal. As Newman's funeral procession journeyed from the Birmingham Oratory to Rednal, thousands lined the streets to pay their last respects. On his memorial plaque at the Birmingham Oratory were words of his own choosing: *Ex umbris et imaginibus in veritatem*—"From Shadows and Images into Truth."

17. BLESSED JOHN HENRY NEWMAN

At the time of Newman's death, the London *Times* remarked that "whether Rome canonizes him or not, he will be canonized in the thoughts of pious people of many creeds in England." In 1907, the future archbishop of Birmingham, John McIntyre (1855–1935), expressed his "hope that our Cardinal will be the first canonised saint of the Second Spring." In 1941, an American Dominican, Fr. Charles Callan, made a similar proposal in *America* magazine. The following year the archbishop of Toronto, James Charles McGuigan (1894–1974) gave an *imprimatur* to the first prayer for Newman's beatification. In 1958, Archbishop Francis Grimshaw (1901–1965) of Birmingham initiated the canonical process for canonization. In 1980, a reconstituted Historical Commission began the task of gathering all the necessary documents for the diocesan part of the process of beatification and forwarded its findings to the Vatican in 1986. In January 1991, Pope John Paul II declared that Newman had exercised all of the Christian virtues in a heroic degree and was henceforth to be known as "Venerable John Henry Newman" (Reading 17.1).

The next requisite in the process of beatification was evidence of a miracle. In 2009, the Vatican recognized the cure in 2001 of the severe spinal disorder of Deacon Jack Sullivan of Marshfield, Massachusetts, as an authentic miracle worked through Newman's intercession. As part of the process for beatification, Newman's grave in the Birmingham Oratory Cemetery at Rednal was opened on October 2, 2008; however, no human remains were found. At Newman's request the wooden coffin in which he was buried was covered with a type of mould intended to speed the process of decomposition; that mould plus the damp soil characteristic of the graveyard had apparently resulted in the complete disintegration of his body. Some soil, along with a few objects recovered from his grave, were placed in a reliquary in the chapel dedicated to his memory at the Birmingham Oratory, which is located about eight miles from Rednal.

On September 19, 2010, Pope Benedict XVI beatified John Henry Newman at Cofton Park, not far from the Oratorian house at Rednal. In his homily at the Mass of Newman's beatification, Pope Benedict XVI emphasized: "In Blessed John Henry, that tradition of gentle scholarship, deep human wisdom, and profound love for the Lord has borne rich fruit, as a sign of the abiding presence of the Holy Spirit deep within the heart of God's people, bringing forth abundant gifts of holiness" (Reading 17.2).

Family, Ealing School, "First Conversion"

1.1. NEWMAN'S DOUBTS ABOUT CHRISTIANITY

Like many teenagers, then and now, Newman had doubts about the Christian faith; perhaps to the surprise of his readers, Newman described the attraction of rationalism in his Apologia pro Vita Sua *(1865):*

When I was fourteen, I read Paine's *Tracts against the Old Testament,* and found pleasure in thinking of the objections which were contained in them. Also, I read some of Hume's Essays; and perhaps that on Miracles. So at least I gave my father to understand; but perhaps it was a brag. Also, I recollect copying out some French verses, perhaps Voltaire's, in denial of the immortality of the soul, and saying to myself something like "How dreadful, but how plausible!" —*Apologia pro Vita Sua,* 3

1.2. NEWMAN'S "FIRST CONVERSION"

In his Apologia pro Vita Sua *(1864), Newman vividly recalled what has been called his "first conversion"—nearly five decades earlier (1816). This experience convinced him that he would persevere in his Christian faith ("the doctrine of final perseverance") and that he was "predestined to salvation." This conversion experience also produced in Newman a "mistrust" of "material phenomena" and a sense of the invisible world—which he described as "the thought of two and two only absolute and luminously self-evident beings, myself and my Creator." His conversion experience seems to have instilled in Newman the dual conviction that Providence was guiding his life and that he had a special work to do as a Christian in the world.*

When I was fifteen, (in the autumn of 1816,) a great change of thought took place in me. I fell under the influences of a definite Creed, and received into my intellect impressions of dogma, which, through God's mercy, have never been effaced or obscured. Above and beyond the conversations and sermons of the excellent man, long dead, the Rev. Walter Mayers, of Pembroke College, Oxford, who was the human means of this beginning of divine faith in me, was the effect of the books which he put into my hands, all of the school of Calvin. One of the first books I read was a work of Romaine's; I neither recollect the title nor the contents, except one doctrine, which of course I do not include among those which I believe to have come from a divine source, viz. the doctrine of final perseverance. I received it at once, and believed that the inward conversion of which I was conscious, (and of which I still am more certain than that I have hands and feet,) would last into the next life, and that I was elected to eternal glory. I have no consciousness that this belief had any tendency whatever to lead me to be careless about pleasing God. I retained it till the age of twenty-one, when it gradually faded away; but I believe that it had some influence on my opinions, in the direction of those childish imaginations which I have already mentioned, viz. in isolating me from the objects which surrounded me, in confirming me in my mistrust of the reality of material phenomena, and making me rest in the thought of two and two only absolute and luminously self-evident beings, myself and my Creator;—for while I considered myself predestined to salvation, my mind did not dwell upon others, as fancying them simply passed over, not predestined to eternal death. I only thought of the mercy to myself.

The detestable doctrine last mentioned is simply denied and abjured, unless my memory strangely deceives me, by the writer who made a deeper impression on my mind than any other, and to whom (humanly speaking) I almost owe my soul,—Thomas Scott of Aston Sandford. I so admired and delighted in his writings, that, when I was an Under-graduate, I thought of making a visit to his Parsonage, in order to see a man whom I so deeply revered. . . .

What, I suppose, will strike any reader of Scott's history and writings, is his bold unworldliness and vigorous independence of mind. He followed truth wherever it led him, beginning with Unitarianism, and ending in a zealous faith in the Holy Trinity. It was he who first planted deep in my mind that fundamental truth of religion. With the assistance of Scott's *Essays*, and the admirable work of Jones of Nayland, I made a collection of Scripture texts in proof of the doctrine, with remarks (I think) of my own upon them, before I was sixteen; and a few months later I drew up a series of texts in support of each verse of the Athanasian Creed. These papers I have still.

Besides his unworldliness, what I also admired in Scott was his resolute opposition to Antinomianism, and the minutely practical character of his writings. They show him to be a true Englishman, and I deeply felt his influence; and for years I used almost as proverbs what I considered to be the scope and issue of his doctrine, *Holiness rather than peace*, and *Growth the only evidence of life*.   —*Apologia pro Vita Sua*, 4–5 ·

> Antinomianism is the heretical belief that some
> Christians are exempt from obeying the commandments.

1.3. NEWMAN'S CALL TO CELIBACY

As a result of his "first conversion," Newman not only came to believe in his own final perseverance and the divine guidance of Providence; he also felt that God was calling him to lead "a single life"—that is a call to celibacy:

I am obliged to mention, though I do it with great reluctance, another deep imagination, which at this time, the autumn of

1816, took possession of me,—there can be no mistake about the fact; viz. that it would be the will of God that I should lead a single life. This anticipation, which has held its ground almost continuously ever since,—with the break of a month now and a month then, up to 1829, and, after that date, without any break at all,—was more or less connected in my mind with the notion, that my calling in life would require such a sacrifice as celibacy involved; as, for instance, missionary work among the heathen, to which I had a great drawing for some years. It also strengthened my feeling of separation from the visible world, of which I have spoken above.   —*Apologia pro Vita Sua*, 7

1.4. "A PARTICULAR PROVIDENCE AS REVEALED IN THE GOSPEL"

It is hardly surprising that Newman's sense of the guidance of Providence in his own life frequently surfaced in his preaching. His Anglican sermon—"A Particular Providence as Revealed in the Gospel," which he originally preached on April 5, 1835— emphasized God's "particular providence" at work in the life of each individual. Using examples from both the Old and New Testaments, Newman characterized God, not as a remote and "unchangeable Creator," but as a "Compassionate Guardian" and "Helper" who is personally interested in each person. In light of God's personal concern for each of us, human rivalries seem petty, and human accomplishments seem secondary.

How gracious is this revelation of God's particular providence to those who seek Him! how gracious to those who have discovered that this world is but vanity, and who are solitary and isolated in themselves, whatever shadows of power and happiness surround them! The multitude, indeed, go on without these thoughts, either from insensibility, as not understanding their own wants, or changing from one idol to another, as each successively fails. But men of keener hearts would be overpowered by despondency, and would even loathe existence, did they suppose themselves under the mere operation of fixed laws, powerless

to excite the pity or the attention of Him who has appointed
them. What should they do especially, who are cast among
persons unable to enter into their feelings, and thus strangers
to them, though by long custom ever so much friends! or who
have perplexities of mind they cannot explain to themselves,
much less remove, and no one to help them; or who have
affections and aspirations pent up within them, because they
have not met with objects to which to devote them; or who
are misunderstood by those around them, and find they have
no words to set themselves right with them, or no principles
in common by way of appeal; or who seem to themselves
to be without place or purpose in the world, or to be in the
way of others; or who have to follow their own sense of duty
without advisers or supporters, nay, to resist the wishes and
solicitations of superiors or relatives; or who have the burden
of some painful secret, or of some incommunicable solitary
grief! In all such cases the Gospel narrative supplies our very
need, not simply presenting to us an unchangeable Creator to
rely upon, but a compassionate Guardian, a discriminating
Judge and Helper.

God beholds thee individually, whoever thou art. He "calls
thee by thy name." He sees thee, and understands thee, as He
made thee. He knows what is in thee, all thy own peculiar feelings and thoughts, thy dispositions and likings, thy strength and
thy weakness. He views thee in thy day of rejoicing, and thy day
of sorrow. He sympathises in thy hopes and thy temptations.
He interests Himself in all thy anxieties and remembrances, all
the risings and fallings of thy spirit. He has numbered the very
hairs of thy head and the cubits of thy stature. He compasses
thee round and bears thee in his arms; He takes thee up and sets
thee down. He notes thy very countenance, whether smiling or
in tears, whether healthful or sickly. He looks tenderly upon thy
hands and thy feet; He hears thy voice, the beating of thy heart,
and thy very breathing. Thou dost not love thyself better than He
loves thee. Thou canst not shrink from pain more than He dis-
likes thy bearing it; and if He puts it on thee, it is as thou would
put it on thyself, if thou art wise, for a greater good afterwards.
Thou art not only His creature (though for the very sparrows

He has a care, and pitied the "much cattle" of Nineveh), thou art man redeemed and sanctified, His adopted son, favoured with a portion of that glory and blessedness which flows from Him everlastingly unto the Only-begotten. Thou art chosen to be His, even above thy fellows who dwell in the East and South. Thou wast one of those for whom Christ offered up His last prayer, and sealed it with His precious blood. What a thought is this, a thought almost too great for our faith! Scarce can we refrain from acting Sarah's part, when we bring it before us, so as to "laugh" from amazement and perplexity. What is man, what are we, what am I, that the Son of God should be so mindful of me? What am I, that He should have raised me from almost a devil's nature to that of an Angel's? that He should have changed my soul's original constitution, new-made me, who from my youth up have been a transgressor, and should Himself dwell personally in this very heart of mine, making me His temple? What am I, that God the Holy Ghost should enter into me, and draw up my thoughts heavenward "with plaints unutterable?"

These are the meditations which come upon the Christian to console him, while he is with Christ upon the holy mount. And, when he descends to his daily duties, they are still his inward strength, though he is not allowed to tell the vision to those around him. They make his countenance to shine, make him cheerful, collected, serene, and firm in the midst of all temptation, persecution, or bereavement. And with such thoughts before us, how base and miserable does the world appear in all its pursuits and doctrines! How truly miserable does it seem to seek good from the creature; to covet station, wealth, or credit; to choose for ourselves, in fancy, this or that mode of life; to affect the manners and fashions of the great; to spend our time in follies; to be discontented, quarrelsome, jealous or envious, censorious or resentful; fond of unprofitable talk, and eager for the news of the day; busy about public matters which concern us not; hot in the cause of this or that interest or party; or set upon gain; or devoted to the increase of barren knowledge! And at the end of our days, when flesh and heart fail, what will be our consolation, though we have made ourselves rich, or have served an office, or been the first man among our equals, or have depressed a rival, or managed things our own way, or have settled splendidly, or have been intimate with the great, or have fared sumptuously, or have gained a name! Say, even if we obtain that which lasts longest, a place in history, yet, after all, what ashes shall we have eaten for bread! And, in that awful hour, when death is in sight, will He, whose eye is now so loving towards us, and whose hand falls on us so gently, will He acknowledge us any more?

—*Parochial and Plain Sermons* 3:123–127

2

Student at Trinity College

2.1. "LOVE OF RELATIONS AND FRIENDS"

The importance of friendships in Newman's life is reflected in his sermons, which presented the people who are mentioned in scripture not merely as historical figures, but as examples for present-day living. On the feast of St. John the Evangelist, December 27, 1831, Newman preached at Oxford on the text from the First Letter of John: "Beloved, let us love one another, for love is of God" (4:7). Emphasizing that John was "the beloved disciple of Jesus," Newman pointed out that Christians need to love their family and friends, who are close at hand, if they are really to obey Christ's command to love everyone.

St. John the Apostle and Evangelist is chiefly and most familiarly known to us as "the disciple whom Jesus loved." He was one of the three or four who always attended our Blessed Lord, and . . . was His bosom friend, as we commonly express ourselves. . . .

Much might be said on this remarkable circumstance. I say *remarkable*, because it might be supposed that the Son of God Most High could not have loved one man more than another; or again, if so, that He would not have had only one friend, but, as being All-holy, He would have loved all men more or less, in proportion to their holiness. Yet we find our Saviour had a private friend; and this shows us, first, how entirely He was a man, as much as any of us, in His wants and feelings; and next, that there is nothing contrary to the spirit of the Gospel, nothing inconsistent with the fulness of Christian love, in having our affections directed in an especial way . . . towards those whom the circumstances of our past life, or some peculiarities of character, have endeared to us. . . . Now I shall here maintain, in opposition to such notions of Christian love, and with our Saviour's pattern before me, that the best preparation for loving the world at large, and loving it duly and wisely, is to cultivate an intimate friendship and affection towards those who are immediately about us.

It has been the plan of Divine Providence to ground what is good and true in religion and morals, on the basis of our good natural feelings. What we are towards our earthly friends in the instincts and wishes of our infancy, such we are to become at length towards God and man in the extended field of our duties as accountable beings. To honour our parents is the first step towards honouring God; to love our brethren according to the flesh, the first step towards considering all men our brethren. . . .

But again, the love of our private friends is the only preparatory exercise for the love of all men. The love of God is not the same thing as the love of our parents, though parallel to it; but the love of mankind in general should be in the main the same habit as the love of our friends, only exercised towards different objects. . . . We are to begin with loving our friends about us, and gradually to enlarge the circle of our affections, till it reaches all Christians, and then all men. Besides, it is obviously impossible to love all men in any strict and true sense. What is meant by loving all men, is, to feel well-disposed to all men, to be ready to assist them, and to act towards those who come in our way, as if we loved them. We cannot love those about whom we know nothing; except indeed we view them in Christ, as the objects of His Atonement, that is, rather in faith than in love. And love, besides, is a habit, and cannot be attained without actual *practice*, which on so large a scale is impossible. We see then how absurd it is, when writers (as is the manner of some who slight the Gospel) talk magnificently about loving the whole human race with a comprehensive affection, of being the friends of all mankind, and the like. Such vaunting professions, what do they come to? that such men have certain benevolent *feelings* towards the world,—feelings and nothing more;—nothing more than unstable feelings, the mere offspring of an indulged imagination, which exist only when their minds are wrought upon, and are sure to fail them in the hour of need. This is not to love men, it is but to talk about love.—The real love of man *must* depend on practice, and therefore, must begin by exercising itself on our friends around us, otherwise it will have no existence. By trying to love our relations and friends, by submitting to their wishes, though contrary to our own, by bearing with their infirmities, by overcoming their occasional waywardness by kindness, by dwelling on their excellences, and trying to copy them, thus it is that we form in our hearts that root of charity, which, though small at first, may, like the mustard seed, at last even overshadow the earth. The vain talkers about philanthropy, just spoken of, usually show the emptiness of their profession, by being morose and cruel in the private relations of life, which they seem to account as subjects beneath their notice. Far different indeed, far different (unless it be a sort of irreverence to contrast such dreamers with the great Apostle, whose memory we are today celebrating), utterly the reverse of this fictitious benevolence was his elevated and enlightened sympathy for all men. We know he is celebrated for his declarations about Christian love. "Beloved, let us love one another, for love is of God. If we love one another, God dwelleth in us, and His love is perfected in us. God is love, and he that dwelleth in love dwelleth in God, and God in him" [1 John 4:7, 12, 16]. Now did he begin with some vast effort at loving on a large scale? Nay, he had the unspeakable privilege of being the *friend of Christ*. Thus he was taught to love others; first his affection was concentrated, then it was expanded. Next he had the solemn and comfortable charge of tending our Lord's Mother, the Blessed Virgin, after His departure. Do we not here discern the secret sources of his especial love of the brethren? Could he, who first was favoured with his Saviour's affection, then trusted with a son's office towards His Mother, could he be other than a memorial and pattern (as far as man can be), of love, deep, contemplative, fervent, unruffled, unbounded? . . .

Those who have not accustomed themselves to love their neighbours whom they have seen, will have nothing to lose or gain, nothing to grieve at or rejoice in, in their larger plans of benevolence. They will take no interest in them for their own sake; rather, they will engage in them, because expedience demands, or credit is gained, or an excuse found for being busy. Hence too we discern how it is, that private virtue is the only sure foundation of public virtue; and that no national good is to be expected (though it may now and then accrue), from men who have not the fear of God before their eyes.

The Ancients thought so much of friendship, that they made it a *virtue*. In a Christian view, it is not quite this; but it is often accidentally a special *test* of our virtue. For consider:—let us say that this man, and that, not bound by any very necessary tie, find their greatest pleasure in living together; say that this continues for years, and that they love each other's society the more, the longer they enjoy it. Now observe what is implied in this. Young people, indeed, readily love each other, for they are cheerful and innocent; more easily yield to each other, and are full of hope;— types, as Christ says, of His true converts. But this happiness does not last; their tastes change. Again, grown persons go on for years as friends; but these do not live together; and, if any accident throws them into familiarity for a while, they find it difficult to restrain their tempers and keep on terms, and discover that they are best friends at a distance. But what is it that can bind two friends together in intimate converse for a course of years, but the participation in something that is Unchangeable and essentially Good, and what is this but religion? Religious tastes alone are unalterable. The Saints of God continue in one way, while the fashions of the world change; and a faithful indestructible friendship may thus be a test of the parties, so loving each other, having the love of God seated deep in their hearts. Not an infallible test certainly; for they may have dispositions remarkably the same, or some engrossing object of this world, literary or other; they may be removed from the temptation to change, or they may have a natural sobriety of temper, which remains contented wherever it finds itself. However, under certain circumstances, it is a lively token of the presence of divine grace in them; and it is always a sort of symbol of it, for there is at first sight something of the nature of virtue in the very notion of constancy, dislike of change being not only the characteristic of a virtuous mind, but in some sense a virtue itself.

Should God call upon us to preach to the world, surely we must obey His call; but at present, let us do what lies before us. Little children, let us love one another. Let us be meek and gentle; let us think before we speak; let us try to improve our talents in private life; let us do good, not hoping for a return, and avoiding all display before men. Well may I so exhort you at this season [of Christmas], when we have so lately partaken together the Blessed Sacrament which binds us to mutual love, and gives us strength to practise it. Let us not forget the promise we then made, or the grace we then received. We are not our own; we are bought with the blood of Christ; we are consecrated to be temples of the Holy Spirit, an unutterable privilege, which is weighty enough to sink us with shame at our unworthiness, did it not the while strengthen us by the aid itself imparts, to bear its extreme costliness. May we live worthy of our calling, and realize in our own persons the Church's prayers and professions for us!   —"Love of Relations and Friends" (excerpts),
Parochial and Plain Sermons 2:51–60

2.2. STUDENT DRINKING

On Trinity Sunday, June 6, 1819, Newman wrote to Rev. Walter Mayers (1790–1828), who was Senior Classical Master at Ealing School (1814–1822) and Newman's spiritual mentor while he was a student there. After going to Oxford, Newman continued to seek spiritual advice from Mayers. Mayers later became curate of Over Worton, where Newman preached his first sermon on June 23, 1824; four years later, Newman preached the sermon at Mayers' funeral.

*In the following letter to Mayers, Newman expressed his con-
cern about the propensity of college students to drunkenness
on the occasion of the college's annual "Gaudy"—a celebra-
tion whose name is derived from the Latin* gaudium *(joy) and
exemplified in the collegiate drinking song—*Gaudeamus igitur
*("Let us rejoice"). Newman felt that drunkenness was extremely
inappropriate behavior for students of a college dedicated to the
Trinity.*

Tomorrow is our Gaudy. If there be one time of the year in which
the glory of our college is humbled, and all appearance of goodness fades away, it is on Trinity Monday. Oh, how the angels
must lament over a whole society throwing off the allegiance
and service of their Maker, which they have pledged the day
before at His table, and showing themselves the sons of Belial!

It is sickening to see what I might call the apostasies of many.
This year it was supposed there would have been no such merry-
making. A quarrel existed among us: the college was divided
into two sets, and no proposition for the usual subscription for
wine was set on foot. Unhappily, a day or two before the time
a reconciliation takes place; the wine party is agreed upon, and
this wicked union, to be sealed with drunkenness, is profanely
joked upon with allusions to one of the expressions in the Athanasian Creed.

To see the secret eagerness with which many wished there
would be no Gaudy; to see how they took hope, as time advanced
and no mention was made of it; but they are all gone, there has
been weakness and fear of ridicule. Those who resisted last year
are going this. I fear even for myself, so great a delusion seems
suddenly to have come over all.

Oh that the purpose of some may be changed before the
time! I know not how to make myself of use. I am intimate with
very few. The Gaudy has done more harm to the college than
the whole year can compensate. An habitual negligence of the
awfulness of the Holy Communion is introduced. How can we
prosper?   —"Autobiographical Memoir," 33

2.3. BACCALAUREATE EXAMINATIONS

During the final weeks of 1820, Newman's family and friends had expected him to excel in the oral examinations for his bachelor's degree as a prelude to a distinguished career in law or government. Called to his examinations a day earlier than expected, Newman's performance was poor; his mediocre showing was not only personally painful, but also a disappointment to his family, who had great expectations for him. On December 1, he informed his father of his failure to gain the honors that he had hoped to achieve:

It is all over, and I have not succeeded. The pain it gives me to be obliged to inform you and my mother of it, I cannot express. What I feel on my own account is indeed nothing at all, compared with the thought that I have disappointed you. And most willingly would I consent to a hundred times the sadness that now overshadows me, if so doing would save my mother and you from feeling vexation. I will not attempt to describe what I have gone through, but it is past away, and I feel quite lightened of a load. The examining masters were as kind as it was possible to be; but my nerves quite forsook me and I failed. I have done everything I could to attain my object; I have spared no labour, and my reputation in my college is as solid as before, if not so splendid. If a man falls in battle after a display of bravery, he is honoured as a hero; ought not the same glory to attend him who falls in the field of literary conflict?

—"Autobiographical Memoir," 40–41

3

Fellow of Oriel College

3.1. "JEREMIAH, A LESSON FOR THE DISAPPOINTED"

It comes as a surprise to many people that Newman experienced many major disappointments—his father's bankruptcy, his failure to graduate from Oxford with honors, etc. In this sermon, which was preached on September 12, 1829, shortly after he had accepted the provost's decision of gradually removing him from his position as tutor by not assigning him any more students, Newman seems to identify himself with the Prophet Jeremiah, who provides "a lesson for the disappointed."

But of all the persecuted prophets Jeremiah is the most eminent; i.e. we know more of his history, of his imprisonments, his wanderings, and his afflictions. He may be taken as a representative of the Prophets; and hence it is that he is an especial type of our Lord and Saviour. All the Prophets were types of the Great Prophet whose way they were preparing; they tended towards and spoke of Christ. In their sufferings they foreshadowed His priesthood, and in their teaching His prophetical office, and in their miracles His royal power. The history of Jeremiah, then, as being drawn out in Scripture more circumstantially than that of the other Prophets, is the most exact type of Christ among them; that is, next to David, who, of course, was the nearest resemblance to Him of all, as a sufferer, an inspired teacher, and

47

a king. Jeremiah comes next to David; I do not say in dignity and privilege, for it was Elijah who was taken up to heaven, and appeared at the Transfiguration; nor in inspiration, for to Isaiah one should assign the higher evangelical gifts; but in typifying Him who came and wept over Jerusalem, and then was tortured and put to death by those He wept over. And hence, when our Lord came, while some thought Him Elijah, and others John the Baptist, risen from the dead, there were others who thought Him Jeremiah. Of Jeremiah, then, I will now speak, as a specimen of all those Prophets whom St. Paul sets before us as examples of faith, and St. James as examples of patience.

Jeremiah's ministry may be summed up in three words, good hope, labour, disappointment. . . .

No prophet commenced his labours with greater encouragement than Jeremiah. A king had succeeded to the throne who was bringing back the times of the man after God's own heart. There had not been a son of David so zealous as Josiah since David himself. The king, too, was young, at most twenty years of age, in the beginning of his reformation. What might not be effected in a course of years, however corrupt and degraded was the existing state of his people? So Jeremiah might think. It must be recollected, too, that religious obedience was under the Jewish covenant awarded with temporal prosperity. There seemed, then, every reason for Jeremiah at first to suppose that bright fortunes were in store for the Church. . . . At first sight, then, it seemed reasonable to anticipate further and permanent improvement. Every one begins with being sanguine; doubtless then, as now, many labourers in God's husbandry entered on their office with more lively hopes than their after fortunes warranted. Whether or not, however, such hope of success encouraged Jeremiah's first exertions, very soon, in his case, this cheerful prospect was overcast, and he was left to labour in the dark. . . .

I call resignation a more blessed frame of mind than sanguine hope of present success, because it is the truer, and the more consistent with our fallen state of being, and the more improving to our hearts; and because it is that for which the most eminent servants of God have been conspicuous. To expect great effects from our exertions for religious objects is natural indeed, and innocent, but it arises from inexperience of the kind of work we have to do,—to change the heart and will of man. It is a far nobler frame of mind, to labour, not with the hope of seeing the fruit of our labour, but for conscience' sake, as a matter of duty; and again, in faith, trusting good *will* be done, though we see it not. Look through the Bible, and you will find God's servants, even though they began with success, end with disappointment; not that God's purposes or His instruments fail, but that the time for reaping what we have sown is hereafter, not here; that here there is no great visible fruit in any one man's lifetime. Moses, for instance, began with leading the Israelites out of Egypt in triumph; he ended at the age of an hundred and twenty years, before his journey was finished and Canaan gained, one among the offending multitudes who were overthrown in the wilderness [1 Cor. 10:5]. . . . Even in the successes of the first Christian teachers, the Apostles, the same rule is observed. After all the great works God enabled them to accomplish, they confessed before their death that what they experienced, and what they saw before them, was reverse and calamity, and that the fruit of their labour would not be seen, till Christ came to open the books and collect His saints from the four corners of the earth. . . .

Now, in the instance of Jeremiah, we have on record that variety and vicissitude of feelings, which this transition from hope to disappointment produces, at least in a sensitive mind. His trials were very great, even in Josiah's reign; but when that pious king's countenance was withdrawn on his early death, he was exposed to persecution from every class of men. At one time we read of the people conspiring against him; at another, of the men of his own city, Anathoth, "seeking his life" [Jer. 9: 21], on account of his prophesying in the Lord's name. At another time he was seized by the priests and the prophets in order to be put to death, from which he was only saved by certain of the princes and elders who were still faithful to the memory of Josiah. Then, again, Pashur, the chief governor of the temple, smote him and tortured him. At another time, the king, Zedekiah, put him in prison. Afterwards, when the army of the Chaldeans had besieged Jerusalem, the Jews accused him of falling away to the enemy, and smote him, and imprisoned him; then they cast him into a dungeon, where he "sunk in the mire," and almost perished from hunger [Jer. 38:6, 9]. When Jerusalem had been taken by the enemy, Jeremiah was forcibly carried down to Egypt by men who at first pretended to reverence and consult him, and there he came to his end—it is believed, a violent end. Nebuchadnezzar, the heathen king of Babylon and conqueror of Jerusalem, was one of the few persons who showed him kindness. This great king, who afterwards honoured Daniel, and was at length brought to acknowledge the God of heaven by a severe chastisement, on the taking of the city delivered Jeremiah from prison, and gave charge to the captain of his guard concerning him, to "look well to him, and to do him no harm; but to do unto him even as he should say. . . . "

Such were his trials: his affliction, fear, despondency, and sometimes even restlessness under them are variously expressed; that succession and tide of feelings which most persons undergo before their minds settle into the calm of resignation. At one time he speaks as astonished at his failure: "O Lord, art not Thine eyes upon the truth? Thou hast stricken them, but they have not grieved; Thou hast consumed them, but they have refused to receive correction." [Jer. 5: 3] . . . These are the sorrows of a gentle and peaceable mind, forced against its will into the troubles of life, and incurring the hatred of those whom it opposes against its nature. . . .

However, of such changes of feelings what was the end?— resignation. He elsewhere uses language which expresses that chastened spirit and weaned heart, which is the termination of all agitation and anxiety in the case of religious minds. He, who at one time could not comfort himself, at another was sent to comfort a brother; and, in comforting Baruch, he speaks in that nobler temper of resignation which takes the place of sanguine hope and harassing fear, and betokens calm and clear-sighted faith and inward peace. "Thus saith the Lord the God of Israel unto thee, O Baruch. Thou didst say, Woe is me now, for the

Lord hath added grief to my sorrow; I fainted in my sighing, and I find no rest . . . Behold, that which I have built will I break down, and that which I have planted I will pluck up, even this whole land. And seekest thou great things for thyself? seek them not: for, behold, I will bring evil upon all flesh; . . . but thy life will I give unto thee for a prey in all places whither thou goest;" that is, seek not success, be not impatient, fret not thyself—be content, if, after all thy labours, thou dost but save thyself, without seeing other fruit of them.

And now, my brethren, does what I have been saying apply to all of us, or only to Prophets? It applies to all of us. For all of us live in a world which promises well, but does not fulfil; and all of us (taking our lives altogether apart from religious prospects) begin with hope, and end with disappointment. Doubtless, there is much difference in our respective trials here, arising from difference of tempers and fortunes. Still it is in our nature to begin life thoughtlessly and joyously; to seek great things in one way or other; to have vague notions of good to come; to love the world, and to believe its promises, and seek satisfaction and happiness from it. And, as it is our nature to hope, so it is our lot, as life proceeds, to encounter disappointment. I know that there are multitudes, in the retired ranks of society, who pass their days without any great varieties of fortune; though, even in such cases, thinking persons will have much more to say of themselves than at first sight might appear. Still, that disappointment in some shape or other is the lot of man (that is, looking at our prospects apart from the next world) is plain, from the mere fact, if nothing else could be said, that we begin life with health and end it with sickness; or in other words, that it *comes* to an *end*, for an end is a failure. And even in the quietest walks of life, do not the old feel regret, more or less vividly, that they are not young? Do not they lament the days gone by, and even with the pleasure of remembrance feel the pain? And why, except that they think that they have lost something which they once had, whereas in the beginning of life, they thought of gaining something they had not? A double disappointment.

Now is it religion that suggests this sad view of things? No, it is experience; it is the *world's* doing; it is fact, from which we cannot escape, though the Bible said not a word about the perishing nature of all earthly pleasures.

Here then it is, that God Himself offers us His aid by His Word, and in His Church. Left to ourselves, we seek good from the world, but cannot find it; in youth we look forward, and in age we look back. It is well we should be persuaded of these things betimes, to gain wisdom and to provide for the evil day. Seek we great things? We must seek them where they really are to be found, and in the way in which they are to be found; we must seek them as He has set them before us, who came into the world to enable us to gain them. We must be willing to give up present hope for future enjoyment, this world for the unseen. The truth is (though it is so difficult for us to admit it heartily), our nature is not at first in a state to enjoy happiness, even if we had it offered to us. We seek for it, and we feel we need it; but (strange though it is to say, still so it is) we are not fitted to be happy. If then at once we rush forward to seek enjoyment, it will be like a child's attempting to walk before his strength is come. If we would gain true bliss, we must cease to seek it as an end; we must postpone the prospect of enjoying it. For we are by nature in an unnatural state; we must be changed from what we are when born, before we can receive our greatest good. And as in sickness sharp remedies are often used, or irksome treatment, so it is with our souls; we must go through pain, we must practise self-denial, we must curb our wills, and purify our hearts, before we are capable of any lasting solid peace. To attempt to gain happiness, except in this apparently tedious and circuitous way, is a labour lost; it is building on the sand; the foundation will soon give way, though the house looks fair for a time. To be gay and thoughtless, to be self-indulgent and self-willed, is quite out of character with our real state. We must learn to know ourselves, and to have thoughts and feelings becoming ourselves. Impetuous hope and undisciplined mirth ill-suit a sinner. Should *he* shrink from low notions of himself, and sharp pain, and mortification of natural wishes, whose guilt called down the Son of

God from heaven to die upon the cross for him? May he live in pleasure here, and call this world his home, while he reads in the Gospel of his Saviour's life-long affliction and disappointment?

It cannot be; let us prepare for suffering and disappointment, which befit us as sinners, and which are necessary for us as saints. Let us not turn away from trial when God brings it on us, or play the coward in the fight of faith. "Watch ye, stand fast in the faith, quit you like men, be strong;" [1 Cor. 16:13] such is St. Paul's exhortation. When affliction overtakes you, remember to accept it as a means of improving your hearts, and pray God for His grace that it may do so. Look disappointment in the face. "Take . . . the Prophets . . . for an example of suffering affliction, and of patience. Behold, we count them happy who endure." Give not over your attempts to serve God, though you see nothing come of them. Watch and pray, and obey your conscience, though you cannot perceive your own progress in holiness. Go on, and you cannot but go forward; believe it, though you do not see it. Do the duties of your calling, though they are distasteful to you. Educate your children carefully in the good way, though you cannot tell how far God's grace has touched their hearts. Let your light shine before men, and praise God by a consistent life, even though others do not seem to glorify their Father on account of it, or to be benefited by your example. . . . Persevere in the narrow way. The Prophets went through sufferings to which ours are mere trifles; violence and craft combined to turn them aside, but they kept right on, and are at rest.

Now, I know full well, that this whole subject is distasteful to many men, who say we ought to be cheerful. . . . You will find that lightness of heart and cheerfulness are quite consistent with that new and heavenly character which He gives us, though to gain it in any good measure, we must for a time be sorrowful, and ever after thoughtful. But I give you fair warning, you must at first take His word on trust; and if you do not, there is no help for it. He says, "Come unto Me, . . . and I will give you rest." You must begin on faith: you cannot see at first whither He is leading you, and how light will rise out of the darkness.

You must begin by denying yourselves your natural wishes,—a painful work; by refraining from sin, by rousing from sloth, by preserving your tongue from insincere words, and your hands from deceitful dealings, and your eyes from beholding vanity; by watching against the first rising of anger, pride, impurity, obstinacy, jealousy; by learning to endure the laugh of irreligious men for Christ's sake; by forcing your minds to follow seriously the words of prayer, though it be difficult to you, and by keeping before you the thought of God all through the day. These things you will be able to do if you do but seek the mighty help of God the Holy Spirit which is given you; and while you follow after them, then, in the Prophet's language, "your light shall rise in obscurity, and your darkness shall be as the noonday. And the Lord shall guide you continually, and satisfy your soul in drought: and you shall be like a watered garden, and like a spring of water, whose waters fail not" [Isa. 63:10, 11].

—*Parochial and Plain Sermons* 8:26–40

3.2. CANDIDATE FOR ORIEL FELLOWSHIP

Convinced that his poor performance on the oral examinations for his bachelor's degree was not a true index of his talents, Newman decided to become a candidate for a fellowship at Oriel College. The Oriel fellowships, then the most prestigious at Oxford, were awarded on the basis of competitive written examinations—and Newman felt that his talents lay more in writing than in speaking. On February 5, 1822, some two months prior to the exam, Newman recorded his ambivalent thoughts in his diary:

Today I called on the Provost of Oriel, and asked his permission to stand at the ensuing election. I cannot help thinking I shall one time or other get a fellowship there: most probably next year. I am glad I am going to stand now; I shall make myself known, and learn the nature of the examination. The principal thing seems to be Latin composition, and a metaphysical turn is a great advantage; general mathematics are also required . . . Last 5th of January [1821], I wrote to my aunt: 'I deprecate the day in which God gives me any repute, or any approach to wealth.' Alas, how I am changed! I am perpetually praying to get into Oriel, and to obtain the prize for my essay. O Lord! dispose of me as will best promote Thy glory, but give me resignation and contentment.   —"Autobiographical Memoir," 59–60

3.3. ELECTION AS ORIEL FELLOW

Newman's election as a fellow of Oriel College on April 12, 1822, not only restored his reputation, which had been tarnished by his poor performance on his baccalaureate examinations; it opened the door to a successful future, either in law or government, or in the Church of England. Newman considered his selection as an Oriel fellow, not only as providing career opportunities for the future, but as nothing less than providential—as he indicated in an autobiographical memoir:

As to Mr. Newman, he ever felt this twelfth of April, 1822, to be the turning-point of his life, and of all days most memorable. It raised him from obscurity and need, to competency and reputation. He never wished anything better or higher than, in the words of the epitaph, 'to live and die a Fellow of Oriel.' Henceforth, his way was clear before him; and he was constant all through his life, as his intimate friends know, in his thankful remembrance year after year of this great mercy of Divine providence. Nor was it in its secular aspect only that it was so unique an event in his history; it opened upon him a theological career, placing him upon the high and broad platform of University society and intelligence, and bringing him across those various influences, personal and intellectual, and the teaching of those various schools of ecclesiastical thought, whereby the religious sentiment in his mind, which had been his blessing from the time he left school, was gradually developed and formed and brought on to its legitimate issues.

—"Autobiographical Memoir," 64

4

Anglican Deacon and Priest

4.1. MEMORIZING SCRIPTURE

After deciding to become a clergyman, Newman began memorizing various books of the Bible, a practice he recommended to his sister Harriet in a letter dated October 13, 1823:

If you have leisure time on Sunday, learn portions of Scripture by heart. The benefit seems to me incalculable. It imbues the mind with good and holy thoughts. It is a resource in solitude, on a journey, and in a sleepless night; and let me press most earnestly upon you and my other dear sisters, as well as on myself, the frequent exhortations in Scripture to prayer.

—"Autobiographical Memoir," 72

4.2. PARISH VISITATION

Although his father considered the practice of parish visitation an intrusion on the privacy of parishioners, Newman felt that the practice was beneficial; as he wrote to his mother on July 28, 1824:

About ten days ago I began my *visitation* of the whole parish, going from house to house, asking the names, numbers, trades, where they went to church, &c. I have got through, as yet, about a third (and the most respectable third) of the population. In general they have been very civil; often expressed gratification that a clergyman should visit them; hoped to see me again, &c. &c. If in the habit of attending the dissenting meeting, they generally excused themselves on the plea of the rector being old, and they could not hear him or the church too small, &c.; but expressed no unwillingness to come back. I rather dread the two-thirds of the parish which are to come; but trust (and do not doubt) I shall be carried through it well, and as I could wish. It will be a great thing done; I shall know my parishioners, and be known by them.   —"Autobiographical Memoir," 75–76

4.3. CHANGING THEOLOGICAL VIEWS

Newman's "first conversion" was imbued with Evangelicalism, even though both in doctrinal content and in its extended timing, it differed from the typical Evangelical conversions of his day; indeed, some Evangelicals maintained that he really had not had a conversion. In any case, although Newman remained grateful to Evangelicalism, both for its personal benefit and for its benefit to Christianity, his pastoral experience, along with his theological discussions as a young fellow of Oriel, led him to the conviction that Evangelicalism did not work in fact:

Up to this time the latter [Newman] took for granted, if not intelligently held, the opinions called Evangelical; and of an Evangelical cast were his early sermons, though mildly such. His first sermon, on "Man goeth forth to his work and to his labour until the evening," implied in its tone a denial of baptismal regeneration; and Mr. Hawkins, to whom he showed it, came down upon it at once on this score. The sermon divided the Christian world into two classes, the one all darkness, the other all light; whereas, said Mr. Hawkins, it is impossible for us, in fact, to draw such a line of demarcation across any body of men, large or small, because difference in religion and moral excellence is one of degree. Men are not either saints or sinners; but they are not as good as they should be, and better than they might be—more or less converted to God, as it may happen. Preachers should follow the example of St. Paul; *he* did not divide his brethren into two, the converted and unconverted, but he addressed them all, as "in Christ," "sanctified in Him," as having had "the Holy Ghost in their hearts," and this while he was rebuking them for the irregularities and scandals that had occurred among them. Criticism such as this, which of course he did not deliver once for all, but as occasions offered, and which, when Newman dissented, he maintained and enforced, had a great, though a gradual, effect upon the latter, when carefully studied in the work from which it was derived, and which Hawkins gave him; this was Sumner's "Apostolical Preaching." This book was successful in the event beyond anything else in rooting out Evangelical doctrines from Mr. Newman's creed. . . .

Though the force of logic and the influence of others had so much to do with Mr. Newman's change of religious opinion, it must not be supposed that the teaching of facts had no part in it. On the contrary, he notes down in memoranda made at the time, his conviction, gained by personal experience, that the religion which he had received from John Newton and Thomas Scott would not work in a parish; that it was unreal; that this he had actually found as a fact, as Mr. Hawkins had told him beforehand; that Calvinism was not a key to the phenomena of human nature, as they occur in the world. And, in truth, much as he owed to the Evangelical teaching, so it was he never had been a genuine Evangelical. That teaching had been a great blessing for England; it had brought home to the hearts of thousands the cardinal and vital truths of Revelation, and to himself among others. The Divine truths about our Lord and His person and offices, His grace, the regeneration of our nature in Him; the supreme duty of living, not only morally, but in his faith, fear, and love; together with the study of Scripture, in which these truths lay, had sheltered and protected him in his most dangerous years, had been his comfort and stay when he was forlorn, and had brought him on in habits of devotion, till the time came when he was to dedicate himself to the Christian ministry. And he ever felt grateful to the good clergyman who introduced them to him, and to the books, such as Scott's "Force of Truth,"

Beveridge's "Private Thoughts," and Doddridge's "Rise and Progress," which insist upon them; but, after all, the Evangelical teaching, considered as a system and in what was peculiar to itself, had from the first failed to find a response in his own religious experience, as afterwards in his parochial. He had, indeed, been converted by it to a spiritual life, and so far his experience bore witness to its truth; but he had not been converted in that special way which it laid down as imperative, but so plainly against rule, as to make it very doubtful in the eyes of normal Evangelicals whether he had really been converted at all. Indeed, at various times of his life, as, for instance, after the publication of his "Apologia," letters, kindly intended, were addressed to him by strangers or anonymous writers, assuring him that he did not yet know what conversion meant, and that the all-important change had still to be wrought in him if he was to be saved.

—"Autobiographical Memoir," 104, 107–108

4.4. NEWMAN'S FATHER'S DEATH

The sudden and unexpected last illness of his father made a deep impression on Newman. Fortunately, there was time for father and son to converse, as well as for the son to minister to his father during the final days of his life; as Newman later reflected:

That dread event has happened. Is it possible? O my Father! I got to town on Sunday morning. He knew me; tried to put out his hand, and said "God bless you!" Towards the evening of Monday he said his last words. He seemed in great peace of mind. He could, however, only articulate "God bless you; thank my God, thank my God!" and, lastly, "My dear." Dr. C. came on Wednesday and pronounced him dying. Towards evening we joined in prayer, commending his soul to God. . . . Of late he had thought his end approaching. One day on the river he told my Mother, "I shall never see another summer." On Thursday he looked beautiful. Such calmness, sweetness, composure, and majesty were in his countenance. Can a man be a materialist who sees a dead body? I had never seen one before. His last

words to me, or all but his last, were to bid me read to him the
53rd chapter of Isaiah.   —"Autobiographical Memoir," 79

4.5. REFLECTIONS ON PREACHING

*As was the Anglican custom at the time, Newman wrote out his
sermons in longhand and then read them to his congregation.
He also sent copies of his written sermons to his mother, who
dutifully critiqued them; Newman felt constrained to reply:*

The sermons I send you were not intended for compositions:
you will find them full of inaccuracies. I am aware they contain
truths which are unpalatable to the generality of mankind; but
the doctrine of Christ crucified is the only spring of real virtue and piety, and the only foundation of peace and comfort.
I know I must do good. I may and shall meet with disappointments, much to distress me, much (I hope) to humble me; but as
God is true, He will go with the doctrine: *magna est veritas et
prævalebit*   —"Autobiographical Memoir," 76

The Latin quotation—"the truth is great and will prevail"—
which is from 1 Esdras 4:41, is also the title of a poem by
Coventry Patmore [1823–1896]

4.6. VISITING THE SICK

*Along with visiting the homes of his parishioners, Newman
made it a point to visit the sick. In his private notes, Newman
recorded one of these visits—which indicates "something of the
matter and manner of his pastoral visiting":*

—John C . . . , perhaps thirty-five: had been a coachman, and all
his life in the society of coachmen. . . . For some months past,
hearing he was in a declining way, I have called from time to
time, and particularly left Doddridge's "Rise and Progress." At
length, the day before yesterday, I was sent for. He seemed very
near his end, and was very desirous of seeing me. He talked of

sin being a heavy burden, of which he wished to be released. "God was most merciful in having spared him; and he ought to be most thankful" (and he said it with energy) "that he was favoured with a clergyman to attend him." Such is the substance of the conversation I had with him yesterday and the day before. Today I found that he had suddenly declared the weight of sin was taken off him, and tears burst from him, and he said he was *so* rejoiced. He seems very humble and earnest, and willingly listened to what I said about the danger of deception. I was indeed much perplexed, fearing to speak against the mysterious working of God (if it was His working), yet equally fearing to make him satisfied with a partial repentance and with emotions, and should do harm to his wife, &c. I spoke *very* strongly on our being sinful and corrupt till death; on the necessity of sin being found a burden *always*, on the fear of self-deception and of falling away even after the most vivid feelings; and on the awful state of those who, *having* left religion for their death-bed, could give no *evidence* of their sincerity. All this he seemed to admit, and thanked me very fervently. I am thinking of the *cause* of this. His mother, I see, is a religious woman. She cannot be indiscreet? Doddridge *could* mislead him—or is it the work of the Holy Spirit even in its suddenness?

—"Autobiographical Memoir," 80–81

Doddridge's *The Rise and Progress of Religion in the Soul* is available at *http://www.ccel.org/d/doddridge/rise/rise.htm*.

4.7. "ACCEPTANCE OF RELIGIOUS PRIVILEGES COMPULSORY"

A decade after his ordination to the Anglican priesthood, Newman on March 22, 1835—during the initial years of the Oxford Movement—preached a sermon, "Acceptance of Religious Privileges Compulsory," which emphasized that the call to the "sacred office" of priesthood was a "fearful undertaking" yet a responsibility which priests could accept with the assurance that an "abundance of heavenly aid would be given them."

Another remarkable instance of the force which was put upon men by the early Church, will be found in the then existing usage of bringing such as had the necessary gifts to ordination, without asking their consent. The primitive Christians looked upon Ordination very differently (alas for ourselves!) very differently from this age. Now the ministerial office is often regarded as a *profession* of this world,—a provision, a livelihood; it is associated in men's minds with a comparatively easy, or at least not a troubled life,—with respectability and comfort, a competency, a position in society. Alas for us! we feel none of those terrors about it, which made the early Christians flee from it! But in their eyes (putting aside the risk of undertaking it in times of persecution) it was so solemn a function, that the holier a man was, the less inclined he felt to undertake it. They felt that it was in some sort to incur the responsibility of other men, and to be put in trust with their salvation; they felt it was scarcely possible to engage in it, without the risk of being besprinkled with the blood of ruined souls. They understood somewhat of St. Paul's language when he said that necessity was laid upon him, and woe to him unless he preached the Gospel. In consequence they shrank from the work, as though (to use a weak similitude) they had been bid dive down for pearls at the bottom of the sea, or scale some precipitous and dizzy cliff. True, they knew that abundance of heavenly aid would be given them, according to their need; but they knew also, that even if any part of the work was to be their own, though they were only called on to cooperate with God, that was in such a case fearful undertaking enough. So they literally fled away in many instances, when they were called to the sacred office; and the Church as literally took them by force, and (after the precedent of St. Paul's own conversion) laid necessity upon them.

—Parochial and Plain Sermons 4:60–61

Tutor of Oriel College

5.1. CONCERN FOR STUDENTS' MORAL DISPOSITIONS

Although Newman as a tutor was concerned about the spiritual well-being of Oriel students, he soon discovered that other Oxford teachers were not:

He [Newman] was especially opposed to young men being compelled, or even suffered as a matter of course, to go terminally [i.e., every term] to communion, and shocked at the reception he met with from those to whom he complained of so gross a profanation of the sacred rite. When he asked one high authority whether there was any obligation upon the undergraduates to communicate, he was cut short with the answer, "That question never, I believe, enters into their heads, and I beg you will not put it into them." When he told another that a certain number of them, after communion, intoxicated themselves at a champagne breakfast, he was answered, "I don't believe it, and, if it is true, I don't want to know it."   —"Autobiographical Memoir," 133

5.2. VIEW OF THE ORIEL TUTORSHIP

During Newman's time at Oxford, the fellows of colleges were expected to be celibate Anglican clergyman. When a fellow

decided to marry, he was required to resign his fellowship,
thereby providing vacancies for the election of new fellows.
Unlike Newman, few fellows considered either their fellowship
or their tutorship permanent positions. Similarly, in contrast
to many college tutors who considered their work as basically
secular, but not incompatible with Anglican orders, Newman,
speaking in the third person, considered his tutorship a spiritual
responsibility:

He [Newman] had as deep a sense of the solemnity of the ordination vow as another could have, but he thought there were
various modes of fulfilling it, and that the tutorial office was
simply one of them. As to that vow he has recorded in his Private
Journal what he calls his terror at the obligation it involved.
He writes the hour after he had received the Diaconate, "It is
over; at first, after the hands were laid on me, my heart shud-
dered within me; the words 'For ever' are so terrible." The next
day he says, "For ever! words never to be recalled. I have the
responsibility of souls on me to the day of my death." He felt he
had left the secular line once for all, that he had entered upon a
Divine ministry, and for the first two years of his clerical life he
connected his sacred office with nothing short of the prospect
of missionary work in heathen countries as the destined fulfilment of it. When then, as time went on, the direct duties of a
college exerted a more urgent claim upon him, and he became
Tutor, it must be understood that, in his view, the tutorial office
was but another way, though not so heroic a way as a mission
to idolaters, of carrying out his vow. To have considered that
office to be merely secular, and yet to have engaged in it, would
have been the greatest of inconsistencies. Nor is this a matter
of mere inference from the sentiments and views recorded in
his Journal. On occasion of his Father's death, three months
after his ordination, he observes, "My Mother said the other
day she hoped to live to see me married, but I think I shall
either die within college walls, or as a missionary in a foreign
land," thus coupling the two lives together, dissimilar as they

were in their character. A few years later we find in his verses a like reference to college engagements, not as a clergyman's accident of life, but as his divinely appointed path of duty. He says that he is "enrolled" in a sacred warfare, and that he would not exchange it for any other employment; that he is a "prisoner" in an Oxford "cell," according to the "High dispose" of Him "who binds on each his part"—that he is like the snapdragon on the college walls, and that such a *habitat* was so high a lot that well might he "in college cloister live and die." And, when it was decided that he was to be one of the Public Tutors, and he was about to enter upon the duties of his new office, he says in his Journal, "May I engage in them, remembering that I am a minister of Christ, and have a commission to preach the Gospel, remembering the worth of souls, and that I shall have to answer for the opportunities given me of benefiting those who are under my care." It will be seen presently why it is necessary thus distinctly to bring out Mr. Newman's view of the substantially religious nature of a college tutorship.

—"Autobiographical Memoir," 131–132

5.3. REFORMING THE TUTORSHIP

From the beginning of his tutorship in 1826, Newman had a double goal in mind: first, like the proverbial new broom, to rid Oriel of those students who were not serious about either their studies or their behavior; second, as a tutor, he wanted to provide religious guidance to his students—a responsibility he described as follows:

It was in Easter term, 1826, that Newman entered upon duties which he felt thus sacred, and he commenced them with an energy proverbial in the instance of "new brooms." He was one of four tutors, and the junior of them, and, though it would be very unjust to say of him that he intentionally departed from the received way of the College, it cannot be denied that there was something unusual and startling in his treatment of the undergraduate members of it who came under his jurisdiction. He began by setting himself fiercely against the gentlemen commoners, young men of birth, wealth, or prospects, whom he considered (of course, with real exceptions) to be the scandal and the ruin of the place. Oriel he considered was losing its high repute through them, and he behaved towards them with a haughtiness which incurred their bitter resentment. He was much annoyed at the favour shown them in high quarters, and did not scruple to manifest as much annoyance with those who favoured as with those who were favoured. He had hardly got through his first month of office when he writes in his Private Journal, "There is much in the system which I think wrong; I think the tutors see too little of the men, and there is not enough of direct religious instruction. It is my wish to consider myself as the minister of Christ. Unless I find that opportunities occur of doing spiritual good to those over whom I am placed, it will become a grave question whether I ought to continue in the tuition."

—"Autobiographical Memoir," 132–133

5.4. TUTORSHIP DISPUTE IN RETROSPECT

Forty years after the tutorship dispute, Newman still seems to have had both strong memories and mixed emotions about the conflict: on the one hand, he was grateful to Edward Hawkins for the assistance he had provided to Newman as a young Oriel fellow; on the other hand, Newman still had mixed emotions about the mutual "provocation" which had occasioned their alienation. As Newman reflected in his Apologia *(1865):*

From 1822 to 1825 I saw most of the present Provost of Oriel, Dr. Hawkins, at that time Vicar of St. Mary's; and, when I took orders in 1824 and had a curacy in Oxford, then, during the Long Vacations, I was especially thrown into his company. I can say with a full heart that I love him, and have never ceased to love him; and I thus preface what otherwise might sound rude, that in the course of the many years in which we were together afterwards, he provoked me very much from time to time, though I am perfectly certain that I have provoked him a great deal more. Moreover, in me such provocation was unbecoming, both because he was the Head of my College, and because, in the first years that I knew him, he had been in many ways of great service to my mind. —*Apologia pro Vita Sua*, 8

5.5. TUTORSHIP LETTERS

In his "Autobiographical Memoir," Newman included excerpts from three letters in regard to his accepting the Oriel tutorship. The first letter to his mother shows his understanding of teaching as a spiritual responsibility:

I have a great undertaking before me in the tutorship here. I trust God may give me grace to undertake it in a proper spirit, and to keep steadily in view that I have set myself apart for His service for ever. There is always the danger of the love of literary pursuits assuming too prominent a place in the thoughts of a college tutor, or his viewing his situation merely as a secular office—a menus of a future provision when he leaves college.

The second excerpt comes from a letter written in June 1826 by one of his new students, Thomas Mozley, who later married Newman's sister Harriet:

Newman—my new tutor—has been very attentive and obliging, and has given me abundance of good advice. He has requested me to consider carefully what information and instruction I require for my course of reading, and also to determine what books to take up, and he will have a little conversation with me before the vacation.

The third excerpt is from a letter written by Newman in November 1826 to his sister Harriet about his students:

. . . I have some trouble with my horses [college pupils], as you may imagine, for whenever they get a new coachman they make an effort to get the reins slack. But I shall be very obstinate, though their curvetting and shyings are very teasing.

—"Autobiographical Writings," 114, 116

6

Vicar of Saint Mary's

6.1. "RELIGIOUS JOY":
DECEMBER 25, 1825

As indicated in his diary entry for the day, Newman's first Christmas as an Anglican priest in 1825 was extraordinarily busy: in addition to attending Sunday school both in the morning and afternoon, he also received the children of two families into the church and buried one person; he preached in the morning on Romans 1:16 and in the afternoon on Luke 2:10–11: "And the angels said unto them, Fear not: for, behold, I bring you good tidings of great joy, which shall be to all people. For unto you is born this day in the city of David a Saviour, which is Christ the Lord."

This sermon invites its audience to imagine themselves as shepherds at Bethlehem on the first Christmas and to experience both their initial loneliness and then their joy at the angelic announcement. This sermon takes the form of a homiletic lectio divina*—an extended reflection on a biblical passage in which repetition of biblical phrases are used to intensify the realism of the event. Underlying this homiletic dramatization of the First Christmas is an important doctrinal premise: the Incarnation of the Divine is intended to effect the Divinization of the* Human.

There are two principal lessons which we are taught on the great Festival which we this day celebrate, lowliness and joy. . . .

First, we are reminded that though this life must ever be a life of toil and effort, yet that, properly speaking, we have not to seek our highest good. It is found, it is brought near us, in the descent of the Son of God from His Father's bosom to this world. It is stored up among us on earth. No longer need men of ardent minds weary themselves in the pursuit of what they fancy may be chief goods; no longer have they to wander about and encounter peril in quest of that unknown blessedness to which their hearts naturally aspire, as they did in heathen times. The text speaks to them and to all, "Unto you," it says, "is born this day in the city of David a Saviour, which is Christ the Lord."

Nor, again, need we go in quest of any of those things which this vain world calls great and noble. Christ altogether dishonoured what the world esteems, when He took on Himself a rank and station which the world despises. No lot could be more humble and more ordinary than that which the Son of God chose for Himself.

So that we have on the Feast of the Nativity these two lessons—instead of anxiety within and despondence without, instead of a weary search after great things,—to be cheerful and joyful; and, again, to be so in the midst of those obscure and ordinary circumstances of life which the world passes over and thinks scorn of. . . .

1. First, what do we read just before the text? that there were certain shepherds keeping watch over their flock by night, and Angels appeared to them. Why should the heavenly hosts appear to these shepherds? What was it in them which attracted the attention of the Angels and the Lord of Angels? Were these shepherds learned, distinguished, or powerful? Were they especially known for piety and gifts? Nothing is said to make us think so. Faith, we may safely say, they had, or some of them, for to him that hath more shall be given; but there is nothing to show that they were holier and more enlightened than other good men of the time, who waited for the consolation of Israel. Nay, there is no reason to suppose that they were better than the common run of men in their circumstances, simple, and fearing God, but without any great advances in piety, or any very formed habits

of religion. Why then were they chosen? for their poverty's sake and obscurity. Almighty God looks with a sort of especial love, or (as we may term it) affection, upon the lowly. . . .

The shepherds, then, were chosen on account of their lowliness, to be the first to hear of the Lord's nativity, a secret which none of the princes of this world knew.

And what a contrast is presented to us when we take into account who were our Lord's messengers to them! The Angels who excel in strength, these did His bidding towards the shepherds. Here the highest and the lowest of God's rational creatures are brought together. A set of poor men, engaged in a life of hardship, exposed at that very time to the cold and darkness of the night, watching their flocks, with the view of scaring away beasts of prey or robbers; they—when they are thinking of nothing but earthly things, counting over the tale of their sheep, keeping their dogs by their side, and listening to the noises over the plain, considering the weather and watching for the day— suddenly are met by far other visitants than they conceived. We know the contracted range of thought, the minute and ordinary objects, or rather the one or two objects, to and fro again and again without variety, which engage the minds of men exposed to such a life of heat, cold, and wet, hunger and nakedness, hardship and servitude. They cease to care much for any thing, but go on in a sort of mechanical way, without heart, and still more without reflection.

To men so circumstanced the Angel appeared, to open their minds, and to teach them not to be downcast and in bondage because they were low in the world. He appeared as if to show them that God had chosen the poor in this world to be heirs of His kingdom, and so to do honour to their lot. "Fear not," he said, "for behold I bring you good tidings of great joy, which shall be to all people. For unto you is born this day in the city of David a Saviour, which is Christ the Lord."

2. And now comes a second lesson, which I have said may be gained from the Festival. The Angel honoured a humble lot by his very appearing to the shepherds; next he taught it to be joyful by his message. He disclosed good tidings so much above

this world as to equalize high and low, rich and poor, one with another. He said, "Fear not." This is a mode of address frequent in Scripture, as you may have observed, as if man needed some such assurance to support him, especially in God's presence. The Angel said, "Fear not," when he saw the alarm which his presence caused among the shepherds. Even a lesser wonder would have reasonably startled them. Therefore the Angel said, "Fear not." We are naturally afraid of any messenger from the other world, for we have an uneasy conscience when left to ourselves, and think that his coming forebodes evil. Besides, we so little realize the unseen world, that were Angel or spirit to present himself before us we should be startled by reason of our unbelief, a truth being brought home to our minds which we never apprehended before. So for one or other reason the shepherds were sore afraid when the glory of the Lord shone around about them. And the Angel said, "Fear not." A little religion makes us afraid; when a little light is poured in upon the conscience, there is a darkness visible; nothing but sights of woe and terror; the glory of God alarms while it shines around. His holiness, the range and difficulties of His commandments, the greatness of His power, the faithfulness of His word, frighten the sinner, and men seeing him afraid, think religion has made him so, whereas he is not yet religious at all. They call him religious, when he is merely conscience-stricken. But religion itself, far from inculcating alarm and terror, says, in the words of the Angel, "Fear not;" for such is His mercy, while Almighty God has poured about us His glory, yet it is a consolatory glory, for it is the light of His glory in the Face of Jesus Christ [2 Cor. 4:6]. Thus the heavenly herald tempered the too dazzling brightness of the Gospel on that first Christmas. The glory of God at first alarmed the shepherds, so he added the tidings of good, to work in them a more wholesome and happy temper. Then they rejoiced.

"Fear not," said the Angel, "for behold I bring you good tidings of great joy, which shall be to all people. For unto you is born this day in the city of David a Saviour, which is Christ the Lord." And then, when he had finished his announcement, "suddenly there was with the Angel a multitude of the heavenly host, praising God and saying, Glory to God in the highest, and on earth peace, good will towards men." Such were the words which the blessed Spirits who minister to Christ and His Saints, spoke on that gracious night to the shepherds, to rouse them out of their cold and famished mood into great joy; to teach them that they were objects of God's love as much as the greatest of men on earth; nay more so, for to them first He had imparted the news of what that night was happening. His Son was then born into the world. Such events are told to friends and intimates, to those whom we love, to those who will sympathize with us, not to strangers. How could Almighty God be more gracious, and show His favour more impressively to the lowly and the friendless, than by hastening (if I may use the term) to confide the great, the joyful secret to the shepherds keeping watch over their sheep by night?

The Angel then gave the first lesson of mingled humility and joyfulness; but an infinitely greater one was behind in the event itself, to which he directed the shepherds, in that birth itself of the Holy Child Jesus. This he intimated in these words: "Ye shall find the babe wrapped in swaddling clothes, lying in a manger." Doubtless, when they heard the Lord's Christ was born into the world, they would look for Him in kings' palaces. They would not be able to fancy that He had become one of themselves, or that they might approach Him; therefore the Angel thus warned them where to find Him, not only as a sign, but as a lesson also.

"The shepherds said one to another, Let us now go even unto Bethlehem, and see this thing which is come to pass, which the Lord hath made known to us." Let us too go with them, to contemplate that second and greater miracle to which the Angel directed them, the Nativity of Christ. St. Luke says of the Blessed Virgin, "She brought forth her first-born Son, and wrapped Him in swaddling clothes, and laid Him in a manger." What a wonderful sign is this to all the world, and therefore the Angel repeated it to the shepherds: "Ye shall find the babe wrapped in swaddling clothes, lying in a manger." The God of heaven and earth, the Divine Word, who had been in glory with the Eternal Father from the beginning, He was at this time born into this world of sin as a little infant. He, as at this time, lay in His mother's arms, to all appearance helpless and powerless, and was wrapped by Mary in an infant's bands, and laid to sleep in a manger. The Son of God Most High, who created the worlds, became flesh, though remaining what He was before. He became flesh as truly as if He had ceased to be what He was, and had actually been changed into flesh. He submitted to be the offspring of Mary, to be taken up in the hands of a mortal, to have a mother's eye fixed upon Him, and to be cherished at a mother's bosom. A daughter of man became the Mother of God—to her, indeed, an unspeakable gift of grace; but in Him what condescension! What an emptying of His glory to become man! and not only a helpless infant, though that were humiliation enough, but to inherit all the infirmities and imperfections of our nature which were possible to a sinless soul. What were His thoughts, if we may venture to use such language or admit such a reflection concerning the Infinite, when human feelings, human sorrows, human wants, first became His? What a mystery is there from first to last in the Son of God becoming man! Yet in proportion to the mystery is the grace and mercy of it; and as is the grace, so is the greatness of the fruit of it.

Let us steadily contemplate the mystery, and say whether any consequence is too great to follow from so marvellous a dispensation; any mystery so great, any grace so overpowering, as that which is already manifested in the incarnation and death of the Eternal Son. Were we told that the effect of it would be to make us as Seraphim, that we were to ascend as high as He descended low—would that startle us after the Angel's news to the shepherds? And this indeed is the effect of it, so far as such words may be spoken without impiety. Men we remain, but not mere men, but gifted with a measure of all those perfections which Christ has in fulness, partaking each in his own degree of His Divine Nature so fully, that the only reason (so to speak) why His saints are not really like Him, is that it is impossible—that He is the Creator, and they His creatures; yet still so, that they are all but Divine, all that they can be made without violating the incommunicable majesty of the Most High. Surely in proportion to His glory is His power of glorifying; so that to say that through Him we shall be made *all but* gods—though it is to say, that we are infinitely below the adorable Creator—still is to say, and truly, that we shall be higher than every other being in the world; higher than Angels or Archangels, Cherubim or Seraphim—that is, not here, or in ourselves, but in heaven and in Christ:—Christ, already the first-fruits of our race, God and man, having ascended high above all creatures, and we through His grace tending to the same high blessedness, having the earnest of His glory given here, and (if we be found faithful) the fulness of it hereafter.

If all these things be so, surely the lesson of joy which the Incarnation gives us is as impressive as the lesson of humility. St. Paul gives us the one lesson in his epistle to the Philippians: "Let this mind be in you, which was also in Christ Jesus: who, being in the form of God, thought it not robbery to be equal with God: but made Himself of no reputation, and took upon Him the form of a servant, and was made in the likeness of men:" and St. Peter gives us the lesson of joyfulness: "whom having not seen, ye love; in whom, though now ye see Him not, yet believing, ye rejoice with joy unspeakable, and full of glory: receiving the end of your faith, even the salvation of your souls" [Phil. 2:5–7; 1 Pet. 1:8–9].

Take these thoughts with you, my brethren, to your homes on this festive day; let them be with you in your family and social meetings. It is a day of joy: it is good to be joyful—it is wrong to be otherwise. For one day we may put off the burden of our polluted consciences, and rejoice in the perfections of our Saviour Christ, without thinking of ourselves, without thinking of our own miserable uncleanness; but contemplating His glory, His righteousness, His purity, His majesty, His overflowing love. We may rejoice in the Lord, and in all His creatures see Him. We may enjoy His temporal bounty, and partake the pleasant things of earth with Him in our thoughts; we may rejoice in our friends for His sake, loving them most especially because He has loved them.

"God has not appointed us unto wrath, but to obtain salvation through our Lord Jesus Christ, who died for us, that whether we wake or sleep, we should live together with Him."

Kind witness, thou wast meet at once to dwell
  On His eternal shore;
    All warning spared,
For none He gives where hearts are for prompt change prepared.

Death wrought in mystery; both complaint and cure
  To human skill unknown:—
God put aside all means, to make us sure
  It was His deed alone;
    Lest we should lay
Reproach on our poor selves, that thou wast caught away.

Death urged as scant of time:—lest, Sister dear,
  We many a lingering day
Had sicken'd with alternate hope and fear,
  The ague of delay;
    Watching each spark
Of promise quench'd in turn, till all our sky was dark.

Death came and went:—that so thy image might
  Our yearning hearts possess,
Associate with all pleasant thoughts and bright,
  With youth and loveliness;
    Sorrow can claim,
Mary, nor lot nor part in thy soft soothing name.

Joy of sad hearts, and light of downcast eyes!
  Dearest thou art enshrined
In all thy fragrance in our memories;
  For we must ever find
    Bare thought of thee
Freshen this weary life, while weary life shall be.

Oxford, April 1828
—*Verses on Various Occasions*, 26–28

Discovery of the Patristic Church

7.1. "THE GREEK FATHERS"

During the summer vacation of 1828, Newman began read-
ing the "Apostolical Fathers"; this reading of the Fathers of the
Church helped him develop a Catholic view of the Church and
its sacraments. His admiration for the Greek Fathers is evident
in the following poem, which he wrote during his Mediterranean
voyage:

> Let heathen sing thy heathen praise,
> Fall'n Greece! the thought of holier days
>   In my sad heart abides;
> For sons of thine in Truth's first hour
> Were tongues and weapons of His power,
> Born of the Spirit's fiery shower,
>   Our fathers and our guides.
>
> All thine is Clement's varied page;
> And Dionysius, ruler sage,
>   In days of doubt and pain;
> And Origen with eagle eye;
> And saintly Basil's purpose high
> To smite imperial heresy,
>   And cleanse the Altar's stain.

From thee the glorious preacher came
With soul of zeal and lips of flame,
   A court's stern martyr-guest;
And thine, O inexhaustive race!
Was Nazianzen's heaven-taught grace;
And royal-hearted Athanase,
   With Paul's own mantle blest.

Off Zante, December 28, 1832
—*Verses on Various Occasions*, 102–103

7.2. "RELIGION A WEARINESS
TO THE NATURAL MAN"

On July 27, 1828, the Eighth Sunday after Pentecost, New-man preached "Religion a Weariness to the Natural Man" at the morning service at St. Mary's Church, Brighton, on the text from Isaiah 53:2: "He hath no form nor comeliness; and when we shall see Him, there is no beauty that we should desire Him." After pointing out that "Religion is a Weariness" to many different types of people—children, youngsters, adults, etc.—New-man emphasized that Christians must change their hearts by giving up this world in order to gain the next.

"Religion is a weariness;" such is the judgment commonly passed, often avowed, concerning the greatest of blessings which Almighty God has bestowed upon us. And when God gave the blessing, He at the same time foretold that such would be the judgment of the world upon it, . . . He declared beforehand, that to man His religion would be uninteresting and distasteful. Not that this prediction excuses our deadness to it; this dislike of the religion given us by God Himself, seen as it is on all sides of us,—of religion in all its parts, whether its doctrines, its precepts, its polity, its worship, its social influence,—this distaste for its very name, must obviously be an insult to the Giver. . . .

Let me then review human life in some of its stages and conditions, in order to impress upon you the fact of this contrariety between ourselves and our Maker: He having one will, we

another; He declaring one thing to be good for us, and we fancying other objects to be our good.

1. "Religion is a weariness;" alas! so feel even children before
they can well express their meaning. Exceptions of course now
and then occur; and of course children are always more open to
religious impressions and visitations than grown persons. They
have many good thoughts and good desires, of which, in after
life, the multitude of men seem incapable. Yet who, after all,
can have a doubt that, in spite of the more intimate presence of
God's grace with those who have not yet learned to resist it, still,
on the whole, religion is a weariness to children? Consider their
amusements, their enjoyments,—what they hope, what they
devise, what they scheme, and what they dream about themselves in time future, when they grow up; and say what place
religion holds in their hearts. Watch the reluctance with which
they turn to religious duties, to saying their prayers, or reading
the Bible; and then judge. Observe, as they get older, the influence which the fear of the ridicule of their companions has in
deterring them even from speaking of religion, or seeming to be
religious. Now the dread of ridicule, indeed, is natural enough;
but why should religion inspire ridicule? What is there absurd
in thinking of God? Why should we be ashamed of worshipping
Him? It is unaccountable, but it is natural. We may call it an
accident, or what we will; still it is an undeniable fact, and that
is what I insist upon. I am not forgetful of the peculiar character of children's minds: sensible objects first meet their observa-
tion; it is not wonderful that they should at first be inclined to
limit their thoughts to things of sense. A distinct profession of
faith, and a conscious maintenance of principle, may imply a
strength and consistency of thought to which they are as yet
unequal. Again, childhood is capricious, ardent, light-hearted;
it cannot think deeply or long on any subject. Yet all this is not
enough to account for the fact in question—why they should
feel this distaste for the very subject of religion. Why should
they be ashamed of paying reverence to an unseen, all-powerful
God, whose existence they do not disbelieve? Yet they do feel
ashamed of it. Is it that they are ashamed of themselves, not of

their religion; feeling the inconsistency of professing what they cannot fully practise? This refinement does not materially alter the view of the case; for it is merely their own acknowledgment that they do not love religion as much as they ought. No; we seem compelled to the conclusion, that there is by nature some strange discordance between what we love and what God loves. So much, then, on the state of boyhood.

2. "Religion is a weariness." I will next take the case of young persons when they first enter into life. Here I may appeal to some perhaps who now hear me. Alas! my brethren, is it not so? Is not religion associated in your minds with gloom, melancholy, and weariness? I am not at present going so far as to reprove you for it, though I might well do so; if I did, perhaps you might at once turn away, and I wish you calmly to think the matter over, and bear me witness that I state the fact correctly. It is so; you cannot deny it. The very terms "religion," "devotion," "piety," "conscientiousness," "mortification," and the like, you find to be inexpressibly dull and cheerless: you cannot find fault with them, indeed, you would if you could; and whenever the words are explained in particulars and realized, then you do find occasion for exception and objection. But though you cannot deny the claims of religion used as a vague and general term, yet how irksome, cold, uninteresting, uninviting, does it at best appear to you! how severe its voice! how forbidding its aspect! With what animation, on the contrary, do you enter into the mere pursuits of time and the world! What bright anticipations of joy and happiness flit before your eyes! How you are struck and dazzled at the view of the prizes of this life, as they are called! How you admire the elegancies of art, the brilliance of wealth, or the force of intellect! According to your opportunities you mix in the world, you meet and converse with persons of various conditions and pursuits, and are engaged in the numberless occurrences of daily life. You are full of news; you know what this or that person is doing, and what has befallen him; what has not happened, which was near happening, what may happen. You are full of ideas and feelings upon all that goes on around you. But, from some cause or other, religion has no part, no

sensible influence, in your judgment of men and things. It is out of your way. Perhaps you have your pleasure parties; you readily take your share in them time after time; you pass continuous hours in society where you know that it is quite impossible even to mention the name of religion. Your heart is in scenes and places when conversation on serious subjects is strictly forbidden by the rules of the world's propriety. I do not say we should discourse on religious subjects, wherever we go; I do not say we should make an effort to discourse on them at any time, nor that we are to refrain from social meetings in which religion does not lie on the surface of the conversation: but I do say, that when men find their pleasure and satisfaction to lie in society which proscribes religion, and when they deliberately and habitually prefer those amusements which have necessarily nothing to do with religion, such persons cannot view religion as God views it. And this is the point: that the feelings of our hearts on the subject of religion are different from the declared judgment of God; that we have a natural distaste for that which He has said is our chief good.

3. Now let us pass to the more active occupations of life. Here, too, religion is confessedly felt to be wearisome, it is out of place. The transactions of worldly business, speculations in trade, ambitious hopes, the pursuit of knowledge, the public occurrences of the day, these find a way directly to the heart; they rouse, they influence. It is superfluous to go about to prove this innate power over us of things of time and sense, to make us think and act. The name of religion, on the other hand, is weak and impotent; it contains no spell to kindle the feelings of man, to make the heart beat with anxiety, and to produce activity and perseverance. The reason is not merely that men are in want of leisure, and are sustained in a distressing continuance of exertion, by their duties towards those dependent on them. They have their seasons of relaxation, they turn for a time from their ordinary pursuits; still religion does not attract them, they find nothing of comfort or satisfaction in it. For a time they allow themselves to be idle. They want an object to employ their minds upon; they pace to and fro in very want of an object; yet their

duties to God, their future hopes in another state of being, the revelation of God's mercy and will, as contained in Scripture, the news of redemption, the gift of regeneration, the sanctities, the devotional heights, the nobleness and perfection which Christ works in His elect, do not suggest themselves as fit subjects to dispel their weariness. Why? Because religion makes them melancholy, say they, and they wish to relax. Religion is a labour, it is a weariness, a greater weariness than the doing nothing at all. . . .

4. But this natural contrariety between man and his Maker is still more strikingly shown by the confession of men of the world who have given some thought to the subject, and have viewed society with somewhat of a philosophical spirit. Such men treat the demands of religion with disrespect and negligence, on the ground of their being unnatural. They say, "It is natural for men to love the world for its own sake; to be engrossed in its pursuits, and to set their hearts on the rewards of industry, on the comforts, luxuries, and pleasures of this life. Man would not be man if he could be made otherwise; he would not be what he was evidently intended for by his Maker." Let us pass by the obvious *answer* that might be given to this objection; it is enough for my purpose that it is *commonly urged*, recognizing as it does the fact of the disagreement existing between the claims of God's word, and the inclinations and natural capacities of man. Many, indeed, of those unhappy men who have denied the Christian faith, treat the religious principle altogether as a mere unnatural, eccentric state of mind, a peculiar untoward condition of the affections to which weakness will reduce a man, whether it has been brought on by anxiety, oppressive sorrow, bodily disease, excess of imagination or the like, and temporary or permanent according to the circumstances of the disposing cause; a state to which we all are liable, as we are liable to any other mental injury, but unmanly and unworthy of our dignity as rational beings. Here again it is enough for our purpose, that it is allowed by these persons that the love of religion is unnatural and inconsistent with the original condition of our minds.

The same remark may be made upon the notions which secretly prevail in certain quarters at the present day, concerning the unsuitableness of Christianity to an enlightened age. Men there are who look upon the inspired word of God with a sort of indulgence, as if it had its use, and had done service in its day; that in times of ignorance it awed and controlled fierce barbarians, whom nothing else could have subdued; but that from its very claim to be divine and infallible, and its consequent unalterableness, it is an obstacle to the improvement of the human race beyond a certain point, and must ultimately fall before the gradual advancement of mankind in knowledge and virtue. In other words, the literature of the day is weary of Revealed Religion.

5. Once more; that religion is in itself a weariness is seen even in the conduct of the better sort of persons, who really on the whole are under the influence of its spirit. So dull and uninviting is calm and practical religion, that religious persons are ever exposed to the temptation of looking out for excitements of one sort or other, to make it pleasurable to them. The spirit of the Gospel is a meek, humble, gentle, unobtrusive spirit. It doth not cry nor lift up its voice in the streets, unless called upon by duty so to do, and then it does it with pain. Display, pretension, conflict, are unpleasant to it. What then is to be thought of persons who are ever on the search after novelties to make religion interesting to them; who seem to find that Christian activity cannot be kept up without unchristian party-spirit, or Christian conversation without unchristian censoriousness? Why, this; that religion is to them as to others, taken by itself, a weariness, and requires something foreign to its own nature to make it palatable. Truly it is a weariness to the natural man to serve God humbly and in obscurity; it is very wearisome, and very monotonous, to go on day after day watching all we do and think, detecting our secret failings, denying ourselves, creating within us, under God's grace, those parts of the Christian character in which we are deficient; wearisome to learn modesty, love of insignificance, willingness to be thought little of, backwardness to clear ourselves when slandered, and readiness to confess

when we are wrong; to learn to have no cares for this world, neither to hope nor to fear, but to be resigned and contented!

I may close these remarks, by appealing to the consciences of all who have ever set about the work of religion in good earnest, whoever they may be, whether they have made less, or greater progress in their noble toil, whether they are matured saints, or feeble strugglers against the world and the flesh. They have ever confessed how great efforts were necessary to keep close to the commandments of God; in spite of their knowledge of the truth, and their faith, in spite of the aids and consolations they receive from above, still how often do their corrupt hearts betray them! Even their privileges are often burdensome to them, even to pray for the grace which in Christ is pledged to them is an irksome task. They know that God's service is perfect freedom, and they are convinced, both in their reason and from their own experience of it, that it is true happiness; still they confess withal the strange reluctance of their nature to love their Maker and His Service. And this is the point in question; not only the mass of mankind, but even the confirmed servants of Christ, witness to the opposition which exists between their own nature and the demands of religion.

This then is the remarkable fact which I proposed to show. Can we doubt that man's will runs contrary to God's will—that the view which the inspired word takes of our present life, and of our destiny, does not satisfy us, as it rightly ought to do? that Christ hath no form nor comeliness in our eyes; and though we see Him, we see no desirable beauty in Him? That holy, merciful, and meek Saviour, the Eternal, the Only-begotten Son of God, our friend and infinite benefactor—He who left the glory of His Father and died for us, who has promised us the overflowing riches of His grace both here and hereafter, He is a light shining in a dark place, and "the darkness comprehendeth it not." "Light is come into the world and men love darkness rather than light." The nature of man is flesh, and that which is born of the flesh is flesh, and ever must so remain; it never can discern, love, accept, the holy doctrines of the Gospel. It will occupy itself in various ways, it will take interest in things of sense and time, but it can never be religious. It is at enmity with God. . . .

It is then plain enough, though Scripture said not a word on the subject, that if we would be happy in the world to come, we must make us new hearts, and begin to love the things we naturally do not love. Viewing it as a practical point, the end of the whole matter is this, we must be changed; for we cannot, we cannot expect the system of the universe to come over to us; the inhabitants of heaven, the numberless creations of Angels, the glorious company of the Apostles, the goodly fellowship of the Prophets, the noble army of Martyrs, the holy Church universal, the Will and Attributes of God, these are fixed. We must go over to them. . . . It is a plain matter of self-interest, to turn our thoughts to the means of changing our hearts, putting out of the question our duty towards God and Christ, our Saviour and Redeemer. . . . It is not His loss that we love Him not, it is our loss. He is All-blessed whatever becomes of us. He is not less blessed because we are far from Him. It is we who are not blessed, except as we approach Him, except as we are like Him, except as we love Him. Woe unto us, if in the day in which He comes from Heaven we see nothing desirable or gracious in His wounds; but instead, have made for ourselves an ideal blessedness, different from that which will be manifested to us in Him. Woe unto us, if we have made pride, or selfishness, or the carnal mind, our standard of perfection and truth; if our eyes have grown dim, and our hearts gross, as regards the true light of men, and the glory of the Eternal Father. May He Himself save us from our self-delusions, whatever they are, and enable us to give up this world, that we may gain the next;—and to rejoice in Him, who had no home of His own, no place to lay His head, who was poor and lowly, and despised and rejected, and tormented and slain!   —*Parochial and Plain Sermons* 7:13–26

8

Mediterranean Pilgrim

8.1. "WANDERINGS"

As the Hermes, *the ship carrying Newman and the Froudes, sailed away from England, the last visible point on the horizon was "The Lizard," a peninsula in southwestern Cornwall—a view that prompted Newman to reflect about leaving home—familial and earthly:*

> Ere yet I left home's youthful shrine,
>   My heart and hope were stored
> I went afar; the world unroll'd
>   Her many-pictured page;
>
> I stored the marvels which she told,
>   And trusted to her gage.
> Her pleasures quaff'd, I sought awhile
>   The scenes I prized before;
>
> But parent's praise and sister's smile
>   Stirr'd my cold heart no more.
> So ever sear, so ever cloy
>   Earth's favours as they fade;
> Since Adam lost for one fierce joy
>   His Eden's sacred shade.
>
> —Off the Lizard, December 8, 1832
> *Verses on Various Occasions,* 75–76

87

8.2. "THE IMMORTALITY OF THE SOUL"

En route to Rome, Newman and the Froudes spent the last two weeks of February in Naples, where Newman preached at the afternoon service in the British Ambassador's Chapel on Sunday February 24, 1833, on the text: "What shall a man give in exchange for his soul?" (Matt. 16:26). Newman's sermon contrasted the pagan view that people should be merry in the present, for "Tomorrow we die," with the basic appeal and promise of Christianity: a future life. Regrettably, however, many Christians forget that they have been regenerated through Baptism and live like pagans, heedless of the immortality of their soul and the fact that God made it.

I suppose there is no tolerably informed Christian but considers he has a correct notion of the difference between our religion and the paganism which it supplanted. Every one, if asked what it is we have gained by the Gospel, will promptly answer, that we have gained the knowledge of our immortality, of our having souls which will live for ever; that the heathen did not know this, but that Christ taught it, and that His disciples know it. Every one will say, and say truly, that this was the great and solemn doctrine which gave the Gospel a claim to be heard when first preached, which arrested the thoughtless multitudes, who were busied in the pleasures and pursuits of this life, awed them with the vision of the life to come, and sobered them till they turned to God with a true heart. It will be said, and said truly, that this doctrine of a future life was the doctrine which broke the power and the fascination of paganism. The poor benighted heathen were engaged in all the frivolities and absurdities of a false ritual, which had obscured the light of nature. They knew God, but they forsook Him for the inventions of men; they made protectors and guardians for themselves; and had "gods many and lords many" [1 Cor. 8:5]. They had their profane worship, their gaudy processions, their indulgent creed, their easy observances, their sensual festivities, their childish extravagances, such as might suitably be the religion of beings who were to live for seventy or eighty years, and then die once for all, never to live again. "Let us eat and drink, for tomorrow we die," was their doctrine and their rule of life. "Tomorrow we die;"—this the Holy Apostles admitted. They taught so far *as* the heathen; "Tomorrow we die;" but then they added, "And after death *the judgment*;"—judgment upon the eternal soul, which lives in spite of the death of the body. And this was the truth, which awakened men to the necessity of having a better and deeper religion than that which had spread over the earth, when Christ came,—which so wrought upon them that they left that old false worship of theirs, and it fell. Yes! though throned in all the power of the world, a sight such as eye had never before seen, though supported by the great and the many, the magnificence of kings, and the stubbornness of people, it fell. Its ruins remain scattered over the face of the earth; the shattered works of its great upholder, that fierce enemy of God, the Pagan Roman Empire. Those ruins are found even among themselves, and show how marvellously great was its power, and therefore how much more powerful was that which broke its power; and this was the doctrine of the immortality of the soul. So entire is the revolution which is produced among men, wherever this high truth is really received.

I have said that every one of us is able fluently to speak of this doctrine, and is aware that the knowledge of it forms the fundamental difference between our state and that of the heathen. And yet, in spite of our being able to speak about it and our "form of knowledge" [Rom. 2:20] (as St. Paul terms it), there seems scarcely room to doubt, that the greater number of those who are called Christians in no true sense realize it in their own minds at all. Indeed, it is a very difficult thing to bring home to us, and to feel, that we have souls; and there cannot be a more fatal mistake than to suppose we see what the doctrine means, as soon as we can use the words which signify it. So great a thing is it to understand that we have souls, that the knowing it, taken in connection with its results, is all one with *being serious*, i.e., truly religious. To discern our immortality is necessarily connected with fear and trembling and repentance, in the case of every Christian. Who is there but would be sobered by an actual sight of the flames of hell fire and the souls therein hopelessly enclosed? Would not all his thoughts be drawn to that awful sight, so that he would stand still gazing fixedly upon it, and forgetting everything else; seeing nothing else, hearing nothing, engrossed with the contemplation of it; and when the sight was withdrawn, still having it fixed in his memory, so that he would be henceforth dead to the pleasures and employments of this world, considered in themselves, thinking of them only in their reference to that fearful vision? This would be the overpowering effect of such a disclosure, whether it actually led a man to repentance or not. And thus absorbed in the thought of the life to come are they who really and heartily receive the words of Christ and His Apostles. Yet to this state of mind, and therefore to this true knowledge, the multitude of men called Christians are certainly strangers; a thick veil is drawn over their eyes; and in spite of their being able to talk of the doctrine, they are as if they never had heard of it. They go on just as the heathen did of old: they eat, they drink; or they amuse themselves in vanities, and live in the world, without fear and without sorrow, just as if God had not declared that their conduct in this life would decide their destiny in the next; just as if they either had no souls, or had nothing or little to do with the saving of them, which was the creed of the heathen.

Now let us consider what it is to bring home to ourselves that we have souls, and in what the especial difficulty of it lies; for this may be of use to us in our attempt to realize that awful truth. We are from our birth apparently dependent on things about us. We see and feel that we could not live or go forward without the aid of man. To a child this world is every thing: he seems to himself a part of this world,—a part of this world, in the same sense in which a branch is part of a tree; he has little notion of his own separate and independent existence: that is, he has no just idea he has a soul. And if he goes through life with his notions unchanged, he has no just notion, even to the end of life, that he has a soul. He views himself merely in his connection with this world, which is his all; he looks to this world for his good, as to an idol; and when he tries to look beyond this life, he is able to discern nothing in prospect, because he has no idea of any thing, nor can fancy any thing, *but* this life. And if he is obliged to fancy something, he fancies this life over again; just as the heathen, when they reflected on those traditions of another life, which were floating among them, could but fancy the happiness of the blessed to consist in the enjoyment of the sun, and the sky, and the earth, as before, only as if these were to be more splendid than they are now.

To understand that we have souls, is to feel our separation from things visible, our independence of them, our distinct existence in ourselves, our individuality, our power of acting for ourselves this way or that way, our accountableness for what we do. These are the great truths which lie wrapped up indeed even in a child's mind, and which God's grace can unfold there in spite of the influence of the external world; but at first this outward world prevails. We look off from self to the things around us, and forget ourselves in them. Such is our state,—a depending for support on the reeds which are no stay, and overlooking our real strength,—at the time when God begins His process of reclaiming us to a truer view of our place in His great system of providence. And when He visits us, then in a little while there is a stirring within us. The unprofitableness and feebleness of the things of this world are forced upon our minds; they promise but cannot perform, they disappoint us. Or, if they do perform what they promise, still (so it is) they do not satisfy us. We still crave for something, we do not well know what; but we are sure it is something which the world has not given us. And then its changes are so many, so sudden, so silent, so continual. It never leaves changing; it goes on to change, till we are quite sick at heart:—then it is that our reliance on it is broken. It is plain we cannot continue to depend upon it, unless we keep pace with it, and go on changing too; but this we cannot do. We feel that, while it changes, we are one and the same; and thus, under God's blessing, we come to have some glimpse of the meaning of our independence of things temporal, and our immortality. And should it so happen that misfortunes come upon us, (as they often do,) then still more are we led to understand the nothing-ness of this world; then still more are we led to distrust it, and are weaned from the love of it, till at length it floats before our eyes merely as some idle veil, which, notwithstanding its many tints, cannot hide the view of what is beyond it;—and we begin, by degrees, to perceive that there are but two beings in the whole universe, our own soul, and the God who made it.

Sublime, unlooked-for doctrine, yet most true! To every one of us there are but two beings in the whole world, himself and God; for, as to this outward scene, its pleasures and pursuits, its honours and cares, its contrivances, its personages, its king-doms, its multitude of busy slaves, what are they to us? noth-ing—no more than a show:— "The world passeth away and the lust thereof." And as to those others nearer to us, who are not to be classed with the vain world, I mean our friends and relations, whom we are right in loving, these, too, after all, are nothing to us here. They cannot really help or profit us; we see them, and they act upon us, only (as it were) at a distance, through the medium of sense; they cannot get at our souls; they cannot enter into our thoughts, or really be companions to us. In the next world it will, through God's mercy, be otherwise; but here we enjoy, not their presence, but the anticipation of what one day shall be; so that, after all, they vanish before the clear vision we have, first, of our own existence, next of the presence of the great God in us, and over us, as our Governor and Judge, who dwells in us by our conscience, which is His representative.

And now consider what a revolution will take place in the mind that is not utterly reprobate, in proportion as it realizes this relation between itself and the most high God. We never in this life can fully understand what is meant by our living for ever, but we can understand what is meant by this world's *not* living for ever; by its dying never to rise again. And learning this, we learn that we owe it no service, no allegiance; it has no claim over us, and can do us no material good nor harm. On the other hand, the law of God written on our hearts bids us serve Him, and partly tells us how to serve Him, and Scripture completes the precepts which nature began. And both Scripture and conscience tell us we are answerable for what we do, and that God is a righteous Judge; and, above all, our Saviour, as our visible Lord God, takes the place of the world as the Only-begotten of the Father, having shown Himself openly, that we may not say that God is hidden. And thus a man is drawn forward by all manner of powerful influences to turn from things temporal to things eternal, to deny himself, to take up his cross and follow Christ. For there are Christ's awful threats and warnings to make him serious, His precepts to attract and elevate him, His promises to cheer him, His gracious deeds and sufferings to humble him to the dust, and to bind his heart once and for ever in gratitude to Him who is so surpassing in mercy. All these things act upon him; and, as truly as St. Matthew rose from the receipt of custom when Christ called, heedless what bystanders would say of him, so they who, through grace, obey the secret voice of God, move onward contrary to the world's way, and careless what mankind may say of them, as understanding that they have souls, which is the one thing they have to care about.

I am well aware that there are indiscreet teachers gone forth into the world, who use language such as I have used, but mean something very different. Such are they who deny the grace of baptism, and think that a man is converted to God all at once. But I have no need now to mention the difference between their teaching and that of Scripture. Whatever their peculiar errors are, so far as they say that we are by nature blind and sinful, and must, through God's grace, and our own endeavours, learn that we have souls and rise to a new life, severing ourselves from the world that is, and walking by faith in what is unseen and future, so far they say true, for they speak the words of Scripture. . . .

Let us, then, seriously question ourselves, and beg of God grace to do so honestly, whether we are loosened from the world; or whether, living as dependent on it, and not on the Eternal Author of our being, we are in fact taking our portion with this perishing outward scene, and ignorant of our having souls. I know very well that such thoughts are distasteful to the minds of men in general. Doubtless many a one there is, who, on hearing doctrines such as I have been insisting on, says in his heart, that religion is thus made gloomy and repulsive; that he would attend to a teacher who spoke in a less severe way; and that in fact Christianity was not intended to be a dark burdensome law, but a religion of cheerfulness and joy. This is what young people think, though they do not express it in this argumentative form. They view a strict life as something offensive and hateful; they turn from the notion of it. And then, as they get older and see more of the world, they learn to defend their opinion, and express it more or less in the way in which I have just put it. They hate and oppose the truth, as it were upon principle; and the more they are told that they have souls, the more resolved they are to live as if they had not souls. But let us take it as a clear point from the first, and not to be disputed, that religion must ever be difficult to those who neglect it. All things that we have to learn are difficult at first; and our duties to God, and to man for His sake, are peculiarly difficult, because they call upon us to take up a new life, and quit the love of this world for the next. It cannot be avoided; we must fear and be in sorrow, before we can rejoice. The Gospel must be a burden before it comforts and brings us peace. No one can have his heart cut away from the natural objects of its love, without pain during the process and throbbings afterwards. This is plain from the nature of the case; and, however true it be, that this or that teacher may be harsh and repulsive, yet he cannot materially alter things. Religion is in itself at first a weariness to the worldly mind, and it requires an effort and a self-denial in every one who honestly determines to be religious.

But there are other persons who are far more hopeful than those I have been speaking of, who, when they hear repentance and newness of life urged on them, are frightened at the thought of the greatness of the work; they are disheartened at being told to do so much. Now let it be well understood, that to realize our own individual accountableness and immortality, of which I have been speaking, is not required of them all at once. I never said a person was not in a hopeful way who did not thus fully discern the world's vanity and the worth of his soul. But a man is truly in a very desperate way who does not wish, who does not try, to discern and feel all this. I want a man on the one hand to confess his immortality with his lips, and on the other, to live as if he tried to understand his own words, and then he is in the way of salvation; he is in the way towards heaven, even though he has not yet fully emancipated himself from the fetters of this world. Indeed none of us (of course) are entirely loosened from this world. We all use words, in speaking of our duties, higher and fuller than we really understand. No one entirely realizes what is meant by his having a soul; even the best of men is but in a state of progress towards the simple truth; and the most weak and ignorant of those who seek after it cannot but be in progress. And therefore no one need be alarmed at hearing that he has much to do before he arrives at a right view of his own condition in God's sight, i.e. at *faith*; for we all have much to do, and the great point is, are we willing to do it?

Oh that there were such an heart in us, to put aside this visible world, to desire to look at it as a mere screen between us and God, and to think of Him who has entered in beyond the veil, and who is watching us, trying us, yes, and blessing, and influencing, and encouraging us towards good, day by day! Yet, alas, how do we suffer the mere varying circumstances of every day to sway us! How difficult it is to remain firm and in one mind under the seductions or terrors of the world! We feel variously according to the place, time, and people we are with. We are serious on Sunday, and we sin deliberately on Monday. We rise in the morning with remorse at our offences and resolutions of amendment, yet before night we have transgressed again. The mere change of society puts us into a new frame of mind; nor do we sufficiently understand this great weakness of ours, or seek for strength where alone it can be found, in the Unchangable God. What will be our thoughts in that day, when at length this outward world drops away altogether, and we find ourselves where we ever have been, in His presence, with Christ standing at His right hand!

On the contrary, what a blessed discovery is it to those who make it, that this world is but vanity and without substance; and that really they are ever in their Saviour's presence. This is a thought which it is scarcely right to enlarge upon in a mixed congregation, where there may be some who have not given their hearts to God; for why should the privileges of the true Christian be disclosed to mankind at large, and sacred subjects, which are his peculiar treasure, be made common to the careless liver? He knows his blessedness, and needs not another to tell it him. He knows in whom he has believed; and in the hour of danger or trouble he knows what is meant by that peace, which Christ did not explain when He gave it to His Apostles, but merely said it was not as the world could give. . . .

—*Parochial and Plain Sermons* 1:15–26

8.3. "LEAD, KINDLY LIGHT"

During his Mediterranean voyage (1832–1833), Newman wrote many poems, which he sent home for publication. While visiting Sicily, Newman became seriously ill; once he had recovered, he hastened to return home, convinced that he had "a work to do in England." En route from Sicily to Marseilles, Newman wrote his best known poem—"The Pillar of the Cloud"—popularly known by its opening lines: "Lead, Kindly Light." This poem expresses Newman's confidence that God's Providence was leading him back to England for a mission, whose dimensions and challenges are still unclear. This poem, which has been set to various musical arrangements— sometimes with additional lyrics—presents the Christian life as a pilgrimage; even though experiencing an "encircling gloom," Christian pilgrims need to be confident that God is guiding them step by step.

THE PILLAR OF THE CLOUD

Lead, Kindly Light, amid the encircling gloom,
    Lead Thou me on!
The night is dark, and I am far from home—
    Lead Thou me on!
Keep Thou my feet; I do not ask to see
    The distant scene—one step enough for me.

I was not ever thus, nor pray'd that Thou
    Shouldst lead me on.
I loved to choose and see my path, but now
    Lead Thou me on!
I loved the garish day, and, spite of fears,
    Pride ruled my will: remember not past years!

So long Thy power hath blest me, sure it still
    Will lead me on,
O'er moor and fen, o'er crag and torrent, till
    The night is gone;
And with the morn those angel faces smile
    Which I have loved long since, and lost awhile.

At Sea, June 16, 1833
—*Verses on Various Occasions*, 156–157

8.4. "HOPE IN GOD—CREATOR"

During his life, Newman wrote many reflections and prayers, which he planned to assemble into a book; however, he never completed this project, which was undertaken by his fellow Oratorian, William Paine Neville (1824–1905), who published Newman's reflections and prayers under the title Meditations and Devotions *in 1893. The following meditation and prayer, which was written by Newman on March 7, 1848, while he was at Maryvale (near Birmingham) and devoting most of his time to the task of establishing the Oratory in England, emphasizes that God as Creator has created each individual for a purpose; each person, in turn as a divine instrument, should trust in God.*

1. God was all-complete, all-blessed in Himself; but it was His will to create a world for His glory. He is Almighty, and might have done all things Himself, but it has been His will to bring about His purposes by the beings He has created. We are all created to His glory—we are created to do His will. I am created to do something or to be something for which no one else is created; I have a place in God's counsels, in God's world, which no

one else has; whether I be rich or poor, despised or esteemed by man, God knows me and calls me by my name.

2. God has created me to do Him some definite service; He has committed some work to me which He has not committed to another. I have my mission—I never may know it in this life, but I shall be told it in the next. Somehow I am necessary for His purposes, as necessary in my place as an Archangel in his—if, indeed, I fail, He can raise another, as He could make the stones children of Abraham. Yet I have a part in this great work; I am a link in a chain, a bond of connexion between persons. He has not created me for naught. I shall do good, I shall do His work; I shall be an angel of peace, a preacher of truth in my own place, while not intending it, if I do but keep His commandments and serve Him in my calling.

3. Therefore I will trust Him. Whatever, wherever I am, I can never be thrown away. If I am in sickness, my sickness may serve Him; in perplexity, my perplexity may serve Him; if I am in sorrow, my sorrow may serve Him. My sickness, or perplexity, or sorrow may be necessary causes of some great end, which is quite beyond us. He does nothing in vain; He may prolong my life, He may shorten it; He knows what He is about. He may take away my friends, He may throw me among strangers, He may make me feel desolate, make my spirits sink, hide the future from me—still He knows what He is about.

O Adonai, O Ruler of Israel, Thou that guidest Joseph like a flock, O Emmanuel, O Sapientia, I give myself to Thee. I trust Thee wholly. Thou art wiser than I—more loving to me than I myself. Deign to fulfil Thy high purposes in me whatever they be—work in and through me. I am born to serve Thee, to be Thine, to be Thy instrument. Let me be Thy blind instrument. I ask not to see—I ask not to know—I ask simply to be used.

—*Meditations and Devotions*, 300–302

9

Early Years of the
Oxford Movement: 1833–1839

9.1. TRACT NUMBER ONE

On July 14, 1833, John Keble preached the "Assize Sermon"—a sermon officially addressed to court officials at the beginning of a new term. Such sermons customarily exhorted the officials to exercise their judiciary functions with equity and justice. Keble, basing his sermon on a verse from the Old Testament—"As for me, God forbid that I should sin against the Lord in ceasing to pray for you: but I will teach you the good and the right way" (1 Sam. 12:23), asked his audience: "What are the symptoms, by which one may judge most fairly, whether or no a nation, as such, is becoming alienated from God and Christ?" Then Keble pointed out omens and tokens of an Apostate Mind in England.

The first of the Tracts for the Times, which was written by Newman though published anonymously, echoed Keble's "Assize Sermon" by calling for people to choose sides in defense of "Apostolical religion." Tract One, which carried the title "Thoughts on the Ministerial Commission: Respectfully Addressed to the Clergy," emphasized that "the times are very evil, yet no one speaks against them." Newman pointed out the need to support the bishops in their struggle against the evils of the day, since the authority of bishops rests, not on their appointment by civil authorities, but by "apostolical descent"; in contrast, the ministers of other churches are not only chosen by the people but are subservient to the people. Viewed in retrospect, Tract One clearly indicated that Newman saw the Church as "Apostolic" both in its ministry and in its doctrine. What Newman did not and could not foresee was that the Anglican bishops would not support his efforts at apostolic ressourcement.

I am but one of yourselves,—a Presbyter; and therefore I conceal my name, lest I should take too much on myself by speaking in my own person. Yet speak I must; for the times are very evil, yet no one speaks against them.

Is this not so? Do not we "look one upon another," yet perform nothing? Do we not all confess the peril into which the Church is come, yet sit still each in his own retirement, as if mountains and seas cut off brother from brother? Therefore suffer me, while I try to draw you forth from those pleasant retreats, which it has been our blessedness hitherto to enjoy, to contemplate the condition and prospects of our Holy Mother in a practical way; so that one and all may unlearn that idle habit, which has grown upon us, of owning the state of things to be bad, yet doing nothing to remedy it.

Consider a moment. Is it fair, is it dutiful, to suffer our Bishops to stand the brunt of the battle without doing our part to support them? Upon them comes "the care of all the Churches." This cannot be helped: indeed it is their glory. Not one of us would wish in the least to deprive them of the duties, the toils, the responsibilities of their high Office. And, black event as it would be for the country, yet, (as far as they are concerned,) we could not wish them a more blessed termination of their course, than in the spoiling of their goods, and martyrdom.

To them then we willingly and affectionately relinquish their high privileges and honours; we encroach not upon the rights of the SUCCESSORS OF THE APOSTLES; we touch not their sword and crosier. Yet surely we may be their shield-bearers in the battle without offence; and by our voice and deeds be to them what Luke and Timothy were to St. Paul.

Now then let me come at once to the subject which leads me to address you. Should the Government and Country so far forget their GOD as to cast off the Church, to deprive it of its temporal honours and substance, *on what* will you rest the claim of respect and attention which you make upon your flocks? Hitherto you have been upheld by your birth, your education, your wealth, your connexions; should these secular advantages cease, on what must CHRIST'S Ministers depend? Is not this a serious practical question? We know how miserable is the state of religious bodies not supported by the State. Look at the Dissenters on all sides of you, and you will see at once that their Ministers, depending simply upon the people, become the *creatures* of the people. Are you content that this should be your case? Alas! can a greater evil befall Christians, than for their teachers to be guided by them, instead of guiding? How can we "hold fast the form of sound words," and "keep that which is committed to our trust," if our influence is to depend simply on our popularity? Is it not our very office to *oppose* the world? can we then allow ourselves to *court* it? to preach smooth things and prophesy deceits? to make the way of life easy to the rich and indolent, and to bribe the humbler classes by excitements and strong intoxicating doctrine? Surely it must not be so;—and the question recurs, on *what* are we to rest our authority, when the State deserts us?

CHRIST has not left His Church without claim of its own upon the attention of men. Surely not. Hard Master He cannot be, to bid us oppose the world, yet give us no credentials for so doing. There are some who rest their divine mission on their own unsupported assertion; others, who rest it upon their popularity; others, on their success; and others, who rest it upon their temporal distinctions. This last case has, perhaps, been too much our own; I fear we have neglected the real ground on which our authority is built,—OUR APOSTOLICAL DESCENT.

We have been born, not of blood, nor of the will of the flesh, nor of the will of man, but of GOD. The LORD JESUS CHRIST gave His SPIRIT to His Apostles; they in turn laid their hands on those who should succeed them; and these again on others; and so the sacred gift has been handed down to our present Bishops, who have appointed us as their assistants, and in some sense representatives.

Now every one of us believes this. I know that some will at first deny they do; still they do believe it. Only, it is not sufficiently practically impressed on their minds. They *do* believe it; for it is the doctrine of the Ordination Service, which they have recognised as truth in the most solemn season of their lives. In order, then, not to prove, but to remind and impress, I entreat your attention to the words used when you were made Ministers of CHRIST'S Church.

The office of Deacon was thus committed to you: "Take thou authority to execute the office of Deacon in the Church of GOD committed unto thee: In the name," &c.

And the priesthood thus: "Receive the HOLY GHOST, for the office and work of a Priest, in the Church of GOD, now committed unto thee by the imposition of our hands. Whose sins thou dost forgive, they are forgiven; and whose sins thou dost retain, they are retained. And be thou a faithful dispenser of the Word of GOD, and of His Holy Sacraments: In the name," &c.

These, I say, were words spoken to us, and received by us, when we were brought nearer to GOD than at any other time of our lives. I know the grace of ordination is contained in the laying on of hands, not in any form of words;—yet in our own case, (as has ever been usual in the Church,) words of blessing have accompanied the act. Thus we have confessed before GOD our belief, that through the Bishop who ordained us, we received the HOLY GHOST, the power to bind and to loose, to administer the Sacraments, and to preach. Now *how* is he able to give these great gifts? *Whence* is his right? Are these words idle, (which would be taking GOD'S name in vain,) or do they express merely a wish, (which surely is very far below their meaning,) or do they not rather indicate that the Speaker is conveying a gift? Surely they can mean nothing short of this. But whence, I ask, his right to do so? Has he any right, except as having received the power from those who consecrated him to be a Bishop? He could not give what he had never received. It is plain then that he but *transmits*; and that the Christian Ministry is a *succession*. And if we trace back the power of ordination from hand to hand, of course we shall come to the Apostles at last. We know we do, as a plain historical fact; and therefore all we, who have been ordained Clergy, in the very form of our ordination acknowledged the doctrine of the APOSTOLICAL SUCCESSION.

And for the same reason, we must necessarily consider none to be *really* ordained who have not thus been ordained. For if ordination is a divine ordinance, it must be necessary; and if it is not a divine ordinance, how dare we use it? Therefore all who use it, all of *us*, must consider it necessary. As well might we pretend the Sacraments are not necessary to Salvation, while we make use of the offices of the Liturgy; for when GOD appoints means of grace, they are *the* means.

I do not see how any one can escape from this plain view of the subject, except, (as I have already hinted,) by declaring, that the words do not mean all that they say. But only reflect what a most unseemly time for random words is that, in which Ministers are set apart for their office. Do we not adopt a Liturgy, *in order to* hinder inconsiderate idle language, and shall we, in the most sacred of all services, write down, subscribe, and use again and again forms of speech, which have not been weighed, and cannot be taken strictly?

Therefore, my dear Brethren, act up to your professions. Let it not be said that you have neglected a gift; for if you have the Spirit of the Apostles on you, surely this *is* a great gift. "Stir up the gift of GOD which is in you." Make much of it. Show your value of it. Keep it before your minds as an honourable badge, far higher than that secular respectability, or cultivation, or polish, or learning, or rank, which gives you a hearing with the many. Tell *them* of your gift. The times will soon drive you to do this, if you mean to be still any thing. But wait not for the times. Do not be compelled, by the world's forsaking you, to recur as if unwillingly to the high source of your authority. Speak out now, before you are forced, both as glorying in your privilege, and to ensure your rightful honour from your people. A notion has gone abroad, that they can take away your power. They think they have given and can take it away. They think it lies in the Church property, and they know that they have politically the power to confiscate that property. They have been deluded into a notion that present palpable usefulness, produceable results, acceptableness to your flocks, that these and such like are the test of your Divine commission. Enlighten them in this matter. Exalt our Holy Fathers, the Bishops, as the Representatives of the Apostles, and the Angels of the Churches; and magnify your office, as being ordained by them to take part in their Ministry.

But, if you will not adopt my view of the subject, which I offer to you, not doubtingly, yet (I hope) respectfully, at all events, CHOOSE YOUR SIDE. To remain neuter much longer will be itself to take a part. *Choose* your side; since side you shortly must, with one or other party, even though you do nothing. Fear to be of those, whose line is decided for them by chance circumstances, and who may perchance find themselves with the enemies of CHRIST, while they think but to remove themselves from worldly politics. Such abstinence is impossible in troublous times. HE THAT IS NOT WITH ME, IS AGAINST ME, AND HE THAT GATHERETH NOT WITH ME SCATTERETH ABROAD.

9.2. "CHRISTIAN ZEAL"

Newman preached this sermon at Oxford in St. Mary's Church on the Feast of Saints Simon and Jude (October 28, 1834) on the text of John 2:17: "The zeal of Thine house hath eaten Me up." In reflecting on the feast day and its texts, Newman pointed out that Christian zeal implies love for the Truth and for the Church; in contrast to those who equate zeal with intolerance, Newman described zeal as an "imperfect virtue" that needs to be complemented by love and faith. Newman concluded with some criticisms of the Roman Church and those who make zeal into a political weapon.

The Apostles commemorated on this Festival direct our attention to the subject of Zeal, which I propose to consider, under the guidance of our Saviour's example, as suggested by the text. St. Simon is called Zelotes, which means the Zealous; a title given him (as is supposed) from his belonging before his conversion to the Jewish sect of Zealots, which professed extraordinary Zeal for the law. Anyhow, the appellation marks him as distinguished for this particular Christian grace. St. Jude's Epistle, which forms part of the service of the day, is almost wholly upon the duty of manifesting Zeal for Gospel Truth, and opens with a direct exhortation to "contend earnestly for the Faith once delivered to the Saints." The Collect also indirectly reminds us of the same duty, for it prays that all the members of the Church may be united in spirit by the Apostles' doctrine; and what are these but the words of Zeal, viz. of a love for the Truth and the Church so strong as not to allow that man should divide what God hath joined together?

However, it will be a more simple account of Zeal, to call it the earnest desire for God's honour, leading to strenuous and bold deeds in His behalf; and that in spite of all obstacles. . . .

1. Now, Zeal is one of the elementary religious qualifications; that is, one of those which are essential in the very notion of a religious man. A man cannot be said to be in earnest in religion, till he magnifies his God and Saviour; till he so far consecrates and exalts the thought of Him in his heart, as an object of praise, and adoration, and rejoicing, as to be pained and grieved at dishonour shown to Him, and eager to avenge Him. In a word, a religious temper is one of loyalty towards God; and we all know what is meant by being loyal from the experience of civil matters. To be loyal is not merely to obey; but to obey with promptitude, energy, dutifulness, disinterested devotion, disregard of consequences. And such is Zeal, except that it is ever attended with that reverential feeling which is due from a creature and a sinner towards his Maker, and towards Him alone. It is the main principle in *all* religious service to love God above all things; now, Zeal is to love Him above all men, above our dearest and most intimate friends. . . .

Zeal is the very consecration of God's Ministers to their office. Accordingly our Blessed Saviour, the One Great High Priest, the Antitype of all Priests who went before Him and the Lord and Strength of all who come after, began His manifestation of

Himself by two acts of Zeal. When twelve years old he deigned to put before us in representation the sacredness of this duty, when He remained in the Temple "while His father and mother sought Him sorrowing," and on their finding Him, returned answer, "Wist ye not that I must be about My Father's business?" And again, at the opening of His public Ministry, He went into the Temple, and "made a scourge of small cords, and drove out the sheep and oxen, and overthrew the changers' tables" [Luke 2:48, 49; John 2:15] that profaned it: thus fulfilling the prophecy contained in the text, "The Zeal of Thine house hath eaten Me up."

Being thus consumed by Zeal Himself, no wonder He should choose His followers from among the Zealous. James and John, whom He called Boanerges, the sons of Thunder, had warm hearts, when He called them, however wanting in knowledge; and felt as if an insult offered to their Lord should have called down fire from Heaven. Peter cut off the right ear of one of those who seized Him. Simon was of the sect of the Zealots. St. Paul's case is still more remarkable. He, in his attachment to the elder Covenant of God, had even fought against Christ; but he did so from earnestness, from being "zealous towards God," though blindly. He "verily thought with himself, that he *ought to do* many things contrary to the name of Jesus of Nazareth," and acted "in ignorance;" [Acts 26:9; 1 Tim. 1:13], so he was spared. . . .

Thus positive misbelief is a less odious state of mind than the temper of those who are indifferent to religion, who say that one opinion is as good as the other, and contemn or ridicule those who are in earnest. Surely, if this world be a scene of contest between good and evil, as Scripture declares, "he that is not with Christ, is against Him." . . .

In fact we have no standard of Truth at all but the Bible, and to that I would appeal. "To the Law and to the Testimony;" if the opinions of the day are conformable to it, let them remain in honour, but if not, however popular they may be at the moment, they will surely come to nought. It is the present fashion to call Zeal by the name of intolerance, and to account intolerance the chief of sins; that is, any earnestness for one opinion above

another concerning God's nature, will, and dealings with man,—
or, in other words, any earnestness for the Faith once delivered
to the Saints, any earnestness for Revelation as such. Surely, in
this sense, the Apostles were the most intolerant of men: what is
it but intolerance in this sense of the word to declare, that "he
that hath the Son hath life, and he that hath not the Son of God
hath not life;" that "they that obey not the Gospel of our Lord
Jesus Christ, shall be punished with everlasting destruction from
the presence of the Lord;" that "neither fornicators, nor idolaters, nor adulterers, nor covetous, nor revilers, nor extortioners,
shall inherit the kingdom of God;" that we must not even "eat"
with a brother who is one of such; that we may not "receive into
our houses," or "bid God speed" to any one who comes to us
without the "doctrine of Christ"? Has not St. Paul, whom many
seem desirous of making an Apostle of less rigid principles than
his brethren, said, even about an individual, "The Lord reward
him according to his works!" [1 John 5:12; 2 Thess. 1:8, 9; 1
Cor. 6:9, 10, 11; 2 John 10, 11; 2 Tim. 4:14]. and though we
of this day have not the spiritual discernment which alone can
warrant such a form of words about this man or that, have we
not here given us a clear evidence, that there are cases in which
God's glory is irreconcilable with the salvation of sinners, and
when, in consequence, it is not unchristian to acquiesce in His
judgments upon them? . . .

   Such is Zeal, a Christian grace to the last, while it is also an
elementary virtue; equally belonging to the young convert and
the matured believer; displayed by Moses at the first, when he
slew the Egyptian, and by St. Paul in his last hours, while he was
reaching forth his hand for his heavenly crown.

   2. On the other hand, Zeal is an imperfect virtue; that is, in
our fallen state, it will ever be attended by unchristian feelings, if
it is cherished by itself. This is the case with many other tempers
of mind which yet are absolutely required of us. Who denies that
it is a duty in the returning sinner to feel abhorrence of his past
offences, and a dread of God's anger? yet such feelings, unless
faith accompany them, lead to an unfruitful remorse, to despair,
to hardened pride; or again, to perverse superstitions. Not that

humiliation is wrong in any sense or degree, but it induces collateral weaknesses or sins, from unduly exciting one side of our imperfect nature. Mercy becomes weakness, when unattended by a sense of justice and firmness: the wisdom of the serpent becomes craft, unless it be received into the harmlessness of the dove. And Zeal, in like manner, though an essential part of a Christian temper, is but a part; and is in itself imperfect, even for the very reason that it is elementary. Hence it appropriately fills so prominent a place in the Jewish Dispensation, which was intended to lay the foundations, as of Christian Faith, so of the Christian character. Whether we read the injunctions delivered by Moses against idolatry and idolaters, or trace the actual history of God's chosen servants, such as Phinehas, Samuel, Elijah, and especially David, we find that the Law was peculiarly a Covenant of Zeal. On the other hand, the Gospel brings out into its full proportions, that perfect temper of mind, which the Law enjoined indeed, but was deficient both in enforcing and creating,—Love; that is, Love or Charity, as described by St. Paul in his first Epistle to the Corinthians, which is not merely brotherly-love (a virtue ever included in the notion of Zeal itself), but a general temper of gentleness, meekness, sympathy, tender consideration, open-heartedness towards all men, brother or stranger, who come in our way. In this sense, Zeal is of the Law, and Love of the Gospel: and Love perfects Zeal, purifying and regulating it. Thus the Saints of God go on unto perfection. . . .

Love, however, is not the only grace which is necessary to the perfection of Zeal; Faith is another. This, at first sight, may sound strange; for what is Zeal, it may be asked, but a result of Faith? who is zealous for that in which he does not trust and delight? Yet, it must be kept in mind, that we have need of Faith not only that we may direct our actions to a right object, but that we may perform them rightly; it guides us in choosing the means, as well as the end. Now, Zeal is very apt to be self-willed; it takes upon itself to serve God in its own way. This is evident from the very nature of it; for, in its ruder form, it manifests itself in sudden and strong emotions at the sight of presumption or irreverence, proceeding to action almost as a matter of feeling, without having time to inquire which way is best. . . . Patience, then, and resignation to God's will, are tempers of mind of which Zeal especially stands in need,—that dutiful Faith, which will take nothing for granted on the mere suggestion of nature, looks up to God with the eyes of a servant towards his master, and, as far as may be, ascertains His will before it acts. If this heavenly corrective be wanting, Zeal, as I have said, is self-willed in its temper: while, by using sanctions, and expecting results of this world, it becomes (what is commonly called) political. Here, again, we see the contrast between the Jewish and the Christian Dispensations. The Jewish Law being a visible system, sanctioned by temporal rewards and punishments, necessarily involved the duty of a political temper on the part of those who were under it. . . . But the Gospel teaches us to "walk by Faith, not by sight;" and Faith teaches us so to be zealous, as still to forbear anticipating the next world, but to wait till the Judge shall come. St. Peter drew his sword, in order (as he thought) to realize at once that good work on which his heart was set, our Lord's deliverance; and, on this very account, he met with that Saviour's rebuke, who presently declared to Pilate, that His Kingdom was not of this world, else would His servants fight. Christian Zeal, therefore, ever bears in mind that the Mystery of Iniquity is to continue on till the Avenger solves it once for all; it renounces all hope of hastening His coming, all desire of intruding upon His work. It has no vain imaginings about the world's real conversion to Him, however men may acknowledge Him outwardly, knowing that "the world lies in wickedness." It has recourse to no officious modes of propagating or strengthening His truth. . . . It plans no intrigues; it recognises no parties; it relies on no arm of flesh. It looks for no essential improvements or permanent reformations, in the dispensation of those precious gifts, which are ever pure in their origin, ever corrupted in man's use of them. It acts according to God's will, this time or that, as it comes, boldly and promptly; yet letting each act stand by itself, as a sufficient service to him, not connecting them in one, or working them into system, further than He commands. In a word, Christian Zeal is not political.

Two reflections arise from considering this last characteristic of the virtue in question; and with a brief notice of these I will conclude.

1. First, it is too evident how grievously the Roman Schools have erred in this part of Christian duty. Let their doctrines be as pure as they would represent, still they have indisputably made their Church an instrument of worldly politics by a "zeal not according to knowledge," and failed in this essential duty of a Christian Witness, viz. in preserving the spiritual character of Christ's kingdom. In saying this, I would not willingly deny the great debt we owe to that Church for her faithful custody of the Faith itself through so many centuries; nor seem unmindful of the circumstances of other times, the gradual growth of religious error, and the external dangers which appeared to place the cause of Christianity itself in jeopardy, and to call for extraordinary measures of defence. Much less would I speak disrespectfully of the great men, who were the agents under Providence in various stages of that mysterious Dispensation, and whom, however our Zeal may burn, we must in very Charity believe to be, what their works and sufferings betoken, single-minded, self-denying servants of their God and Saviour.

2. The Roman Church then has become political; but let us of the present day beware of running into the other extreme, and of supposing that, because Christ's Kingdom is not based upon this world, that it is not connected with it. Surely it was established here for the sake of this world, and must ever act in it, as if a part of it, though its origin is from above. Like the Angels which appeared to the Patriarchs, it is a heavenly Messenger in human form. In its Polity, its Public Assemblies, its Rules and Ordinances, its Censures, and its Possessions, it is a visible body, and, to appearance, an institution of this world. It is no faulty zeal to labour to preserve it in the form in which Christ gave it.

And further, it should ever be recollected, that, though the Church is not of this world, yet we have assurance from God's infallible word, that there *are* in the world temporal and present Dispensers of His Eternal Justice. . . . Hence, as being gifted with a portion of God's power, they hold an office of a priestly nature, and are armed with the fearful sanction, that "they that resist them, shall receive to themselves Judgment." On this ground, religious Rulers have always felt it to be their duty to act as in God's place for the promulgation of the Truth; and the Church, on the other hand, has seen her obligation not only to submit to them, in things temporal, but zealously to co-operate with them in her own line, towards those sacred objects which they have both in common. . . . May Almighty God, for His dear Son's sake, lead us safely through these dangerous times; so that, while we never lay aside our Zeal for His honour, we may sanctify it by Faith and Charity, neither staining our garments by wrath or violence, nor soiling them with the dust of a turbulent world!

—*Parochial and Plain Sermons* 2:379–392

9.3. "LIBERALISM"

Although Newman was influenced by religious "Liberalism" in his early years as a fellow at Oriel College, by the beginning of the Oxford Movement in 1833, as this poem indicates, he had parted ways with "Liberalism"; this poem, which Newman wrote in Sicily a month before he returned to England from his Mediterranean voyage, is prefaced by an excerpt from the Old Testament (2 Kings 10:28–29).

"Jehu destroyed Baal out of Israel. Howbeit from the sins of Jeroboam Jehu departed not from after them, to wit, the golden calves that were in Bethel, and that were in Dan." [shortened]

> Ye cannot halve the Gospel of God's grace;
> > Men of presumptuous heart! I know you well.
> > Ye are of those who plan that we should dwell,
> Each in his tranquil home and holy place;
> Seeing the Word refines all natures rude,
> And tames the stirrings of the multitude.

And ye have caught some echoes of its lore,
    As heralded amid the joyous choirs;
    Ye mark'd it spoke of peace, chastised desires,
Good-will and mercy,—and ye heard no more;
But, as for zeal and quick-eyed sanctity,
And the dread depths of grace, ye pass'd them by.

And so ye halve the Truth; for ye in heart,
    At best, are doubters whether it be true,
    The theme discarding, as unmeet for you,
Statesmen or Sages. O new-compass'd art
Of the ancient Foe!—but what, if it extends
O'er our own camp, and rules amid our friends?

Palermo, June 5, 1833
—*Verses on Various Occasions*, 144–145

10

Crisis Years of the Oxford Movement: 1839–1945

10.1. "LOVE, THE ONE THING NEEDFUL"

On Quinquagesima Sunday, February 10, 1839, Newman preached on the text "Though I speak with the tongues of men and of angels, and have not charity, I am become as sounding brass, or a tinkling cymbal" (1 Cor. 13:1). Newman began this pre-Lenten sermon by pointing out that love is not to be confused with sacrifice or spiritual discernment or faith or almsgiving or even martyrdom. Emphasizing that "man is made to love," Newman recommended that his audience observe Lent by seeking love through self-discipline, especially fasting.

I suppose the greater number of persons who try to live Christian lives, and who observe themselves with any care, are dissatisfied with their own state on this point, viz. that, whatever their religious attainments may be, yet they feel that their motive is not the highest;—that the love of God, and of man for His sake, is not their ruling principle. They may do much, nay, if it so happen, they may suffer much; but they have little reason to think that they love much, that they do and suffer for love's sake. I do not mean that they thus express themselves exactly, but that they are dissatisfied with themselves, and that when this dissatisfaction is examined into, it will be found ultimately to come to this, though they will give different accounts of it. They may call themselves cold, or hard-hearted, or fickle, or double-minded, or doubting, or dim-sighted, or weak in resolve, but they mean pretty much the same thing, that their affections do not rest on Almighty God as their great Object. And this will be found to be the complaint of religious men among ourselves, not less than others; their reason and their heart not going together; their reason tending heavenwards, and their heart earthwards.

I will now make some remarks on the defect I have described, as thinking that the careful consideration of it may serve as one step towards its removal.

Love, and love only, is the fulfilling of the Law, and they only are in God's favour in whom the righteousness of the Law is fulfilled. This we know full well; yet, alas! at the same time, we cannot deny that whatever good thing we have to show, whether activity, or patience, or faith, or fruitfulness in good works, love to God and man is not ours, or, at least, in very scanty measure; not at all proportionately to our apparent attainments. . . .

In the first place, love clearly does not consist merely in great sacrifices. We can take no comfort to ourselves that we are God's own, merely on the ground of great deeds or great sufferings. The greatest sacrifices without love would be nothing worth, and that they are great does not necessarily prove they are done with love. St. Paul emphatically assures us that his acceptance with God did not stand in any of those high endowments, which strike us in him at first sight, and which, did we actually see him, doubtless would so much draw us to him. One of his highest gifts, for instance, was his spiritual knowledge. He shared, and felt the sinfulness and infirmities of human nature; he had a deep insight into the glories of God's grace, such as no natural man can have. He had an awful sense of the realities of heaven, and of the mysteries revealed. He could have answered ten thousand questions on theological subjects, on all those points about which the Church has disputed since his time, and which we now long to ask him. He was a man whom one could not come near, without going away from him wiser than one came; a fount of knowledge and wisdom ever full, ever approachable, ever flowing, from which all who came in faith, gained a measure of the gifts which God had lodged in him. His presence inspired resolution, confidence, and zeal, as one who was the keeper of secrets, and the revealer of the whole counsel of God; and who, by look, and word, and deed encompassed, as it were, his brethren with God's mercies and judgments, spread abroad and reared aloft the divine system of doctrine and precept, and seated himself and them securely in the midst of it. Such was this great servant of Christ and Teacher of the Gentiles; yet he says, "Though I speak with the tongues of men and of Angels, though I have the gift of prophecy, and understand all mysteries, and all knowledge, and have not charity, I am become as sounding brass, or a tinkling cymbal . . . I am nothing." Spiritual discernment, an insight into the Gospel covenant, is no evidence of love.

Another distinguishing mark of his character, as viewed in Scripture, is his faith, a prompt, decisive, simple assent to God's word, a deadness to motives of earth, a firm hold of the truths of the unseen world, and keenness in following them out; yet he says of his faith also, "Though I have all faith, so that I could remove mountains, and have not charity, I am nothing." Faith is no necessary evidence of love.

A tender consideration of the temporal wants of his brethren is another striking feature of his character, as it is a special characteristic of every true Christian; yet he says, "Though I bestow all my goods to feed the poor, and have not charity, it profiteth me nothing." Self-denying alms-giving is no necessary evidence of love.

Once more. He, if any man, had the spirit of a martyr; yet he implies that even martyrdom, viewed in itself, is no passport into the heavenly kingdom. "Though I give my body to be burned, and have not charity, it profiteth me nothing." Martyrdom is no necessary evidence of love.

I do not say that at this day we have many specimens or much opportunity of such high deeds and attainments; but in our degree we certainly may follow St. Paul in them,—in spiritual discernment, in faith, in works of mercy, and in confessorship. We may, we ought to follow him. Yet though we do, still, it may be, we are not possessed of the one thing needful, of the spirit of love, or in a very poor measure; and this is what serious men feel in their own case.

Let us leave these sublimer matters, and proceed to the humbler and continual duties of daily life; and let us see whether these too may not be performed with considerable exactness, yet with deficient love. Surely they may; and serious men complain of themselves here, even more than when they are exercised on greater subjects. Our Lord says, "If ye love Me, keep My commandments;" but they feel that though they are, to a certain point, keeping God's commandments, yet love is not proportionate, does not keep pace, with their obedience; that obedience springs from some source short of love. This they perceive; they feel themselves to be hollow; a fair outside, without a spirit within it.

I mean as follows:—It is possible to obey, not from love towards God and man, but from a sort of conscientiousness short of love; from some notion of acting up to a *law*; that is, more from the fear of God than from love of Him. Surely this is what, in one shape or other, we see daily on all sides of us; the case of men, living to the world, yet not without a certain sense of religion, which acts as a restraint on them. They pursue ends of this world, but not to the full; they are checked, and go a certain way only, because they dare not go further. This external restraint acts with various degrees of strength on various persons. They all live to this world, and act from the love of it; they all allow their love of the world a certain range; but, at some particular point, which is often quite arbitrary, this man stops, and that man stops. Each stops at a different point in the course of the world, and thinks every one else profane who goes further, and superstitious who does not go so far,—laughs at the latter, is shocked at the former. And hence those few who are miserable enough to have rid themselves of all scruples, look with great contempt on such of their companions as have any, be those scruples more or less, as being inconsistent and absurd. They scoff at the principle of mere fear, as a capricious and fanciful principle; proceeding on no rule, and having no evidence of its authority, no claim on our respect; as a weakness in our nature, rather than an essential portion of that nature, viewed in its perfection and entireness. And this being all the notion which their experience gives them of religion, as not knowing really religious men, they think of religion, only as a principle which interferes with our enjoyments unintelligibly and irrationally. Man is made to love. So far is plain. They see that clearly and truly; but religion, as far as they conceive of it, is a system destitute of objects of love; a system of fear. It repels and forbids, and thus seems to destroy the proper function of man, or, in other words, to be unnatural. And it is true that this sort of fear of God, or rather slavish dread, as it may more truly be called, *is* unnatural; but then it is not religion, which really consists, not in the mere fear of God, but in His love; or if it be religion, it is but the religion of devils, who believe and tremble; or of idolaters, whom devils have seduced, and whose worship is superstition,—the attempt to appease beings whom they love not; and, in a word, the religion of the children of this world, who would, if possible, serve God and Mammon, and, whereas religion consists of love *and* fear, give to God their fear, and to Mammon their love.

And what takes place so generally in the world at large, this, I say, serious men will feel as happening, in its degree, in their own case. They will understand that even strict obedience is no evidence of fervent love, and they will lament to perceive that they obey God far more than they love Him. They will recollect the instance of Balaam, who was even exemplary in his obedience, yet had not love; and the thought will come over them as a perplexity, what proof they have that they are not, after all, deceiving themselves, and thinking themselves religious when they are not. They will indeed be conscious to themselves of the sacrifice they make of their own wishes and pursuits to the will of God; but they are conscious also that they sacrifice them because they know they *ought* to do so, not simply from love of God. And they ask, almost in a kind of despair, How are we to learn, not merely to obey, but to love?

. . . And this would seem an especial difficulty in the case of those who live among men, whose duties lie amid the engagements of this world's business, whose thoughts, affections, exertions, are directed towards things which they see, things present and temporal. In their case it seems to be a great thing, even if their *rule* of life is a heavenly one, if they *act* according to God's will; but how can they hope that heavenly Objects should fill their heart, when there is no room left for them? how shall things absent displace things present, things unseen the things that are visible? Thus they seem to be reduced, as if by a sort of necessity, to . . . the state of men of the world, that of having their hearts set on the world, and being only restrained outwardly by religious rules.

. . . Generally speaking, men will be able to bring against themselves positive charges of want of love, more unsatisfactory still. I suppose most men, or at least a great number of men, have to lament over their hardness of heart, which, when analysed, will be found to be nothing else but the absence of love. I mean that hardness which, for instance, makes us unable to repent as we wish. No repentance is truly such without love; it is love which gives it its efficacy in God's sight. Without love there may be remorse, regret, self-reproach, self-condemnation, but there is not saving penitence. There may be conviction of the reason, but not conversion of the heart. Now, I say, a great many men lament in themselves this want of love in repenting; they are hard-hearted; they are deeply conscious of their sins; they abhor them; and yet they can take as lively interest in what goes on around them, as if they had no such consciousness; or they mourn this minute, and the next are quite impenetrable. Or, though, as they think and believe, they fear God's anger, and are full of confusion at themselves, yet they find (to their surprise, I may say) that they cannot abstain from any indulgence ever so trivial, which would be (as their reason tells them) a natural way of showing sorrow. They eat and drink with as good a heart, as if they had no distress upon their minds; they find no difficulty in entering into any of the recreations or secular employments which come in their way. They sleep as soundly; and, in spite of their grief, perhaps find it most difficult to persuade themselves to rise early to pray for pardon. These are signs of want of love.

Or, again, without reference to the case of penitence, they have a general indisposition towards prayer and other exercises of devotion. They find it most difficult to get themselves to pray; most difficult, too, to rouse their minds to attend to their prayers. At very best they do but feel satisfaction in devotion *while* they are engaged in it. Then perhaps they find a real pleasure in it, and wonder they can ever find it irksome; yet if any chance throws them out of their habitual exercises, they find it most difficult to return to them. They do not like them well enough to seek them *from* liking them. They are kept in them by habit, by regularity in observing them; not by love. When the regular course is broken, there is no inward principle to act at once in repairing the mischief. In wounds of the body, nature works towards a recovery, and, left to itself, would recover; but we have no spiritual principle strong and healthy enough to set religious matters right in us when they have got disordered, and to supply for us the absence of rule and custom. Here, again, is obedience, more or less mechanical, or without love.

Again:—a like absence of love is shown in our proneness to be taken up and engrossed with trifles. Why is it that we are so open to the power of excitement? why is it that we are looking out for novelties? why is it that we complain of want of variety in a religious life? why that we cannot bear to go on in an ordinary round of duties year after year? why is it that lowly duties, such as condescending to men of low estate, are distasteful and irksome? why is it that we need powerful preaching, or interesting and touching books, in order to keep our thoughts and feelings on God? why is it that our faith is so dispirited and weakened by hearing casual objections urged against the doctrine of Christ? why is it that we are so impatient that objections should be answered? why are we so afraid of worldly events, or the opinions of men? why do we so dread their censure or ridicule?—Clearly because we are deficient in love. He who loves, cares little for any thing else. The world may go as it will; he sees and hears it not, for his thoughts are drawn another way; he is solicitous mainly to walk with God, and to be found with God; and is in perfect peace because he is stayed in Him.

And here we have an additional proof how weak our love is; viz. when we consider how little adequate our professed principles are found to be, to support us in affliction. I suppose it often happens to men to feel this, when some reverse or unexpected distress comes upon them. They indeed most especially will feel it, of course, who have let their words, nay their thoughts, much outrun their hearts; but numbers will feel it too, who have tried to make their reason and affections keep pace with each other. We are told of the righteous man, that "he will not be afraid of any evil tidings, for his heart standeth fast, and believeth in the Lord. His heart is established, and will not shrink" [Ps. 112:7, 8]. Such must be the case of every one who realizes his own words, when he talks of the shortness of life, the wearisomeness of the world, and the security of heaven. Yet how cold and dreary do all such topics prove, when a man comes into trouble? and why, except that he has been after all set upon things visible, not on God, while he has been speaking of things invisible? There has been much profession and little love.

These are some of the proofs which are continually brought home to us, if we attend to ourselves, of our want of love to God; and they will readily suggest others to us. If I must, before concluding, remark upon the mode of overcoming the evil, I must say plainly this, that, fanciful though it may appear at first sight to say so, the comforts of life are the main cause of it; and, much as we may lament and struggle against it, till we learn to dispense with them in good measure, we shall not overcome it. Till we, in a certain sense, detach ourselves from our bodies, our minds will not be in a state to receive divine impressions, and to exert heavenly aspirations. A smooth and easy life, an uninterrupted enjoyment of the goods of Providence, full meals, soft raiment, well-furnished homes, the pleasures of sense, the feeling of security, the consciousness of wealth,—these, and the like, if we are not careful, choke up all the avenues of the soul, through which the light and breath of heaven might come to us. A hard life is, alas! no certain method of becoming spiritually minded, but it is one out of the means by which Almighty God makes us so. We must, at least at seasons, defraud ourselves of nature, if we would not be defrauded of grace. If we attempt to force our minds into a loving and devotional temper, without this preparation, it is too plain what will follow,—the grossness and coarseness, the affectation, the effeminacy, the unreality, the presumption, the hollowness, (suffer me, my brethren, while I say plainly, but seriously, what I mean,) in a word, what Scripture calls the Hypocrisy, which we see around us; that state of mind in which the reason, seeing what we should be, and the conscience enjoining it, and the heart being unequal to it, some or other pretence is set up, by way of compromise, that men may say, "Peace, peace, when there is no peace."

And next, after enjoining this habitual preparation of heart, let me bid you cherish, what otherwise it were shocking to attempt, a constant sense of the love of your Lord and Saviour in dying on the cross for you. "The love of Christ," says the Apostle, "constraineth us;" not that gratitude leads to love, where there is no sympathy, (for, as all know, we often reproach ourselves with not loving persons who yet have loved us,) but where hearts are in their degree renewed after Christ's image, there, under His grace, gratitude to Him will increase our love of Him, and we shall rejoice in that goodness which has been so good to us. Here, again, self-discipline will be necessary. It makes the heart tender as well as reverent. Christ showed His love in deed, not in word, and you will be touched by the thought of His cross far more by bearing it after Him, than by glowing accounts of it. All the modes by which you bring it before you must be simple and severe; "excellency of speech," or "enticing words," to use St. Paul's language, is the worst way of any. Think of the Cross when you rise and when you lie down, when you go out and when you come in, when you eat and when you walk and when you converse, when you buy and when you sell, when you labour and when you rest, consecrating and sealing all your doings with this one mental action, the thought of the Crucified. Do not talk of it to others; be silent, like the penitent woman, who showed her love in deep subdued acts. She "stood at His feet behind Him weeping, and began to wash His feet with tears, and did wipe them with the hairs of her head, and kissed His feet, and anointed them with the Ointment." And Christ said of her, "Her sins, which are many, are forgiven her, for she loved much; but to whom little is forgiven, the same loveth little" [Luke 7:38, 47].

And, further, let us dwell often upon those His manifold mercies to us and to our brethren, which are the consequence of His coming upon earth; His adorable counsels, as manifested in our personal election,—how it is that we are called and others not; the wonders of His grace towards us, from our infancy until now; the gifts He has given us; the aid He has vouchsafed; the answers He has accorded to our prayers. And, further, let us, as far as we have the opportunity, meditate upon His dealings with His Church from age to age; on His faithfulness to His promises, and the mysterious mode of their fulfilment; how He has ever led His people forward safely and prosperously on the whole amid so many enemies; what unexpected events have worked His purposes; how evil has been changed into good; how His sacred truth has ever been preserved unimpaired; how Saints have been brought on to their perfection in the darkest times. And, further, let us muse over the deep gifts and powers lodged in the Church: what thoughts do His ordinances raise in the believing mind!—what wonder, what awe, what transport, when duly dwelt upon!

It is by such deeds and such thoughts that our services, our repentings, our prayers, our intercourse with men, will become instinct with the spirit of love. Then we do everything thankfully and joyfully, when we are temples of Christ, with His Image set up in us. Then it is that we mix with the world without loving it, for our affections are given to another. We can bear to look on the world's beauty, for we have no heart for it. We are not disturbed at its frowns, for we live not in its smiles. We rejoice in the House of Prayer, because He is there "whom our soul loveth." We can condescend to the poor and lowly, for they are the presence of Him who is Invisible. We are patient in bereavement, adversity, or pain, for they are Christ's tokens.

Thus let us enter the Forty Days of Lent now approaching. For Forty Days we seek after love by means of fasting. May we find it more and more, the older we grow, till death comes and gives us the sight of Him who is at once its Object and its Author.   —*Parochial and Plain Sermons* 5:327–340

10.2. THE "VISIBLE CHURCH":
TRACT XC §4

From his Oriel mentor, Richard Whately, Newman learned the importance of "the Visible Church"; during the Oxford Movement, he began considering the relationship of the Church of England to the Roman Catholic Church. For Newman, the question was not merely theoretical or abstract, but concrete and actual: where is the Church of the Apostles to be found today? In Tract XC (1841), *he took the position that the Anglican doctrinal statement, the* Thirty-Nine Articles, *is basically compatible with the teachings of the Roman Catholic Church. The following excerpt from* Tract XC *is Newman's commentary on the Nineteenth Article: "the Visible Church."*

Article XIX: "The visible Church of CHRIST is a congregation of faithful men (cœtus fidelium), in the which the pure Word of GOD is preached, and the Sacraments be duly ministered, according to CHRIST'S ordinance, in all those things that of necessity are requisite to the same."

This is not an abstract definition of *a* Church, but a description of *the* actually existing One Holy Catholic Church diffused throughout the world; as if it were read, "The Church is a certain existing society of the faithful," &c. This is evident from the mode of describing the Catholic Church familiar to all writers from the first ages down to the age of this Article. For instance, St. Clement of Alexandria says, "I mean by the Church, not a place, but the *congregation of the elect*." Origen: "The Church, the *assembly of all the faithful*." St. Ambrose: "*One congregation*, one Church." St. Isidore: "The Church is a *congregation of saints*, collected on a certain faith, and the best conduct of life." St. Augustin: "The Church is *the people of God* through all ages." Again: "The Church is *the multitude* which is spread over the whole earth." St Cyril: "When we speak of the Church, we denote the most holy *multitude of the pious*." Theodoret: "The Apostle calls the Church the *assembly of the faithful*."

Pope Gregory: "The Church, a *multitude of the faithful* collected of both sexes." Bede: "The Church is the *congregation of all saints.*" Alcuin: "The Holy Catholic Church,—in Latin, the *congregation of the faithful.*" Amalarius: "The Church is *the people* called together by the Church's ministers." Pope Nicholas I.: "The Church, that is, the *congregation of Catholics.*" St. Bernard: "What is the Spouse, but *the congregation of the just?*" Peter the Venerable: "The Church is called *a congregation,* but not of all things, not of cattle, but *of men, faithful,* good, just. Though bad among these good, and just among the unjust, are revealed or concealed, yet it is called a Church." Hugo Victorinus: "The Holy Church, that is, *the university of the faithful.*" Arnulphus: "The Church is called *the congregation of the faithful.*" Albertus Magnus: "The Greek word Church means in Latin convocation; and whereas works and callings belong to rational animals, and reason in man is inward faith, therefore it is called the *congregation of the faithful.*" Durandus: "The Church is in one sense material, in which divers offices are celebrated; in another spiritual, which is the *collection of the faithful.*" Alvarus: "The Church is the *multitude of the faithful,* or the university of Christians." Pope Pius II.: "The Church is the *multitude of the faithful* dispersed through all nations." Estius, Chancellor of Douay: "There is a controversy between Catholics and heretics as to what the word 'Church' means. John Huss and the heretics of our day who follow him, define the Church to be the university of the predestinate; Catholics define it to be the *Society of those who are joined to each other by a right faith and the Sacraments.*"

These illustrations of the phraseology of the Article may be multiplied in any number. And they plainly show that it is not laying down any logical definition *what* a Church is, but is describing, and, as it were, pointing to the Catholic Church diffused throughout the world; which, being but one, cannot possibly be mistaken, and requires no other account of it beyond this single and majestic one. The ministration of the Word and Sacraments is mentioned as a further note of it. As to the question of its limits, whether Episcopal Succession or whether intercommunion with the whole be necessary to each part of it,—these are questions, most important indeed, but of detail, and are not expressly treated of in the Articles.

This view is further illustrated by the following passage from the Homily for Whitsunday:—

> "Our Saviour CHRIST departing out of the world unto His FATHER, promised His Disciples to send down another COMFORTER, that should continue with them for ever, and direct them into all truth. Which thing, to be faithfully and truly performed, the Scriptures do sufficiently bear witness. Neither must we think that this COMFORTER was either promised, or else given, only to the Apostles, but also to *the universal Church of* CHRIST, *dispersed through the whole world*. . . . The true Church is *an universal congregation or fellowship of* GOD'S *faithful and elect people*, built upon the foundation of the Apostles and Prophets, JESUS CHRIST Himself being the head corner-stone. And it hath always three notes or marks, whereby it is known: pure and sound doctrine, the Sacraments ministered according to CHRIST'S holy institution, and the right use of ecclesiastical discipline," &c.

This passage is quoted in that respect in which it claims attention, viz. as far as it is an illustration of the Article. It is speaking of the one Catholic Church, not of an abstract Church which may have concrete fulfilments many or few; and it uses the same terms of it which the Article does of "the visible Church." It says that "the true Church is an *universal* congregation or fellowship of GOD'S faithful and elect people," &c., which as closely corresponds to the *cœtus fidelium*, or "congregation of faithful men" of the Article, as the above descriptions from Fathers or Divines do. Therefore, the *cœtus fidelium* spoken of in the Article is not a definition, which kirk, or connexion, or other communion may, successfully or not, be made to fall under, but the enunciation and pointing out of a fact. —*Via Media* 2:288–290

10.3. "THE PARTING OF FRIENDS"

By 1843, Newman had serious doubt about whether the Church of England could really claim to be the Church of the Apostles and so whether he could continue in good faith to officiate as an Anglican cleric. On September 18, he submitted his resignation as Vicar of St. Mary's and, a week later, preached his final Anglican sermon at the village church in Littlemore—a church which had been dedicated seven years earlier. Preaching on verse 23 of Psalm 104—"Man goeth forth to his work and to his labour until the evening"—Newman cited many biblical examples of "parting."

When the Son of Man, the First-born of the creation of God, came to the evening of His mortal life, He parted with His disciples at a feast. He had borne "the burden and heat of the day;" yet, when "wearied with His journey," He had but stopped at the well's side, and asked a draught of water for His thirst; for He had "meat to eat which" others "knew not of." His meat was "to do the will of Him that sent Him, and to finish His work;" "I must work the works of Him that sent Me," said He, "while it is day; the night cometh, when no man can work" [John 4:6, 34; 9:4]. Thus passed the season of His ministry; and if at any time He feasted with Pharisee or publican, it was in order that He might do the work of God more strenuously. But "when the even was come He sat down with the Twelve." "And He said unto them, With desire have I desired to eat this Passover with you, before I suffer" [Matt. 26:20]. He was about to suffer more than man had ever suffered or shall suffer. But there is nothing gloomy, churlish, violent, or selfish in His grief; it is tender, affectionate, social. He calls His friends around Him, though He was as Job among the ashes; He bids them stay by Him, and see Him suffer; He desires their sympathy; He takes refuge in their love. He first feasted them, and sung a hymn with them, and washed their feet; and when His long trial began, He beheld them and kept them in His presence, till they in terror shrank from it. Yet, on St. Mary and St. John, His Virgin Mother and His Virgin Disciple, who remained, His eyes still rested; and in St. Peter, who was denying Him in the distance, His sudden glance wrought a deep repentance. O wonderful pattern, the type of all trial and of all duty under it, while the Church endures.

We indeed today have no need of so high a lesson and so august a comfort. We have no pain, no grief which calls for it; yet, considering it has been brought before us in this morning's service, we are naturally drawn to think of it, though it be infinitely above us, under certain circumstances of this season and the present time. For now are the shades of evening falling upon the earth, and the year's labour is coming to its end. . . .

"To every thing there is a season, and a time to every purpose under heaven; a time to be born and a time to die; a time to plant and a time to pluck up that which is planted; a time to kill and a time to heal; a time to break down and a time to build up; . . . a time to get and a time to lose; a time to keep and a time to cast away" [Eccles. 3:1–6]. And time, and matter, and motion, and force, and the will of man, how vain are they all, except as instruments of the grace of God, blessing them and working with them! How vain are all our pains, our thought, our care, unless God uses them, unless God has inspired them! how worse than fruitless are they, unless directed to His glory, and given back to the Giver! . . .

We too, at this season, year by year, have been allowed in our measure, according to our work and our faith, to rejoice in God's Presence, for this sacred building which He has given us to worship Him in. It was a glad time when we first met here,— many of us now present recollect it; nor did our rejoicing cease, but was renewed every autumn, as the day came round. It has been "a day of gladness and feasting, and a good day, and of sending portions one to another" [Esther 9:19]. We have kept the feast heretofore with merry hearts; we have kept it seven full years unto "a perfect end;" now let us keep it, even though in haste, and with bitter herbs, and with loins girded, and with a staff in our hand, as they who have "no continuing city, but seek one to come" [Heb. 13:14]. . . .

[*After recalling many examples of partings in the Bible, Newman continued:*]

And what are all these instances but memorials and tokens of the Son of Man, when His work and His labour were coming to an end? Like Jacob, like Ishmael, like Elisha, like the Evangelist whose day is just passed, He kept feast before His departure; and, like David, He was persecuted by the rulers in Israel; and, like Naomi, He was deserted by His friends; and, like Ishmael, He cried out, "I thirst" in a barren and dry land; and at length, like Jacob, He went to sleep with a stone for His pillow, in the evening. And, like St. Paul, He had "finished the work which God gave Him to do," and had "witnessed a good confession;" and, beyond St. Paul, "the Prince of this world had come, and had nothing in Him" [1 Tim. 6:13; John 14:30]. "He was in the world, and the world was made by Him, and the world knew Him not. He came unto His own, and His own received Him not" [John 1:10, 11]. Heavily did He leave, tenderly did He mourn over the country and city which rejected Him. "When He was come near, He beheld the city, and wept over it, saying, If thou hadst known, even thou, at least in this thy day, the things which belong unto thy peace! but now they are hid from thine eyes." And again: "O Jerusalem, Jerusalem, which killest the prophets, and stonest them that are sent unto thee, how often would I have gathered thy children together, as a hen doth gather her brood under her wings, and ye would not! Behold, your house is left unto you desolate" [Luke 14:41, 42; 13:34, 35].

A lesson surely, and a warning to us all, in every place where He puts His Name, to the end of time; lest we be cold towards His gifts, or unbelieving towards His word, or jealous of His workings, or heartless towards His mercies. . . . O mother of saints! O school of the wise! O nurse of the heroic! of whom went forth, in whom have dwelt, memorable names of old, to spread the truth abroad, or to cherish and illustrate it at home! O thou, from whom surrounding nations lit their lamps! O virgin of Israel! wherefore dost thou now sit on the ground and keep silence, like one of the foolish women who were without oil on the coming of the Bridegroom? Where is now the ruler in Sion, and the doctor in the Temple, and the ascetic on Carmel, and the herald in the wilderness, and the preacher in the market-place? where are thy "effectual fervent prayers," offered in secret, and thy alms and good works coming up as a memorial before God? How is it, O once holy place, that "the land mourneth, for the corn is wasted, the new wine is dried up, the oil languisheth, . . . because joy is withered away from the sons of men?" "Alas for the day! . . . how do the beasts groan! the herds of cattle are perplexed, because they have no pasture, yea, the flocks of sheep are made desolate." "Lebanon is ashamed and hewn down; Sharon is like a wilderness, and Bashan and Carmel shake off their fruits" [Joel 1:10–18; Isa. 33:9]. O my mother, whence is this unto thee, that thou hast good things poured upon thee and canst not keep them, and bearest children, yet darest not own them? why hast thou not the skill to use their services, nor the heart to rejoice in their love? how is it that whatever is generous in purpose, and tender or deep in devotion, thy flower and thy promise, falls from thy bosom and finds no home within thine arms? Who hath put this note upon thee, to have "a miscarrying womb, and dry breasts," to be strange to thine own flesh, and thine eye cruel towards thy little ones? Thine own offspring, the fruit of thy womb, who love thee and would toil for thee, thou dost gaze upon with fear, as though a portent, or thou dost loathe as an offence;—at best thou dost but endure, as if they had no claim but on thy patience, self-possession, and vigilance, to be rid of them as easily as thou mayest. Thou makest them "stand all the day idle," as the very condition of thy bearing with them; or thou biddest them be gone, where they will be more welcome; or thou sellest them for nought to the stranger that passes by. And what wilt thou do in the end thereof? . . .

Scripture is a refuge in any trouble; only let us be on our guard against seeming to use it further than is fitting, or doing more than sheltering ourselves under its shadow. Let us use it according to our measure. It is far higher and wider than our need; and its language veils our feelings while it gives expression to them. It is sacred and heavenly; and it restrains and purifies, while it sanctions them. . . .

And, O my brethren, O kind and affectionate hearts, O loving friends, should you know any one whose lot it has been, by writing or by word of mouth, in some degree to help you thus to act; if he has ever told you what you knew about yourselves, or what you did not know; has read to you your wants or feelings, and comforted you by the very reading; has made you feel that there was a higher life than this daily one, and a brighter world than that you see; or encouraged you, or sobered you, or opened a way to the inquiring, or soothed the perplexed; if what he has said or done has ever made you take interest in him, and feel well inclined towards him; remember such a one in time to come, though you hear him not, and pray for him, that in all things he may know God's will, and at all times he may be ready to fulfil it.

—*Sermons on Subject of the Day*, Sermon 26, 395–409

10.4. "TO LIVE IS TO CHANGE"

In order to determine whether the Church of the Apostles continued to exist—and if so, where it was to be found—Newman explored the hypothesis that Christian Doctrine had developed since Apostolic times; not only was this hypothesis original, the very idea of development was original in the middle of the nineteenth century. In An Essay on the Development of Christian Doctrine *(1845), Newman utilized a variety of images and comparisons from nature to illustrate the phenomenon of development; in the following passage, he compared development to a "stream":*

But whatever be the risk of corruption from intercourse with the world around, such a risk must be encountered if a great idea is duly to be understood, and much more if it is to be fully exhibited. It is elicited and expanded by trial, and battles into perfection and supremacy. Nor does it escape the collision of opinion even in its earlier years, nor does it remain truer to itself, and with a better claim to be considered one and the same, though

externally protected from vicissitude and change. It is indeed
sometimes said that the stream is clearest near the spring. Whatever use may fairly be made of this image, it does not apply to
the history of a philosophy or belief, which on the contrary is
more equable, and purer, and stronger, when its bed has become
deep, and broad, and full. It necessarily rises out of an existing
state of things, and for a time savours of the soil. Its vital element
needs disengaging from what is foreign and temporary, and is
employed in efforts after freedom which become more vigorous
and hopeful as its years increase. Its beginnings are no measure
of its capabilities, nor of its scope. At first no one knows what it
is, or what it is worth. It remains perhaps for a time quiescent;
it tries, as it were, its limbs, and proves the ground under it, and
feels its way. From time to time it makes essays which fail, and
are in consequence abandoned. It seems in suspense which way
to go; it wavers, and at length strikes out in one definite direction. In time it enters upon strange territory; points of controversy alter their bearing; parties rise and fall around it; dangers
and hopes appear in new relations; and old principles reappear
under new forms. It changes with them in order to remain the
same. In a higher world it is otherwise, but here below to live
is to change, and to be perfect is to have changed often.

—*An Essay on the Development of*
Christian Doctrine, 39–40

10.5. "ATHANASIUS AND AMBROSE"

In trying to determine whether the Church of the Apostles con-
tinued to exist—and if so, where it was to be found—Newman
not only considered the theoretical aspects of doctrinal devel-
opment, but also posed the question in existential terms: What
church would St. Athanasius and St. Ambrose attend if they
came back to life?

And this general testimony to the oneness of Catholicism
extends to its past teaching relatively to its present, as well as

11

Oratorian

11.1. "FAREWELL TO OXFORD"

Newman left Oxford on February 22, 1846, for Maryvale and then for Rome in September. During his stay in Rome, Newman wrote his first novel, Loss and Gain *(1848), which is the conversion story of a young Oxford student, Charles Reding. Although Newman claimed that "the principal characters are imaginary," the description of Reding's nostalgic departure from Oxford seems comparable to Newman's own:*

There lay old Oxford before him, with its hills as gentle and its meadows as green as ever. At the first view of that beloved place he stood still with folded arms, unable to proceed. Each college, each church—he counted them by their pinnacles and turrets. The silver Isis, the grey willows, the far-stretching plains, the dark groves, the distant range of Shotover, the pleasant village where he had lived with Carlton and Sheffield—wood, water, stone, all so calm, so bright, they might have been his, but his they were not. Whatever he was to gain by becoming a Catholic, this he had lost; whatever he was to gain higher and better, at least this and such as this he never could have again. He could not have another Oxford, he could not have the friends of his boyhood and youth in the choice of his manhood. He mounted the well-known gate on the left, and proceeded down into the plain. There was no one to greet him, to sympathise with him; there was no one to believe he needed sympathy; no one to believe he had given up anything; no one to take interest in him, to feel tender towards him, to defend him. He had suffered much, but there was no one to believe that he had suffered. He would be thought to be inflicting merely, not undergoing, suffering. He might indeed say that he had suffered; but he would be rudely told that every one follows his own will, and that if he had given up Oxford, it was for a whim which he liked better than it. But rather, there was no one to know him; he had been virtually three years away; three years is a generation; Oxford had been his place once, but his place knew him no more. He recollected with what awe and transport he had at first come to the University, as to some sacred shrine; and how from time to time hopes had come over him that some day or other he should have gained a title to residence on one of its ancient foundations. One night in particular came across his memory, how a friend and he had ascended to the top of one of its many towers with the purpose of making observations on the stars; and how, while his friend was busily engaged with the pointers, he, earthly-minded youth, had been looking down into the deep, gas-lit, dark-shadowed quadrangles, and wondering if he should ever be fellow of this or that College, which he singled out from the mass of academical buildings. All had passed as a dream, and he was a stranger where he had hoped to have had a home. . . .

Reding's pathos at losing Oxford was intensified by the chance reading of an article, while he was waiting to meet a friend:

The servant lighted candles in the inner room, and Charles sat down at the fire. For awhile he sat in reflection; then he looked about for something to occupy him. His eye caught an Oxford paper; it was but a few days old. "Let us see how the old place goes on," he said to himself, as he took it up. He glanced from one article to another, looking who were the University-preachers of the week, who had taken degrees, who were public examiners, &c., &c., when his eye was arrested by the following paragraph:—

"DEFECTION FROM THE CHURCH.—We understand that another victim has lately been added to the list of those whom the venom of Tractarian principles has precipitated into the bosom of the Sorceress of Rome. Mr. Reding of St. Saviour's, the son of a respectable clergyman of the Establishment, deceased, after eating the bread of the Church all his life, has at length avowed himself the subject and slave of an Italian Bishop. Disappointment in the schools is said to have been the determining cause of this infatuated act. It is reported that legal measures are in progress for directing the penalties of the Statute of Præmunire against all the seceders; and a proposition is on foot for petitioning her Majesty to assign the sum thereby realised by the Government to the erection of a 'Martyrs' Memorial' in the sister University."

—*Loss and Gain*, Part 3, Chapter 3, 353–357

11.2. ST. PHILIP NERI

Soon after his entrance into the Roman Catholic Church (1845), Newman began considering, not only the priesthood, but also the religious life. He visited a number of different religious communities and considered their way of life both in terms of his own particular gifts and ministerial experience, as well as their suitability for the "English Mission"; eventually he decided to become an Oratorian, the community of St. Philip Neri. In concluding his essay "Duties of the Church towards Knowledge" in his Idea of a University, *Newman described the ministry of St. Philip Neri in a way that not only provides a biographical portrait of St. Philip, but also a vignette of Newman's own ministry as an Oratorian:*

He [St. Philip] lived in an age as traitorous to the interests of Catholicism as any that preceded it, or can follow it. He lived at a time when pride mounted high, and the senses held rule; a

time when kings and nobles never had more of state and homage,
and never less of personal responsibility and peril; when medi-
eval winter was receding, and the summer sun of civilization
was bringing into leaf and flower a thousand forms of luxurious
enjoyment; when a new world of thought and beauty had opened
upon the human mind, in the discovery of the treasures of classic literature and art. He saw the great and the gifted, dazzled by
the Enchantress, and drinking in the magic of her song; he saw
the high and the wise, the student and the artist, painting, and
poetry, and sculpture, and music, and architecture, drawn within
her range, and circling round the abyss: he saw heathen forms
mounting thence, and forming in the thick air:—all this he saw,
and he perceived that the mischief was to be met, not with argument, not with science, not with protests and warnings, not by the
recluse or the preacher, but by means of the great counter-fasci-
nation of purity and truth. He was raised up to do a work almost
peculiar in the Church,—not to be a Jerome Savonarola, though
Philip had a true devotion towards him and a tender memory of
his Florentine house; not to be a St. Charles, though in his beam-
ing countenance Philip had recognized the aureole of a saint; not
to be a St. Ignatius, wrestling with the foe, though Philip was
termed the Society's bell of call, so many subjects did he send to
it; not to be a St. Francis Xavier, though Philip had longed to shed
his blood for Christ in India with him; not to be a St. Caietan, or
hunter, of souls, for Philip preferred, as he expressed it, tranquilly
to cast in his net to gain them; he preferred to yield to the stream,
and direct the current, which he could not stop, of science, literature, art, and fashion, and to sweeten and to sanctify what God
had made very good and man had spoilt.

And so he contemplated as the idea of his mission, not the
propagation of the faith, nor the exposition of doctrine, nor the
catechetical schools; whatever was exact and systematic pleased
him not; he put from him monastic rule and authoritative speech,
as David refused the armour of his king. No; he would be but an
ordinary individual priest as others: and his weapons should be
but unaffected humility and unpretending love. All he did was to
be done by the light, and fervour, and convincing eloquence of

his personal character and his easy conversation. He came to the Eternal City and he sat himself down there, and his home and his family gradually grew up around him, by the spontaneous accession of materials from without. He did not so much seek his own as draw them to him. He sat in his small room, and they in their gay worldly dresses, the rich and the wellborn, as well as the simple and the illiterate, crowded into it. In the mid-heats of summer, in the frosts of winter, still was he in that low and narrow cell at San Girolamo, reading the hearts of those who came to him, and curing their souls' maladies by the very touch of his hand. It was a vision of the Magi worshipping the infant Saviour, so pure and innocent, so sweet and beautiful was he; and so loyal and so dear to the gracious Virgin Mother. And they who came remained gazing and listening, till at length, first one and then another threw off their bravery, and took his poor cassock and girdle instead: or, if they kept it, it was to put haircloth under it, or to take on them a rule of life, while to the world they looked as before.

In the words of his biographer [Pietro Giacomo Bacci], "he was all things to all men. He suited himself to noble and ignoble, young and old, subjects and prelates, learned and ignorant; and received those who were strangers to him with singular benignity, and embraced them with as much love and charity as if he had been a long while expecting them. When he was called upon to be merry he was so; if there was a demand upon his sympathy he was equally ready. He gave the same welcome to all: caressing the poor equally with the rich, and wearying himself to assist all to the utmost limits of his power. In consequence of his being so accessible and willing to receive all comers, many went to him every day, and some continued for the space of thirty, nay forty years, to visit him very often both morning and evening, so that his room went by the agreeable nickname of the Home of Christian mirth. Nay, people came to him, not only from all parts of Italy, but from France, Spain, Germany, and all Christendom; and even the infidels and Jews, who had ever any communication with him, revered him as a holy man."

—*The Idea of a University*, 234–237

11.3. "MEN, NOT ANGELS,
THE PRIESTS OF THE GOSPEL"

As an Anglican, Newman wrote out and read his sermons and later published many of them. Although he often preached from notes in later years, during his first years as a Roman Catholic, he prepared some of his sermons for publication and dedicated his first book of eighteen sermons—Discourses to Mixed Congregations—*to Bishop Nicholas Wiseman. The following excerpt from the third "discourse" highlights the humanness of ordained ministers.*

... He has sent forth for the ministry of reconciliation, not Angels, but men; He has sent forth your brethren to you, not beings of some unknown nature and some strange blood, but of your own bone and your own flesh, to preach to you. "Ye men of Galilee, why stand ye gazing up into heaven?" Here is the royal style and tone in which Angels speak to men, even though these men be Apostles; it is the tone of those who, having never sinned, speak from their lofty eminence to those who have. But such is not the tone of those whom Christ has sent; for it is your brethren whom He has appointed, and none else,—sons of Adam, sons of your nature, the same by nature, differing only in grace,—men, like you, exposed to temptations, to the same temptations, to the same warfare within and without; with the same three deadly enemies—the world, the flesh, and the devil; with the same human, the same wayward heart: differing only as the power of God has changed and rules it. So it is; we are not Angels from Heaven that speak to you, but men, whom grace, and grace alone, has made to differ from you. Listen to the Apostle:—When the barbarous Lycaonians, seeing his miracle, would have sacrificed to him and St. Barnabas, as to gods, he rushed in among them, crying out, "O men, why do ye this? we also are mortals, men like unto you;" or, as the words run more forcibly in the original Greek, "We are of like passions with you." And again to the Corinthians he writes, "We preach not ourselves, but Jesus Christ our Lord; and ourselves your servants through Jesus. God, who commanded the light to shine out of darkness, He hath shined in our hearts, to give the light of the knowledge of the glory of God in the face of Christ Jesus: but we hold this treasure in earthen vessels." And further, he says of himself most wonderfully, that, "lest he should be exalted by the greatness of the revelations," there was given him "an angel of Satan" in his flesh "to buffet him." Such are your Ministers, your Preachers, your Priests, O my brethren; not Angels, not Saints, not sinless, but those who would have lived and died in sin except for God's grace, and who, though through God's mercy they be in training for the fellowship of Saints hereafter, yet at present are in the midst of infirmity and temptation, and have no hope, except from the unmerited grace of God, of persevering unto the end.

—*Discourses to Mixed Congregations*, 44–46

11.4. "THE SECOND SPRING"

Newman was invited to preach at the first Provincial Synod of the newly restored Roman Catholic hierarchy, which met at St. Mary's, Oscott, in 1852. As his text—"Arise, make haste, my love, my dove, my beautiful one, and come. For the winter is now past, the rain is over and gone. The flowers have appeared in our land" (Cant., 2:10–12)—Newman used the image of seasonal changes to describe "the Second Spring" that Roman Catholicism in England was experiencing after the persecution and prejudice that had been the case since the Reformation.

We have familiar experience of the order, the constancy, the perpetual renovation of the material world which surrounds us. Frail and transitory as is every part of it, restless and migratory as are its elements, never-ceasing as are its changes, still it abides. It is bound together by a law of permanence, it is set up in unity; and, though it is ever dying, it is ever coming to life again. Dissolution does but give birth to fresh modes of organization, and one death is the parent of a thousand lives. Each hour, as it comes, is but a testimony, how fleeting, yet how secure, how certain, is the great whole. It is like an image on the waters, which is ever the same, though the waters ever flow. Change upon change—yet one change cries out to another, like the alternate Seraphim, in praise and in glory of their Maker. The sun sinks to rise again; the day is swallowed up in the gloom of the night, to be born out of it, as fresh as if it had never been quenched. Spring passes into summer, and through summer and autumn into winter, only the more surely, by its own ultimate return, to triumph over that grave, towards which it resolutely hastened from its first hour. We mourn over the blossoms of May, because they are to wither; but we know, withal, that May is one day to have its revenge upon November, by the revolution of that solemn circle which never stops—which teaches us in our height of hope, ever to be sober, and in our depth of desolation, never to despair.

And forcibly as this comes home to every one of us, not less forcible is the contrast which exists between this material world, so vigorous, so reproductive, amid all its changes, and the moral world, so feeble, so downward, so resourceless, amid all its aspirations. That which ought to come to nought, endures; that which promises a future, disappoints and is no more. The same sun shines in heaven from first to last, and the blue firmament, the everlasting mountains, reflect his rays; but where is there upon earth the champion, the hero, the lawgiver, the body politic, the sovereign race, which was great three hundred years ago, and is great now? Moralists and poets, often do they descant upon this innate vitality of matter, this innate perishableness of mind. Man rises to fall: he tends to dissolution from the moment he begins to be; he lives on, indeed, in his children, he lives on in his name, he lives not on in his own person. He is, as regards the manifestations of his nature here below, as a bubble that breaks, and as water poured out upon the earth. He was young, he is old, he is never young again. This is the lament over him, poured forth in verse and in prose, by Christians and by heathen. The greatest work of God's hands under the sun, he, in all the manifestations of his complex being, is born only to die.

His bodily frame first begins to feel the power of this constraining law, though it is the last to succumb to it. We look at the bloom of youth with interest, yet with pity; and the more graceful and sweet it is, with pity so much the more; for, whatever be its excellence and its glory, soon it begins to be deformed and dishonoured by the very force of its living on. It grows into exhaustion and collapse, till at length it crumbles into that dust out of which it was originally taken.

So is it, too, with our moral being, a far higher and diviner portion of our natural constitution; it begins with life, it ends with what is worse than the mere loss of life, with a living death. How beautiful is the human heart, when it puts forth its first leaves, and opens and rejoices in its spring-tide. Fair as may be the bodily form, fairer far, in its green foliage and bright blossoms, is natural virtue. It blooms in the young, like some rich flower, so delicate, so fragrant, and so dazzling. Generosity and lightness of heart and amiableness, the confiding spirit, the gentle temper, the elastic cheerfulness, the open hand, the pure affection, the noble aspiration, the heroic resolve, the romantic pursuit, the love in which self has no part,—are not these beautiful? and are they not dressed up and set forth for admiration in their best shapes, in tales and in poems? and ah! what a prospect of good is there! who could believe that it is to fade! and yet, as night follows upon day, as decrepitude follows upon health, so surely are failure, and overthrow, and annihilation, the issue of this natural virtue, if time only be allowed to it to run its course. There are those who are cut off in the first opening of this excellence, and then, if we may trust their epitaphs, they have lived like angels; but wait a while, let them live on, let the course of life proceed, let the bright soul go through the fire and water of the world's temptations and seductions and corruptions and transformations; and, alas for the insufficiency of nature! alas for its powerlessness to persevere, its waywardness in disappointing its own promise! Wait till youth has become age; and not more different is the miniature which we have of him when a boy, when every feature spoke of hope, put side by side of the large portrait painted to his honour, when he is old, when his limbs are shrunk, his eye dim, his brow furrowed, and his hair grey, than differs the moral grace of that boyhood from the forbidding and repulsive aspect of his soul, now that he has lived to the age of man. For moroseness, and misanthropy, and selfishness, is the ordinary winter of that spring.

Such is man in his own nature, and such, too, is he in his works. The noblest efforts of his genius, the conquests he has made, the doctrines he has originated, the nations he has civilized, the states he has created, they outlive himself, they outlive him by many centuries, but they tend to an end, and that end is dissolution. Powers of the world, sovereignties, dynasties, sooner or later come to nought; they have their fatal hour. . . . Thus man and all his works are mortal; they die, and they have no power of renovation.

But what is it, my Fathers, my Brothers, what is it that has happened in England just at this time? Something strange is passing over this land, by the very surprise, by the very commotion, which it excites. Were we not near enough the scene of action to be able to say what is going on,—were we the inhabitants of some sister planet possessed of a more perfect mechanism than this earth has discovered for surveying the transactions of another globe,—and did we turn our eyes thence towards England just at this season, we should be arrested by a political phenomenon as wonderful as any which the astronomer notes down from his physical field of view. It would be the occurrence of a national commotion, almost without parallel, more violent than has happened here for centuries,—at least in the judgments and intentions of men, if not in act and deed. We should note it down, that soon after St. Michael's day, 1850, a storm arose in the moral world, so furious as to demand some great explanation, and to rouse in us an intense desire to gain it. We should observe it increasing from day to day, and spreading from place to place, without remission, almost without lull, up to this very hour, when perhaps it threatens worse still, or at least gives no sure prospect of alleviation. Every party in the body politic undergoes its influence,—from the Queen upon her throne, down to the little ones in the infant or day school. The ten thousands of the constituency, the sum-total of Protestant sects, the aggregate of religious societies and associations, the great body of established clergy in town and country, the bar, even the medical profession, nay, even literary and scientific circles, every class, every interest, every fireside, gives tokens of this ubiquitous storm. This would be our report of it, seeing it from the distance, and we should speculate on the cause. What is it all about? against what is it directed? what wonder has happened upon earth? what prodigious, what preternatural event is adequate to the burden of so vast an effect?

We should judge rightly in our curiosity about a phenomenon like this; it must be a portentous event, and it is. It is an innovation, a miracle, I may say, in the course of human events. The physical world revolves year by year, and begins again; but the political order of things does not renew itself, does not return; it continues, but it proceeds; there is no retrogression. This is so well understood by men of the day, that with them progress is idolized as another name for good. The past never returns— it is never good;—if we are to escape existing ills, it must be by going forward. The past is out of date; the past is dead. As well may the dead live to us, well may the dead profit us, as the past return. *This*, then, is the cause of this national transport, this national cry, which encompasses us. The past *has* returned, the dead lives. Thrones are overturned, and are never restored; States live and die, and then are matter only for history. Babylon was great, and Tyre, and Egypt, and Nineve, and shall never be great again. The English Church was, and the English Church was not, and the English Church is once again. This is the portent, worthy of a cry. It is the coming in of a Second Spring; it is a restoration in the moral world, such as that which yearly takes place in the physical.

Three centuries ago, and the Catholic Church, that great creation of God's power, stood in this land in pride of place. It had the honours of near a thousand years upon it; it was enthroned on some twenty sees up and down the broad country; it was based in the will of a faithful people; it energized through ten thousand instruments of power and influence; and it was ennobled by a host of Saints and Martyrs. The churches, one by one, recounted and rejoiced in the line of glorified intercessors, who were the respective objects of their grateful homage. . . .

But it was the high decree of heaven, that the majesty of that presence should be blotted out. It is a long story, my Fathers and Brothers—you know it well. I need not go through it. The vivifying principle of truth, the shadow of St. Peter, the grace of the Redeemer, left it. That old Church in its day became a corpse (a marvellous, an awful change!); and then it did but corrupt the air which once it refreshed, and cumber the ground which once it beautified. So all seemed to be lost; and there was a struggle for a time, and then its priests were cast out or martyred. There were sacrileges innumerable. Its temples were profaned or destroyed; its revenues seized by covetous nobles, or squandered upon the ministers of a new faith. The presence of Catholicism was at length simply removed,—its grace disowned,—its power despised,—its name, except as a matter of history, at length almost unknown. It took a long time to do this thoroughly; much time, much thought, much labour, much expense; but at last it was done. Oh, that miserable day, centuries before we were born! What a martyrdom to live in it and see the fair form of Truth, moral and material, hacked piecemeal, and every limb and organ carried off, and burned in the fire, or cast into the deep! But at last the work was done. Truth was disposed of, and shovelled away, and there was a calm, a silence, a sort of peace;—and such was about the state of things when we were born into this weary world.

My Fathers and Brothers, *you* have seen it on one side, and some of us on another; but one and all of us can bear witness to the fact of the utter contempt into which Catholicism had fallen by the time that we were born. You, alas, know it far better than I can know it; but it may not be out of place, if by one or two tokens, as by the strokes of a pencil, I bear witness to you from without, of what you can witness so much more truly from within. No longer the Catholic Church in the country; nay, no longer, I may say, a Catholic community;—but a few adherents of the Old Religion, moving silently and sorrowfully about, as memorials of what had been. "The Roman Catholics;"—not a sect, not even an interest, as men conceived of it, —not a body, however small, representative of the Great Communion abroad,—but a mere handful of individuals, who might be counted, like the pebbles and *detritus* of the great deluge, and who, forsooth, merely happened to retain a creed which, in its day indeed, was the profession of a Church. Here a set of poor Irishmen, coming and going at harvest time, or a colony of them lodged in a miserable quarter of the vast metropolis. There, perhaps an elderly person, seen walking in the streets, grave and solitary, and strange, though noble in bearing, and said to be of good family, and a "Roman Catholic." An old-fashioned house of gloomy appearance, closed in with high walls, with an iron gate, and yews, and the report attaching to it that "Roman Catholics" lived there; but who they were, or what they did, or what was meant by calling them Roman Catholics, no one could tell;—though it had an unpleasant sound, and told of form and superstition. . . .

Such was about the sort of knowledge possessed of Christianity by the heathen of old time, who persecuted its adherents from the face of the earth, and then called them a *gens lucifuga*, a people who shunned the light of day. Such were Catholics in England, found in corners, and alleys, and cellars, and the housetops, or in the recesses of the country; cut off from the populous world around them, and dimly seen, as if through a mist or in twilight, as ghosts flitting to and fro, by the high Protestants, the lords of the earth. At length so feeble did they become, so utterly contemptible, that contempt gave birth to pity; and the more generous of their tyrants actually began to wish to bestow on them some favour, under the notion that their opinions were simply too absurd ever to spread again, and that they themselves, were they but raised in civil importance, would soon unlearn and be ashamed of them. And thus, out of mere kindness to us, they began to vilify our doctrines to the Protestant world, that so our very idiocy or our secret unbelief might be our plea for mercy.

A *great* change, an *awful* contrast, between the time-honoured Church of St. Augustine and St. Thomas, and the poor remnant of their children in the beginning of the nineteenth century! It was a miracle, I might say, to have pulled down that lordly power; but there was a greater and a truer one in store. No one could have prophesied its fall, but still less would any one have ventured to prophesy its rise again. The fall was wonderful; still after all it was in the order of nature;—all things come to nought: its rise again would be a different sort of wonder, for it is in the order of grace,—and who can hope for miracles, and such a miracle as this? Has the whole course of history a like to show? I must speak cautiously and according to my knowledge, but I recollect no parallel to it. . . . The inspired word seems to imply the almost impossibility of such a grace as the renovation of those who have crucified to themselves again, and trodden under foot, the Son of God. Who then could have dared to hope that, out of so sacrilegious a nation as this is, a people would have been formed again unto their Saviour? What signs did it show that it was to be singled out from among the nations? Had it been prophesied some fifty years ago, would not the very notion have seemed preposterous and wild? . . .

What! those few scattered worshippers, *the* Roman Catholics, to form a Church! Shall the past be rolled back? Shall the grave open? Shall the Saxons live again to God? Shall the shepherds, watching their poor flocks by night, be visited by a multitude of the heavenly army, and hear how their Lord has been new-born in their own city? Yes; for grace can, where nature cannot. The world grows old, but the Church is ever young. She can, in any time, at her Lord's will, "inherit the Gentiles, and inhabit the desolate cities. . . . "

O Mary, my hope, O Mother undefiled, fulfil to us the promise of this Spring. A second temple rises on the ruins of the old. Canterbury has gone its way, and York is gone, and Durham is gone, and Winchester is gone. It was sore to part with them. We clung to the vision of past greatness, and would not believe it could come to nought; but the Church in England has died, and the Church lives again. Westminster and Nottingham, Beverley and Hexham, Northampton and Shrewsbury, if the world lasts, shall be names as musical to the ear, as stirring to the heart, as the glories we have lost; and Saints shall rise out of them, if God so will, and Doctors once again shall give the law to Israel, and Preachers call to penance and to justice, as at the beginning.

Yes, my Fathers and Brothers, and if it be God's blessed will, not Saints alone, not Doctors only, not Preachers only, shall be ours—but Martyrs, too, shall reconsecrate the soil to God. We know not what is before us, ere we win our own; we are engaged in a great, a joyful work, but in proportion to God's grace is the fury of His enemies. They have welcomed us as the lion greets his prey. Perhaps they may be familiarized in time with our appearance, but perhaps they may be irritated the more. To set up the Church again in England is too great an act to be done in a corner. We have had reason to expect that such a boon would not be given to us without a cross. It is not God's way that great blessings should descend without the sacrifice first of great sufferings. If the truth is to be spread to any wide extent among this people, how can we dream, how can we hope, that trial and trouble shall not accompany its going forth? And we have already, if it may be said without presumption, to commence our work withal, a large store of merits. We have no slight outfit for our opening warfare. Can we religiously suppose that the blood of our martyrs, three centuries ago and since, shall never receive its recompense? . . .

Are Thy martyrs to cry from under Thine altar for their loving vengeance on this guilty people, and to cry in vain? Shall they lose life, and not gain a better life for the children of those who persecuted them? Is this Thy way, O my God, righteous and true? Is it according to Thy promise, O King of saints, if I may dare talk to Thee of justice? Did not Thou Thyself pray for Thine enemies upon the cross, and convert them? Did not Thy first Martyr [St. Stephen] win Thy great Apostle [St. Paul], then a persecutor, by his loving prayer? And in that day of trial and desolation for England, when hearts were pierced through and through with Mary's woe, at the crucifixion of Thy body mystical, was not every tear that flowed, and every drop of blood that was shed, the seeds of a future harvest, when they who sowed in sorrow were to reap in joy?

And as that suffering of the Martyrs is not yet recompensed, so, perchance, it is not yet exhausted. Something, for what we know, remains to be undergone, to complete the necessary sacrifice. May God forbid it, for this poor nation's sake! But still could we be surprised, my Fathers and my Brothers, if the winter even now should not yet be quite over? Have we any right to take it strange, if, in this English land, the spring-time of the Church should turn out to be an English spring, an uncertain, anxious time of hope and fear, of joy and suffering,—of bright promise and budding hopes, yet withal, of keen blasts, and cold showers, and sudden storms?

One thing alone I know,—that according to our need, so will be our strength. One thing I am sure of, that the more the enemy rages against us, so much the more will the Saints in Heaven plead for us; the more fearful are our trials from the world, the more present to us will be our Mother Mary, and our good Patrons and Angel Guardians; the more malicious are the devices of men against us, the louder cry of supplication will ascend from the bosom of the whole Church to God for us. We shall not be left orphans; we shall have within us the strength of the Paraclete, promised to the Church and to every member of it. My Fathers, my Brothers in the priesthood, I speak from my heart when I declare my conviction, that there is no one among you here present but, if God so willed, would readily become a martyr for His sake. I do not say you would wish it; I do not say that the natural will would not pray that that chalice might pass away; I do not speak of what you can do by any strength of yours;—but in the strength of God, in the grace of the Spirit, in the armour of justice, by the consolations and peace of the Church, by the blessing of the Apostles Peter and Paul, and in the name of Christ, you would do what nature cannot do. By the intercession of the Saints on high, by the penances and good works and the prayers of the people of God on earth, you would be forcibly borne up as upon the waves of the mighty deep, and carried on out of yourselves by the fulness of grace, whether nature wished it or no. I do not mean violently, or with unseemly struggle, but calmly, gracefully, sweetly, joyously, you would mount up and ride forth to the battle, as on the rush of Angels' wings, as your fathers did before you, and gained the prize. You, who day by day offer up the Immaculate Lamb of God, you who hold in your hands the Incarnate Word under the visible tokens which He has ordained, you who again and again drain the chalice of the Great Victim; who is to make you fear? what is to startle you? what to seduce you? who is to stop you, whether you are to suffer or to do, whether to lay the foundations of the Church in tears, or to put the crown upon the work in jubilation?

My Fathers, my Brothers, one word more. It may seem as if I were going out of my way in thus addressing you; but I have some sort of plea to urge in extenuation. When the English College at Rome was set up by the solicitude of a great Pontiff in the beginning of England's sorrows, and missionaries were trained there for confessorship and martyrdom here, who was it that saluted the fair Saxon youths as they passed by him in the streets of the great city, with the salutation, "Salvete flores martyrum"? And when the time came for each in turn to leave that peaceful home, and to go forth to the conflict, to whom did they betake themselves before leaving Rome, to receive a blessing which might nerve them for their work? They went for a Saint's blessing; they went to a calm old man, who had never seen blood, except in penance; who had longed indeed to die for Christ, what time the great St. Francis opened the way to the far East, but who had been fixed as if a sentinel in the holy city, and walked up and down for fifty years on one beat, while his brethren were in the battle. Oh! the fire of that heart, too great for its frail tenement, which tormented him to be kept at home when the whole Church was at war! and therefore came those bright-haired strangers to him, ere they set out for the scene of their passion, that the full zeal and love pent up in that burning breast might find a vent, and flow over, from him who was kept at home, upon those who were to face the foe. Therefore one by one, each in his turn, those youthful soldiers came to the old man; and one by one they persevered and gained the crown and the palm,—all but one, who had not gone, and would not go, for the salutary blessing.

My Fathers, my Brothers, that old man was my own St. Philip. Bear with me for his sake. If I have spoken too seriously, his sweet smile shall temper it. As he was with you three centuries ago in Rome, when our Temple fell, so now surely when it is rising, it is a pleasant token that he should have even set out on his travels to you; and that, as if remembering how he interceded for you at home, and recognizing the relations he then formed with you, he should now be wishing to have a name among you, and to be loved by you, and perchance to do you a service, here in your own land.   —Sermon 10, *Sermons Preached on Various Occasions*, 163–182

12

Educator

12.1. "INTELLECT, INSTRUMENT OF RELIGIOUS TRAINING"

In his sermon "Intellect, the Instrument of Religious Training," which Newman preached on the Feast of St. Monica, May 1, 1856, in the University Church in Dublin, Newman commented on the Gospel text: "And when He came nigh to the gate of the city, behold, a dead man was carried out, the only son of his mother: and she was a widow" (Luke 7:2). Newman used the story of St. Augustine's conversion through the prayers of his mother, Monica, as a model for both the Church and the university. The university needs to be an alma mater, *where students can be nourished both intellectually and religiously.*

This day we celebrate one of the most remarkable feasts in the calendar. We commemorate a Saint who gained the heavenly crown by prayers indeed and tears, by sleepless nights and weary wanderings, but not in the administration of any high office in the Church, not in the fulfilment of some great resolution or special counsel; not as a preacher, teacher, evangelist, reformer, or champion of the faith; not as Bishop of the flock, or temporal governor; not by eloquence, by wisdom, or by controversial success; not in the way of any other saint whom we invoke in the circle of the year; but as a mother, seeking and gaining by her penances the conversion of her son. It was for no ordinary son

151

that she prayed, and it was no ordinary supplication by which she gained him. When a holy man saw its vehemence, ere it was successful, he said to her, "Go in peace; the son of such prayers cannot perish." The prediction was fulfilled beyond its letter; not only was that young man converted, but after his conversion he became a saint; not only a saint, but a doctor also, and "instructed many unto justice." St. Augustine was the son for whom she prayed; and if he has been a luminary for all ages of the Church since, many thanks do we owe to his mother, St. Monica, who having borne him in the flesh, travailed for him in the spirit.

The Church, in her choice of a gospel for this feast, has likened St. Monica to the desolate widow whom our Lord met at the gate of the city, as she was going forth to bury the corpse of her only son. He saw her, and said, "Weep not;" and he touched the bier, and the dead arose. St. Monica asked and obtained a more noble miracle. Many a mother who is anxious for her son's bodily welfare, neglects his soul. So did not the Saint of today; her son might be accomplished, eloquent, able, and distinguished; all this was nothing to her while he was dead in God's sight, while he was the slave of sin, while he was the prey of heresy. She desired his true life. She wearied heaven with prayer, and wore out herself with praying; she did not at once prevail. He left his home; he was carried forward by his four bearers, ignorance, pride, appetite, and ambition; he was carried out into a foreign land, he crossed over from Africa to Italy. She followed him, she followed the corpse, the chief, the only mourner; she went where he went, from city to city. It was nothing to her to leave her dear home and her native soil; she had no country below; her sole rest, her sole repose, her *Nunc dimittis*, was his new birth. So while she still walked forth in her deep anguish and isolation, and her silent prayer, she was at length rewarded by the long-coveted miracle. . . .

This, I say, is not a history of past time merely, but of every age. Generation passes after generation, and there is on the one side the same doleful, dreary wandering, the same fever-ish unrest, the same fleeting enjoyments, the same abiding and hopeless misery; and on the other, the same anxiously beating heart of impotent affection. Age goes after age, and still Augustine rushes forth again and again, with his young ambition, and his intellectual energy, and his turbulent appetites; educated, yet untaught; with powers strengthened, sharpened, refined by exercise, but unenlightened and untrained,—goes forth into the world, ardent, self-willed, reckless, headstrong, inexperienced, to fall into the hands of those who seek his life, and to become the victim of heresy and sin. And still, again and again does hapless Monica weep; weeping for that dear child who grew up with her from the womb, and of whom she is now robbed; of whom she has lost sight; wandering with him in his wanderings, following his steps in her imagination, cherishing his image in her heart, keeping his name upon her lips, and feeling withal, that, as a woman, she is unable to cope with the violence and the artifices of the world. And still again and again does Holy Church take her part and her place, with a heart as tender and more strong, with an arm, and an eye, and an intellect more powerful than hers, with an influence more than human, more sagacious than the world, and more religious than home, to restrain and reclaim those whom passion, or example, or sophistry is hurrying forward to destruction.

My Brethren, there is something happy in the circumstance, that the first Sunday of our academical worship should fall on the feast of St. Monica. For is not this one chief aspect of a University, and an aspect which it especially bears in this sacred place, to supply that which that memorable Saint so much desiderated, and for which she attempted to compensate by her prayers? Is it not one part of our especial office to receive those from the hands of father and mother, whom father and mother can keep no longer? Thus, while professing all sciences, and speaking by the mouths of philosophers and sages, a University delights in the in a state of tumult, sedition, or rebellion, certain portions break off from the whole and from the central government, and set up for themselves; so is it with the soul of man. So is it, I say, with the soul, long ago,—that a number of small kingdoms, independent of each other and at war with each other, have arisen in it, such and so many as to reduce the original sovereignty to a circuit of territory and to an influence not more considerable than they have themselves. . . . Hence you find in one man, or one set of men, the reign, I may call it, the acknowledged reign of passion or appetite; among others, the avowed reign of brute strength and material resources; among others, the reign of intellect; and among others (and would they were many!) the more excellent reign of virtue. Such is the state of things, as it shows to us, when we cast our eyes abroad into the world; and every one, when he comes to years of discretion, and begins to think, has all these separate powers warring in his own breast,—appetite, passion, secular ambition, intellect, and conscience, and trying severally to get possession of him. And when he looks out of himself, he sees them all severally embodied on a grand scale, in large establishments and centres, outside of him, one here and another there, in aid of that importunate canvass, so to express myself, which each of them is carrying on within him. And thus, at least for a time, he is in a state of internal strife, confusion, and uncertainty, first attracted this way, then that, not knowing how to choose, though sooner or later choose he must; or rather, he must choose soon, and cannot choose late, for he cannot help thinking, speaking, and acting; and to think, speak, and act, is to choose.

This is a very serious state of things; and what makes it worse is, that these various faculties and powers of the human mind have so long been separated from each other, so long cultivated and developed each by itself, that it comes to be taken for granted that they cannot be united; and it is commonly thought, because some men follow duty, others pleasure, others glory, and

well-known appellation of "Alma Mater." She is a mother who,
after the pattern of that greatest and most heavenly of mothers,
is, on the one hand, "Mater Amabilis," [Lovable Mother] and
"Causa nostræ lætitiæ," [Cause of Our Joy] and on the other,
"Sedes Sapientiæ" [Seat of Wisdom] also. She is a mother, living,
not in the seclusion of the family, and in the garden's shade, but
in the wide world, in the populous and busy town, claiming, like
our great Mother, the meek and tender Mary, . . . because she
alone . . . in every department of human learning, is able to con-
fute and put right those who would set knowledge against itself,
and would make truth contradict truth, and would persuade the
world that, to be religious, you must be ignorant, and to be intellectual, you must be unbelieving.

My meaning will be clearer, if I revert to the nature and condition of the human mind. The human mind, as you know, my
Brethren, may be regarded from two principal points of view, as
intellectual and as moral. As intellectual, it apprehends truth; as
moral, it apprehends duty. The perfection of the intellect is called
ability and talent; the perfection of our moral nature is virtue.
And it is our great misfortune here, and our trial, that, as things
are found in the world, the two are separated, and independent
of each other; that, where power of intellect is, there need not be
virtue; and that where right, and goodness, and moral greatness
are, there need not be talent. It was not so in the beginning; not
that our nature is essentially different from what it was when
first created; but that the Creator, upon its creation, raised it
above itself by a supernatural grace, which blended together all
its faculties, and made them conspire into one whole, and act
in common towards one end; so that, had the race continued
in that blessed state of privilege, there never would have been
distance, rivalry, hostility between one faculty and another. It is
otherwise now; so much the worse for us;—the grace is gone;
the soul cannot hold together; it falls to pieces; its elements
strive with each other. And as, when a kingdom has long been

others intellect, therefore that one of these things excludes the other; that duty cannot be pleasant, that virtue cannot be intellectual, that goodness cannot be great, that conscientiousness cannot be heroic; and the fact is often so, I grant, that there *is* a separation, though I deny its necessity. I grant, that, from the disorder and confusion into which the human mind has fallen, too often good men are not attractive, and bad men are; too often cleverness, or wit, or taste, or richness of fancy, or keenness of intellect, or depth, or knowledge, or pleasantness and agreeableness, is on the side of error and not on the side of virtue. Excellence, as things are, does lie, I grant, in more directions than one, and it is ever easier to excel in one thing than in two. If then a man has more talent, there is the chance that he will have less goodness; if he is careful about his religious duties, there is the chance he is behind-hand in general knowledge; and in matter of fact, in particular cases, persons may be found, correct and virtuous, who are heavy, narrow-minded, and unintellectual, and again, unprincipled men, who are brilliant and amusing. And thus you see, my Brethren, how that particular temptation comes about, of which I speak, when boyhood is past, and youth is opening;—not only is the soul plagued and tormented by the thousand temptations which rise up within it, but it is exposed moreover to the sophistry of the Evil One, whispering that duty and religion are very right indeed, admirable, supernatural,—who doubts it?—but that, somehow or other, religious people are commonly either very dull or very tiresome: nay, that religion itself after all is more suitable to women and children, who live at home, than to men. . . .

Instead of uniting knowledge and religion, as you might have done, did you not set one against the other? For instance, was it not one of the first voluntary exercises of your mind, to indulge a wrong curiosity?—a curiosity which you confessed to yourselves to be wrong, which went against your conscience, while you indulged it. You desired to know a number of things, which it could do you no good to know. This is how boys begin; as soon as their mind begins to stir, it looks the wrong way, and runs upon what is evil. This is their first wrong step; and their next use of their intellect is to put what is evil into words: this is their second wrong step. They form images, and entertain thoughts, which should be away, and they stamp them upon themselves and others by expressing them. And next, the bad turn which they do to others, others retaliate on them. One wrong speech provokes another; and thus there grows up among them from boyhood that miserable tone of conversation,—hinting and suggesting evil, jesting, bantering on the subject of sin, supplying fuel for the inflammable imagination,—which lasts through life, which is wherever the world is, which is the very breath of the world, which the world cannot do without, which the world "speaks out of the abundance of its heart," and which you may prophesy will prevail in every ordinary assemblage of men, as soon as they are at their ease and begin to talk freely,—a sort of vocal worship of the Evil One, to which the Evil One listens with special satisfaction, because he looks on it as the preparation for worse sin; for from bad thoughts and bad words proceed bad deeds.

Bad company creates a distaste for good; and hence it happens that, when a youth has gone the length I have been supposing, he is repelled, from that very distaste, from those places and scenes which would do him good. He begins to lose the delight he once had in going home. By little and little he loses his enjoyment in the pleasant countenances, and untroubled smiles, and gentle ways, of that family circle which is so dear to him still. At first he says to himself that he is not worthy of them, and therefore keeps away; but at length the routine of home is tiresome to him. He has aspirations and ambitions which home does not satisfy. He wants more than home can give. His curiosity now takes a new turn; he listens to views and discussions which are inconsistent with the sanctity of religious faith. At first he has no temptation to adopt them; only he wishes to know what is "said." As time goes on, however, living with companions who have no fixed principle, and who, if they do not oppose, at least do not take for granted, any the most elementary truths; or worse, hearing or reading what is directly against religion, at length, without being conscious of it, he admits a sceptical influence upon his mind. He does not know it, he does not recognize it, but there it is; and, *before* he recognizes it, it leads him to a fretful, impatient way of speaking of the persons, conduct, words, and measures of religious men or of men in authority. This is the way in which he relieves his mind of the burden which is growing heavier and heavier every day. And so he goes on, approximating more and more closely to sceptics and infidels, and feeling more and more congeniality with their modes of thinking, till some day suddenly, from some accident, the fact breaks upon him, and he sees clearly that he is an unbeliever himself.

He can no longer conceal from himself that he does not believe, and a sharp anguish darts through him, and for a time he is made miserable; next, he *laments* indeed that former undoubting faith, which he has lost, but as some pleasant dream;—a dream, though a pleasant one, from which he has been awakened, but which, however pleasant, *he* forsooth, cannot help *being* a dream. And his next stage is to experience a great expansion and elevation of mind; for his field of view is swept clear of all that filled it from childhood, and now he may build up for himself anything he pleases instead. So he begins to form his own ideas of things, and these please and satisfy him for a time; then he gets used to them, and tires of them, and he takes up others; and now he has begun that everlasting round of seeking and never finding: at length, after various trials, he gives up the search altogether, and decides that nothing can be known, and there is no such thing as truth, and that if anything is to be professed, the creed he started from is as good as any other, and has more claims;—however, that really nothing is true, nothing is certain. Or, if he be of a more ardent temperature, or, like Augustine, the object of God's special mercy, then he cannot give up the inquiry, though he has no chance of solving it, and he roams about, "walking through dry places, seeking rest, and finding none." Meanwhile poor Monica sees the change in its effects, though she does not estimate it in itself, or know exactly what it is, or how it came about: nor, even though it be told her, can she enter into it, or understand how one, so dear to her, can be subjected to it. But a dreadful change there is, and she perceives it too clearly; a dreadful change for him and for her; a wall of separation has grown up between them: she cannot throw it down again; but she can turn to her God, and weep and pray. . . .

Young men feel a consciousness of certain faculties within them which demand exercise, aspirations which must have an object, for which they do not commonly find exercise or object in religious circles. This want is no excuse for them, if they think, say, or do anything against faith or morals: but still it is the occasion of their sinning. It is the fact, they are not only moral, they are intellectual beings; but, ever since the fall of man, religion is here, and philosophy is there; each has its own centres of influence, separate from the other; intellectual men desiderate something in the homes of religion, and religious men desiderate something in the schools of science.

Here, then, I conceive, is the object of the Holy See and the Catholic Church in setting up Universities; it is to reunite things which were in the beginning joined together by God, and have been put asunder by man. Some persons will say that I am thinking of confining, distorting, and stunting the growth of the intellect by ecclesiastical supervision. I have no such thought. Nor have I any thought of a compromise, as if religion must give up something, and science something. I wish the intellect to range with the utmost freedom, and religion to enjoy an equal freedom; but what I am stipulating for is, that they should be found in one and the same place, and exemplified in the same persons.

I want to destroy that diversity of centres, which puts everything into confusion by creating a contrariety of influences. I wish the same spots and the same individuals to be at once oracles of philosophy and shrines of devotion. It will not satisfy me, what satisfies so many, to have two independent systems, intellectual and religious, going at once side by side, by a sort of division of labour, and only accidentally brought together. It will not satisfy me, if religion is here, and science there, and young men converse with science all day, and lodge with religion in the evening. It is not touching the evil, to which these remarks have been directed, if young men eat and drink and sleep in one place, and think in another: I want the same roof to contain both the intellectual and moral discipline. Devotion is not a sort of finish given to the sciences; nor is science a sort of feather in the cap, if I may so express myself, an ornament and set-off to devotion. I want the intellectual layman to be religious, and the devout ecclesiastic to be intellectual.

This is no matter of terms, nor of subtle distinctions. Sanctity has its influence; intellect has its influence; the influence of sanctity is the greater on the long run; the influence of intellect is greater at the moment. Therefore, in the case of the young, whose education lasts a few years, where the intellect is, *there* is the influence. Their literary, their scientific teachers, really have the forming of them. Let both influences act freely, and then, as a general rule, no system of mere religious guardianship which neglects the Reason, will in matter of fact succeed against the School. Youths need a masculine religion, if it is to carry captive their restless imaginations, and their wild intellects, as well as to touch their susceptible hearts.

Look down then upon us from Heaven, O blessed Monica, for we are engaged in supplying that very want which called for thy prayers, and gained for thee thy crown. Thou who didst obtain thy son's conversion by the merit of thy intercession, continue that intercession for us, that we may be blest, as human instruments, in the use of those human means by which ordinarily the Holy Cross is raised aloft, and religion commands the world. Gain for us, first, that we may intensely feel that God's grace is all in all, and that we are nothing; next, that, for His greater glory, and for the honour of Holy Church, and for the good of man, we may be "zealous for all the better gifts," and may excel in intellect as we excel in virtue.

—Sermon 1, *Sermons Preached on Various Occasions*, 1–14

12.2. "THE RELIGION OF THE PHARISEE, THE RELIGION OF MANKIND"

Newman preached this sermon in the University Church, Dublin, on the Tenth Sunday after Pentecost, 1856. Reflecting on the Gospel text "O God, be merciful to me, a sinner" (Luke 18:13), Newman contrasted the "heathen idea of religion" with true Christian faith by emphasizing that the superficial religion of the present day is more like that of the Pharisee than of the Christian.

These words set before us what may be called the characteristic mark of the Christian Religion, as contrasted with the various forms of worship and schools of belief, which in early or in later times have spread over the earth. They are a confession of sin and a prayer for mercy. Not indeed that the notion of transgression and of forgiveness was introduced by Christianity, and is unknown beyond its pale; on the contrary, most observable it is, the symbols of guilt and pollution, and rites of deprecation and expiation, are more or less common to them all; but what is peculiar to our divine faith, as to Judaism before it, is this, that confession of sin enters into the idea of its highest saintliness, and that its pattern worshippers and the very heroes of its history are only, and can only be, and cherish in their hearts the everlasting memory that they are, and carry with them into heaven the rapturous avowal of their being, redeemed, restored transgressors. Such an avowal is not simply wrung from the lips of the neophyte, or of the lapsed; it is not the cry of the common run of men alone, who are buffeting with the surge of temptation in the wide world; it is the hymn of saints, it is the triumphant ode sounding from the heavenly harps of the Blessed before the Throne, who sing to their Divine Redeemer, "Thou wast slain, and hast redeemed us to God in Thy blood, out of every tribe, and tongue, and people, and nation."

And what is to the Saints above a theme of never-ending thankfulness, is, while they are yet on earth, the matter of their perpetual humiliation. Whatever be their advance in the spiritual life, they never rise from their knees, they never cease to beat their breasts, as if sin could possibly be strange to them while they were in the flesh. Even our Lord Himself, the very Son of God in human nature, and infinitely separate from sin,—even His Immaculate Mother, encompassed by His grace from the first beginnings of her existence, and without any part of the original stain,—even they, as descended from Adam, were subjected at least to death, the direct, emphatic punishment of sin. And much more, even the most favoured of that glorious company, whom He has washed clean in His Blood; they never forget what they were by birth; they confess, one and all, that they are children of Adam, and of the same nature as their brethren, and compassed with infirmities while in the flesh, whatever may be the grace given them and their own improvement of it. Others may look up to them, but they ever look up to God; others may speak of their merits, but they only speak of their defects. The young and unspotted, the aged and most mature, he who has sinned least, he who has repented most, the fresh innocent brow, and the hoary head, they unite in this one litany, "O God, be merciful to me, a sinner."

So it was with St. Aloysius; so, on the other hand, was it with St. Ignatius; so was it with St. Rose, the youngest of the saints, who, as a child, submitted her tender frame to the most amazing penances; so was it with St. Philip Neri, one of the most aged, who, when some one praised him, cried out, "Begone! I am a devil, and not a saint;" and when going to communicate, would protest before his Lord, that he "was good for nothing, but to do evil." Such utter self-prostration, I say, is the very badge and token of the servant of Christ;—and this indeed is conveyed in His own words, when He says, "I am not come to call the just, but sinners;" and it is solemnly recognized and inculcated by Him, in the words which follow the text, "Every one that exalt-eth himself, shall be humbled, and he that humbleth himself, shall be exalted."

This, you see, my Brethren, is very different from that merely general acknowledgment of human guilt, and of the need of expiation, contained in those old and popular religions, which have before now occupied, or still occupy, the world. In them, guilt is an attribute of individuals, or of particular places, or of particular acts of nations, of bodies politic or their rulers, for whom, in consequence, purification is necessary. Or it is the purification of the worshipper, not so much personal as ritual, before he makes his offering, and an act of introduction to his religious service. All such practices indeed are remnants of true religion, and tokens and witnesses of it, useful both in them-selves and in their import; but they do not rise to the explicitness and the fulness of the Christian doctrine. . . . The disciples of other worships and other philosophies thought and think, that the many indeed are bad, but the few are good. As their thoughts passed on from the ignorant and erring multitude to the select specimens of mankind, they left the notion of guilt behind, and they pictured for themselves an idea of truth and wisdom, per-fect, indefectible, and self-sufficient. It was a sort of virtue with-out imperfection, which took pleasure in contemplating itself, which needed nothing, and which was, from its own internal excellence, sure of a reward. Their descriptions, their stories of good and religious men, are often beautiful, and admit of an instructive interpretation; but in themselves they have this great blot, that they make no mention of sin, and that they speak as if shame and humiliation were no properties of the virtuous. . . .

Now perhaps you will ask me, my Brethren, whether this heathen idea of religion be not really higher than that which I have called pre-eminently Christian; for surely to obey in simple tranquillity and unsolicitous confidence, is the noblest conceivable state of the creature, and the most acceptable worship he can pay to the Creator. Doubtless it is the noblest and most acceptable worship; such has ever been the worship of the angels; such is the worship now of the spirits of the just made perfect; such will be the worship of the whole company of the glorified after the general resurrection. But we are engaged in considering the actual state of man, as found in this world; and I say, considering what he is, any standard of duty, which does not convict him of real and multiplied sins, and of incapacity to please God of his own strength, is untrue; and any rule of life, which leaves him contented with himself, without fear, without anxiety, without humiliation, is deceptive; it is the blind leading the blind: yet such, in one shape or other, is the religion of the whole earth, beyond the pale of the Church.

The natural conscience of man, if cultivated from within, if enlightened by those external aids which in varying degrees are given him in every place and time, would teach him much of his duty to God and man, and would lead him on, by the guidance both of Providence and grace, into the fulness of religious knowledge; but, generally speaking, he is contented that it should tell him very little, and he makes no efforts to gain any juster views than he has at first, of his relations to the world around him and to his Creator. Thus he apprehends part, and part only, of the moral law; has scarcely any idea at all of sanctity; and, instead of tracing actions to their source, which is the motive, and judging them thereby, he measures them for the most part by their effects and their outward aspect. Such is the way with the multitude of men everywhere and at all times; they do not see the Image of Almighty God before them, and ask themselves what He wishes: if once they did this, they would begin to see how much He requires, and they would earnestly come to Him, both to be pardoned for what they do wrong, and for the power to do better. And, for the same reason that they do not please Him, they succeed in pleasing themselves. For that contracted, defective range of duties, which falls so short of God's law, is just what they can fulfil; or rather they choose it, and keep to it, *because* they can fulfil it. Hence, they become both self-satisfied and self-sufficient;—they think they know just what they ought to do, and that they do it all; and in consequence they are very well content with themselves, and rate their merit very high, and have no fear at all of any future scrutiny into their conduct, which may befall them, though their religion mainly lies in certain outward observances, and not a great number even of them.

So it was with the Pharisee in this day's gospel. He looked upon himself with great complacency, for the very reason that the standard was so low, and the range so narrow, which he assigned to his duties towards God and man. He used, or misused, the traditions in which he had been brought up, to the purpose of persuading himself that perfection lay in merely answering the demands of society. He professed, indeed, to pay thanks to God, but he hardly apprehended the existence of any direct duties on his part towards his Maker. He thought he did all that God required, if he satisfied public opinion. To be religious, in the Pharisee's sense, was to keep the peace towards others, to take his share in the burdens of the poor, to abstain from gross vice, and to set a good example. His alms and fastings were not done in penance, but because the world asked for them; penance would have implied the consciousness of sin; whereas it was only Publicans, and such as they, who had anything to be forgiven. And these indeed were the outcasts of society, and despicable; but no account lay against men of well-regulated minds such as his: men who were well-behaved, decorous, consistent, and respectable. He thanked God he was a Pharisee, and not a penitent.

Such was the Jew in our Lord's day; and such the heathen was, and had been. Alas! I do not mean to affirm that it was common for the poor heathen to observe even any religious rule at all; but I am speaking of the few and of the better sort: and these, I say, commonly took up with a religion like the Pharisee's, more beautiful perhaps and more poetical, but not at all deeper or truer than his. They did not indeed fast, or give alms, or observe the ordinances of Judaism; they threw over their meagre observances a philosophical garb, and embellished them with the refinements of a cultivated intellect; still their notion of moral and religious duty was as shallow as that of the Pharisee, and the sense of sin, the habit of self-abasement, and the desire of contrition, just as absent from their minds as from his. They framed a code of morals which they could without trouble obey; and then they were content with it and with themselves. Virtue, according to Xenophon, one of the best principled and most religious of their writers, and one who had seen a great deal of the world, and had the opportunity of bringing together in one the highest thoughts of many schools and countries,—virtue, according to him, consists mainly in command of the appetites and passions, and in serving others in order that they may serve us. He says, in the well known Fable, called the choice of Hercules, that Vice has no real enjoyment even of those pleasures which it aims at; that it eats before it is hungry, and drinks before it is thirsty, and slumbers before it is wearied. It never hears, he says, that sweetest of voices, its own praise; it never sees that greatest luxury among sights, its own good deeds. It enfeebles the bodily frame of the young, and the intellect of the old. Virtue, on the other hand, rewards young men with the praise of their elders, and it rewards the aged with the reverence of youth; it supplies them pleasant memories and present peace; it secures the favour of heaven, the love of friends, a country's thanks, and, when death comes, an everlasting renown. In all such descriptions, virtue is something external; it is not concerned with motives or intentions; it is occupied in deeds which bear upon society, and which gain the praise of men; it has little to do with conscience and the Lord of conscience; and knows nothing of shame, humiliation, and penance. It is in substance the Pharisee's religion, though it be more graceful and more interesting.

Now this age is as removed in distance, as in character, from that of the Greek philosopher; yet who will say that the religion which it acts upon is very different from the religion of the heathen? Of course I understand well, that it might know, and that it will say, a great many things foreign and contrary to heathenism. I am well aware that the theology of this age is very different from what it was two thousand years ago. I know men profess a great deal, and boast that they are Christians, and speak of Christianity as being a religion of the heart; but, when we put aside words and professions, and try to discover what their religion is, we shall find, I fear, that the great mass of men in fact get rid of all religion that is inward; that they lay no stress on acts of faith, hope, and charity, on simplicity of intention, purity of motive, or mortification of the thoughts; that they confine themselves to two or three virtues, superficially practised; that they know not the words contrition, penance, and pardon; and that they think and argue that, after all, if a man does his duty in the world, according to his vocation, he cannot fail to go to heaven, however little he may do besides, nay, however much, in other matters, he may do that is undeniably unlawful. Thus a soldier's duty is loyalty, obedience, and valour, and he may let other matters take their chance; a trader's duty is honesty; an artisan's duty is industry and contentment; of a gentleman are required veracity, courteousness, and self-respect; of a public man, high-principled ambition; of a woman, the domestic virtues; of a minister of religion, decorum, benevolence, and some activity. Now, all these are instances of mere Pharisaical excellence; because there is no apprehension of Almighty God, no insight into His claims on us, no sense of the creature's shortcomings, no self-condemnation, confession, and deprecation, nothing of those deep and sacred feelings which ever characterize the religion of a Christian, and more and more, not less and less, as he mounts up from mere ordinary obedience to the perfection of a saint.

And such, I say, is the religion of the natural man in every age and place;—often very beautiful on the surface, but worthless in God's sight; good, as far as it goes, but worthless and hopeless, because it does not go further, because it is based on self-sufficiency, and results in self-satisfaction. I grant, it may be beautiful to look at, as in the instance of the young ruler whom our Lord looked at and loved, yet sent away sad; it may have all the delicacy, the amiableness, the tenderness, the religious sentiment, the kindness, which is actually seen in many a father of a family, many a mother, many a daughter, in the length and breadth of these kingdoms, in a refined and polished age like this; but still it is rejected by the heart-searching God, because all such persons walk by their own light, not by the True Light of men, because self is their supreme teacher, and because they pace round and round in the small circle of their own thoughts and of their own judgments, careless to know what God says to them, and fearless of being condemned by Him, if only they stand approved in their own sight. . . .

Yes, my Brethren, it is the ignorance of our understanding, it is our spiritual blindness, it is our banishment from the presence of Him who is the source and the standard of all Truth, which is the cause of this meagre, heartless religion of which men are commonly so proud. Had we any proper insight into things as they are, had we any real apprehension of God as He is, of ourselves as we are, we should never dare to serve Him without fear,

or to rejoice unto Him without trembling. And it is the removal
of this veil which is spread between our eyes and heaven, it is the
pouring in upon the soul of the illuminating grace of the New
Covenant, which makes the religion of the Christian so different
from that of the various human rites and philosophies, which
are spread over the earth. The Catholic saints alone confess sin,
because the Catholic saints alone see God. That awful Creator
Spirit, of whom the Epistle of this day speaks so much, He it is
who brings into religion the true devotion, the true worship, and
changes the self-satisfied Pharisee into the broken-hearted, self-
abased Publican. It is the sight of God, revealed to the eye of faith,
that makes us hideous to ourselves, from the contrast which we
find ourselves to present to that great God at whom we look.
It is the vision of Him in His infinite gloriousness, the All-holy,
the All-beautiful, the All-perfect, which makes us sink into the
earth with self-contempt and self-abhorrence. We are contented
with ourselves till we contemplate Him. Why is it, I say, that the
moral code of the world is so precise and well-defined? Why is
the worship of reason so calm? Why was the religion of classic
heathenism so joyous? Why is the framework of civilized society
all so graceful and so correct? Why, on the other hand, is there so
much of emotion, so much of conflicting and alternating feeling,
so much that is high, so much that is abased, in the devotion of
Christianity? It is because the Christian, and the Christian alone,
has a revelation of God; it is because he has upon his mind, in his
heart, on his conscience, the idea of one who is Self-dependent,
who is from Everlasting, who is Incommunicable. He knows
that One alone is holy, and that His own creatures are so frail in
comparison of Him, that they would dwindle and melt away in
His presence, did He not uphold them by His power. He knows
that there is One whose greatness and whose blessedness are
not affected, the centre of whose stability is not moved, by the
presence or the absence of the whole creation with its innumerable beings and portions; whom nothing can touch, nothing can

increase or diminish; who was as mighty before He made the worlds as since, and as serene and blissful since He made them as before. He knows that there is just One Being, in whose hand lies his own happiness, his own sanctity, his own life, and hope, and salvation. He knows that there is One to whom he owes every thing, and against whom he can have no plea or remedy. All things are nothing before Him; the highest beings do but worship Him the more; the holiest beings are such, only because they have a greater portion of Him.

Ah! what has he to pride in now, when he looks back upon himself? Where has fled all that comeliness which heretofore he thought embellished him? What is he but some vile reptile, which ought to shrink aside out of the light of day? This was the feeling of St. Peter, when he first gained a glimpse of the greatness of his Master, and cried out, almost beside himself, "Depart from me, for I am a sinful man, O Lord!" . . . This then, my Brethren, is the reason why every son of man, whatever be his degree of holiness, whether a returning prodigal or a matured saint, says with the Publican, "O God, be merciful to me;" it is because created natures, high and low, are all on a level in the sight and in comparison of the Creator, and so all of them have one speech, and one only, whether it be the thief on the cross, Magdalen at the feast, or St. Paul before his martyrdom:—not that one of them may not have, what another has not, but that one and all have nothing but what comes from Him, and are as nothing before Him, who is all in all.

For us, my dear Brethren, whose duties lie in this seat of learning and science, may we never be carried away by any undue fondness for any human branch of study, so as to be forgetful that our true wisdom, and nobility, and strength, consist in the knowledge of Almighty God. Nature and man are our studies, but God is higher than all. It is easy to lose Him in His works. It is easy to become over-attached to our own pursuit, to substitute it for religion, and to make it the fuel of pride. Our secular attainments will avail us nothing, if they be not subordinate to religion. The knowledge of the sun, moon, and stars, of the earth and its three kingdoms, of the classics, or of history, will never bring us to heaven. We may "thank God," that we are not as the illiterate and the dull; and those whom we despise, if they do but know how to ask mercy of Him, know what is very much more to the purpose of getting to heaven, than all our letters and all our science. Let this be the spirit in which we end our session. Let us thank Him for all that He has done for us, for what He is doing by us; but let nothing that we know or that we can do, keep us from a personal, individual adoption of the great Apostle's words, "Christ Jesus came into this world to save sinners, of whom I am the chief."   —Sermon 2, *Sermons Preached on Various Occasions*, 15–30

12.3. RELATIONSHIP BETWEEN TEACHERS AND STUDENTS

In 1854, Newman published a series of articles about various aspects of university life in the Catholic University Gazette, *a journal that was intended to gain support for the new institution. The following excerpt reflects Newman's experience as a tutor at Oriel and his ideals for the relationships of teachers and students at the Catholic University in Dublin.*

I say then, that the personal influence of the teacher is able in some sort to dispense with an academical system, but that the system cannot in any sort dispense with personal influence. With influence there is life, without it there is none; if influence is deprived of its due position, it will not by those means be got rid of, it will only break out irregularly, dangerously. An academical system without the personal influence of teachers upon pupils, is an arctic winter; it will create an ice-bound, petrified, cast-iron University, and nothing else. You will not call this any new notion of mine; and you will not suspect, after what happened to me a long twenty-five years ago, that I can ever be induced to think otherwise. No! I have known a time in a great School of Letters, when things went on for the most part by mere routine, and form took the place of earnestness. I have experienced a state of things, in which teachers were cut off from the taught as by an insurmountable barrier; when neither party entered into the thoughts of the other; when each lived by and in itself; when the tutor was supposed to fulfil his duty, if he trotted on like a squirrel in his cage, if at a certain hour he was in a certain room, or in hall, or in chapel, as it might be; and the pupil did his duty too, if he was careful to meet his tutor in that same room, or hall, or chapel, at the same certain hour; and when neither the one nor the other dreamed of seeing each other out of lecture, out of chapel, out of academical gown. I have known places where a stiff manner, a pompous voice, coldness and condescension, were the teacher's attributes, and where he neither knew, nor wished to know, and avowed he did not wish to know, the private irregularities of the youths committed to his charge.

—*The Rise and Progress of Universities*
in *Historical Sketches* 3:74–75

13

Advocate for the Laity

13.1. KNOWLEDGE AND THE LAITY

As an educator, Newman wanted to bring out the best in every student. In the conclusion of his discourse "Knowledge Viewed in Relation to Professional Skill" at the Catholic University in Dublin, Newman emphasized that the purpose of education is the cultivation of the mind; accordingly, he wanted the Catholic laity to assume positions of leadership both in society and in the Church.

Today I have confined myself to saying that that training of the intellect, which is best for the individual himself, best enables him to discharge his duties to society. The Philosopher, indeed, and the man of the world differ in their very notion, but the methods, by which they are respectively formed, are pretty much the same. The Philosopher has the same command of matters of thought, which the true citizen and gentleman has of matters of business and conduct. If then a practical end must be assigned to a University course, I say it is that of training good members of society. Its art is the art of social life, and its end is fitness for the world. It neither confines its views to particular professions on the one hand, nor creates heroes or inspires genius on the other. Works indeed of genius fall under no art; heroic minds come under no rule; a University is not a birthplace of poets or of immortal authors, of founders of schools, leaders of colonies, or conquerors of nations. It does not promise a generation of Aristotles or Newtons, of Napoleons or Washingtons, of Raphaels or Shakespeares, though such miracles of nature it has before now contained within its precincts. Nor is it content on the other hand with forming the critic or the experimentalist, the economist or the engineer, though such too it includes within its scope. But a University training is the great ordinary means to a great but ordinary end; it aims at raising the intellectual tone of society, at cultivating the public mind, at purifying the national taste, at supplying true principles to popular enthusiasm and fixed aims to popular aspiration, at giving enlargement and sobriety to the ideas of the age, at facilitating the exercise of political power, and refining the intercourse of private life. It is the education which gives a man a clear conscious view of his own opinions and judgments, a truth in developing them, an eloquence in expressing them, and a force in urging them. It teaches him to see things as they are, to go right to the point, to disentangle a skein of thought, to detect what is sophistical, and to discard what is irrelevant. It prepares him to fill any post with credit, and to master any subject with facility. It shows him how to accommodate himself to others, how to throw himself into their state of mind, how to bring before them his own, how to influence them, how to come to an understanding with them, how to bear with them. He is at home in any society, he has common ground with every class; he knows when to speak and when to be silent; he is able to converse, he is able to listen; he can ask a question pertinently, and gain a lesson seasonably, when he has nothing to impart himself; he is ever ready, yet never in the way; he is a pleasant companion, and a comrade you can depend upon; he knows when to be serious and when to trifle, and he has a sure tact which enables him to trifle with gracefulness and to be serious with effect. He has the repose of a mind which lives in itself, while it lives in the world, and which has resources for its happiness at home when it cannot go abroad. He has a gift which serves him in public, and supports him in retirement, without which good fortune is but vulgar, and with which failure and disappointment have a charm. The art which tends to make a man all this, is in the object which it pursues as useful as the art of wealth or the art of health, though it is less susceptible of method, and less tangible, less certain, less complete in its result.   —*The Idea of a University*, 177–178

13.2. *SENSUS FIDELIUM*

In the July 1859 issue of The Rambler, *Newman published an essay,"On Consulting the Faithful in Matters of Doctrine," which emphasized that Pope Pius IX prior to proclaiming the dogma of the Immaculate Conception (1854) had consulted the faithful about their belief in this doctrine; the theological significance of such consultation rests on the fact that the laity are witnesses to the traditioning of revelation and, as such, have sometimes been better witnesses than the bishops.*

A question has arisen among persons of theological knowledge and fair and candid minds, about the wording and the sense of a passage in the *Rambler* for May. It admits to my own mind of so clear and satisfactory an explanation, that I should think it unnecessary to intrude myself, an anonymous person, between the conductors and readers of this Magazine, except that, as in dogmatic works the replies made to objections often contain the richest matter, so here too, plain remarks on a plain subject may open to the minds of others profitable thoughts, which are more due to their own superior intelligence than to the very words of the writer.

The *Rambler*, then, has these words . . . "in the preparation of a dogmatic definition, the faithful are consulted, as lately in the instance of the Immaculate Conception." Now two questions bearing upon doctrine have been raised on this sentence, putting aside the question of fact as regards the particular instance cited, which must follow the decision on the doctrinal questions: viz. first, whether it can, with doctrinal correctness, be said that an *appeal* to the faithful is one of the preliminaries of a definition of doctrine; and secondly, granting that the faithful are taken into account, still, whether they can correctly be said to be *consulted*.

I shall remark on both these points, and I shall begin with the second.

Now doubtless, if a divine were expressing himself formally, and in Latin, he would not commonly speak of the laity being "consulted" among the preliminaries of a dogmatic definition, because the technical, or even scientific, meaning of the word "consult" is to "consult *with*," or to "take *counsel*." But the English word "consult," in its popular and ordinary use, is not so precise and narrow in its meaning; it is doubtless a word expressive of trust and deference, but not of submission. It includes the idea of inquiring into a matter of *fact*, as well as asking a judgment. Thus we talk of "consulting our barometer" about the weather:—the barometer only attests the *fact* of the state of the atmosphere. In like manner, we may consult a watch or a sundial about the time of day. A physician consults the pulse of his patient; but not in the same sense in which his patient consults *him*. It is but an index of the state of his health. Ecclesiastes says, "Qui *observat* ventum, non seminat;" we might translate it, "he who consults," without meaning that we ask the wind's opinion. This being considered, it was, I conceive, quite allowable for a writer, who was not teaching or treating theology, but, as it were, conversing, to say, as in the passage in question, "In the preparation of a dogmatic definition, the faithful are consulted." Doubtless their advice, their opinion, their judgment on the question of definition is not asked; but the matter of fact, viz. their belief, *is* sought for, as a testimony to that apostolical tradition, on which alone any doctrine whatsoever can be defined. In like manner, we may "consult" the liturgies or the rites of the Church; not that they speak, not that they can take any part whatever in the definition, for they are documents or customs; but they are witnesses to the antiquity or universality of the doctrines which they contain, and about which they are "consulted." And, in like manner, I certainly understood the writer in the *Rambler* to mean (and I think any lay reader might so understand him) that the *fidelium sensus* [understanding of the faithful] and *consensus* is a branch of evidence which it is natural or it necessary for the Church to regard and consult, before she proceeds to any definition, from its intrinsic cogency; and by consequence, that it ever has been so regarded and consulted. . . .

Now I shall go on presently to remark on the proposition itself which is conveyed in the words on which I have been commenting; here, however, I will first observe, that such misconceptions as I have been setting right will and must occur, from the nature of the case, whenever we speak on theological subjects in the vernacular; and if we do not use the vernacular, I do not see how the bulk of the Catholic people are to be catechised or taught at all. English has innovated on the Latin sense of its own Latin words; and if we are to speak according to the conditions of the language, and are to make ourselves intelligible to the multitude, we shall necessarily run the risk of startling those who are resolved to act as mere critics and scholastics in the process of popular instruction. . . .

The conclusion I would draw from all I have been saying is this: Without deciding whether or not it is advisable to introduce points of theology into popular works, and especially whether it is advisable for laymen to do so, still, if this actually is done, we are not to expect in them that perfect accuracy of expression which I demanded in a Latin treatise or a lecture *ex cathedrâ*; and if there be a want of this exactness, we must not at once think it proceeds from self-will and undutifulness in the writers.

Now I come to the *matter* of what the writer in the *Rambler* really said, putting aside the question of the *wording*; and I begin by expressing my belief that, whatever he may be willing to admit on the score of theological Latinity in the use of the word "consult" when applied to the faithful, yet one thing he cannot deny, viz. that in using it, he implied, from the very force of the term, that they are treated by the Holy See, on occasions such as that specified, with attention and consideration.

Then follows the question, Why? and the answer is plain, viz. because the body of the faithful is one of the witnesses to the fact of the tradition of revealed doctrine, and because their *consensus* through Christendom is the voice of the Infallible Church.

I think I am right in saying that the tradition of the Apostles, committed to the whole Church in its various constituents and functions *per modum unius* [as a unit], manifests itself variously at various times: sometimes by the mouth of the episcopacy, sometimes by the doctors, sometimes by the people, sometimes by liturgies, rites, ceremonies, and customs, by events, disputes, movements, and all those other phenomena which are comprised under the name of history. It follows that none of these channels of tradition may be treated with disrespect; granting at the same time fully, that the gift of discerning, discriminating, defining, promulgating, and enforcing any portion of that tradition resides solely in the *Ecclesia docens* [teaching Church].

One man will lay more stress on one aspect of doctrine, another on another; for myself, I am accustomed to lay great stress on the *consensus fidelium*, and I will say how it has come about. . . .

A year or two passed, and the Bishop of Birmingham [Ullathorne] published his treatise on the doctrine. I close this portion of my paper with an extract from his careful view of the argument. "Nor should the universal conviction of pious Catholics be passed over, as of small account in the general argument; for that pious belief, and the devotion which springs from it, are the *faithful reflection* of the pastoral teaching" (p. 172). Reflection; that is, the people are a *mirror*, in which the Bishops see themselves. Well, I suppose a person may *consult* his glass, and in that way may know things about himself which he can learn in no other way. . . .

His lordship proceeds: "The more devout the faithful grew, the more devoted they showed themselves towards this mystery. And it is the devout who have the surest instinct in discerning the mysteries of which the Holy Spirit breathes the grace through the Church, and who, with as sure a tact, reject what is alien from her teaching. The common accord of the faithful has weighed much as an argument even with the most learned divines. St. Augustine says, that amongst many things which most justly held him in the bosom of the Catholic Church, was the 'accord of populations and of nations.' In another work he says, 'It seems that I have believed nothing but the confirmed opinion and the exceedingly wide-spread report of populations and of nations.' Elsewhere he says: 'In matters whereupon the Scripture has not spoken clearly, the custom of the people of God, or the institutions of our predecessors, are to be held as law.' In the same spirit St. Jerome argues, whilst defending the use of relics against Vigilantius: 'So the people of all the Churches who have gone out to meet holy relics, and have received them with so much joy, are to be accounted foolish'" (pp. 172, 173).

And here I might come to an end; but, having got so far, I am induced, before concluding, to suggest an historical instance of the same great principle, which Father Perrone does not draw out.

First, I will set down the various ways in which theologians put before us the bearing of the Consent of the faithful upon the manifestation of the tradition of the Church. Its *consensus* is to be regarded: 1. as a testimony to the fact of the apostolical dogma; 2. as a sort of instinct, or [*phronēma*], deep in the bosom of the mystical body of Christ; 3. as a direction of the Holy Ghost; 4. as an answer to its prayer; 5. as a jealousy of error, which it at once feels as a scandal.

After short explanations of the first four points, Newman discussed the fifth point:

The fifth is enlarged upon in Dr. Newman's second *Lecture on Anglican Difficulties*, from which I quote a few lines: "We know that it is the property of life to be impatient of any foreign substance in the body to which it belongs. It will be sovereign in its own domain, and it conflicts with what it cannot assimilate into itself, and *is irritated and disordered* till it has expelled it. Such expulsion, then, is emphatically a test of uncongeniality, for it shows that the substance ejected, not only is not one with the body that rejects it, but cannot be made one with it; that its introduction is not only useless or superfluous, adventitious, but that it is intolerable." Presently he continues: "The religious life of a people is of a certain quality and direction, and these are tested by the mode in which it encounters the various opinions, customs, and institutions which are submitted to it. Drive a stake into a river's bed, and you will at once ascertain which way it is running, and at what speed; throw up even a straw upon the air, and you will see which way the wind blows; submit your heretical and Catholic principle to the action of the multitude, and you will be able to pronounce at once whether it is imbued with Catholic truth or with heretical falsehood." . . .

Here, of course, I must explain:—in saying this, then, undoubtedly I am not denying that the great body of the Bishops were in their internal belief orthodox; nor that there were numbers of clergy who stood by the laity, and acted as their centres and guides; nor that the laity actually received their faith, in the first instance, from the Bishops and clergy; nor that some portions of the laity were ignorant, and other portions at length corrupted, by the Arian teachers, who got possession of the sees and ordained an heretical clergy;—but I mean still, that in that time of immense confusion the divine dogma of our Lord's divinity was proclaimed, enforced, maintained, and (humanly speaking) preserved, far more by the "Ecclesia docta" [the Church taught = laity] than by the "Ecclesia docens;" [Church teaching = hierarchy] that the body of the episcopate was unfaithful to its commission, while the body of the laity was faithful to its baptism; that at one time the Pope, at other times the patriarchal, metropolitan, and other great sees, at other times general councils, said what they should not have said, or did what obscured and compromised revealed truth; while, on the other hand, it was the Christian people who, under Providence, were the ecclesiastical strength of Athanasius, Hilary, Eusebius of Vercellæ, and other great solitary confessors, who would have failed without them.

I see, then, in the Arian history a palmary example of a state of the Church, during which, in order to know the tradition of the Apostles, we must have recourse to the faithful; for I fairly own, that if I go to writers, since I must adjust the letter of Justin, Clement, and Hippolytus with the Nicene Doctors, I get confused; and what revives and re-instates me, as far as history goes, is the faith of the people. For I argue that, unless they had been catechised, as St. Hilary says, in the orthodox faith from the time of their baptism, they never could have had that horror, which they show, of the heterodox Arian doctrine. Their voice, then, is the voice of tradition; and the instance comes to us with still greater emphasis, when we consider—1. that it occurs in the very beginning of the history of the "Ecclesia docens," [teaching Church] for there can scarcely be said to be any history of her teaching till the age of martyrs was over; 2. that the doctrine in controversy was so momentous, being the very foundation of the Christian system; 3. that the state of controversy and disorder lasted over the long space of sixty years; and that it involved serious persecutions, in life, limb, and property, to the faithful whose loyal perseverance decided it.

It seems, then, as striking an instance as I could take in fulfilment of Father Perrone's statement, that the voice of tradition may in certain cases express itself, not by Councils, nor Fathers, nor Bishops, but the "communis fidelium sensus" [common understanding of the faithful].

I shall set down some authorities for the two points successively, which I have to enforce, viz. that the Nicene dogma was maintained during the greater part of the 4th century, (1) not by the unswerving firmness of the Holy See, Councils, or Bishops, but (2) by the "consensus fidelium" [consensus of the faithful].

I. On the one hand, then, I say, that there was a temporary suspense of the functions of the "Ecclesia docens" [teaching Church]. The body of Bishops failed in the confession of the faith. They spoke variously, one against another; there was nothing, after Nicæa, of firm, unvarying, consistent testimony, for nearly sixty years. There were untrustworthy Councils, unfaithful Bishops; there was weakness, fear of consequences, misguidance, delusion, hallucination, endless, hopeless, extending itself into nearly every corner of the Catholic Church. The comparatively few who remained faithful were discredited and driven into exile; the rest were either deceivers or were deceived. . . .

II. Now we come secondly to the proofs of the fidelity of the laity, and the effectiveness of that fidelity, during that domination of imperial heresy to which the foregoing passages have related. I have abridged the extracts which follow, but not, I hope, to the injury of their sense. . . .

Now I know quite well what will be said to so elaborate a collection of instances as I have been making. The "lector benevolus" [benevolent reader] will quote against me the words of Cicero; "Utitur in re non dubiâ testibus non necessariis" [Witnesses are really unnecessary in a matter beyond doubt.] This is sure to befall a man, when he directs the attention of a friend to any truth which hitherto he has thought little of. At first, he seems to be hazarding a paradox, and at length to be committing a truism. The hearer is first of all startled, and then disappointed; he ends by asking, "Is this all?" It is a curious phenomenon in the philosophy of the human mind, that we often do not know whether we hold a point or not, though we hold it; but when our attention is once drawn to it, then forthwith we find it so much part of ourselves, that we cannot recollect when we began to hold it, and we conclude (with truth), and we declare, that it has always been our belief. . . . A man holds an opinion or a truth, yet without holding it with a simple consciousness and a direct recognition; and thus, though he has never denied, he has never gone so far as to profess it.

As to the particular doctrine to which I have here been directing my view, and the passage in history by which I have been illustrating it, I am not supposing that such times as the Arian will ever come again. As to the present, certainly, if there ever was an age which might dispense with the testimony of the faithful, and leave the maintenance of the truth to the pastors of the Church, it is the age in which we live. Never was the Episcopate of Christendom so devoted to the Holy See, so religious, so earnest in the discharge of its special duties, so little disposed to innovate, so superior to the temptation of theological sophistry. And perhaps this is the reason why the "consensus fidelium" [consensus of the faithful] has, in the minds of many, fallen into the background. Yet each constituent portion of the Church has its proper functions, and no portion can safely be neglected. Though the laity be but the reflection or echo of the clergy in matters of faith, yet there is something in the "pastorum et fidelium *conspiratio*" [agreement of the pastors and the faithful], which is not in the pastors alone. The history of the definition of the Immaculate Conception shows us this; and it will be one among the blessings which the Holy Mother, who is the subject of it, will gain for us, in repayment of the definition, that by that very definition we are all reminded of the part which the laity have had in the preliminaries of its promulgation. Pope Pius has given us a pattern, in his manner of defining, of the duty of considering the sentiments of the laity upon a point of tradition, in spite of whatever fullness of evidence the Bishops had already thrown upon it.

In most cases when a definition is contemplated, the laity will have a testimony to give; but if ever there be an instance when they ought to be consulted, it is in the case of doctrines which bear directly upon devotional sentiments. Such is the Immaculate Conception, of which the *Rambler* was speaking in the sentence which has occasioned these remarks. The faithful people have ever a special function in regard to those doctrinal truths which relate to the Objects of worship. Hence it is, that, while the Councils of the fourth century were traitors to our Lord's divinity, the laity vehemently protested against its impugners. . . . And the Blessed Virgin is preeminently an object of devotion; and therefore it is, I repeat, that though Bishops had already spoken in favour of her absolute sinlessness, the Pope was not content without knowing the feelings of the faithful.

Father Dalgairns gives us another case in point; and with his words I conclude:

> While devotion in the shape of a dogma issues from the high places of the Church, in the shape of devotion . . . it starts from below. . . . Place yourselves, in imagination, in a vast city of the East in the fifth century. Ephesus, the capital of Asia Minor, is all in commotion; for a council is to be held there, and Bishops are flocking in from all parts of the world. There is anxiety painted on every face; so that you may easily see that the question is one of general interest. . . . Ask the very children in the streets what is the

matter; they will tell you that wicked men are coming to make out that their own mother is not the Mother of God. And so, during a live-long day of June, they crowd around the gates of the old cathedral-church of St. Mary, and watch with anxious faces each Bishop as he goes in. Well might they be anxious; for it is well known that Nestorius has won the court over to his side. It was only the other day that he entered the town, with banners displayed and trumpets sounding, surrounded by the glittering files of the emperor's body-guard, with Count Candidianus, their general and his own partisan, at their head. Besides which, it is known for certain, that at least eighty-four Bishops are ready to vote with him; and who knows how many more? He is himself the patriarch of Constantinople, the rival of Rome, the imperial city of the East; and then John of Antioch is hourly expected with his quota of votes; and he, the patriarch of the see next in influence to that of Nestorius, is, if not a heretic, at least of that wretched party which, in ecclesiastical disputes, ever hovers between the two camps of the devil and of God. The day wears on, and still nothing issues from the church; it proves, at least, that there is a difference of opinion; and as the shades of evening close around them, the weary watchers grow more anxious still. At length the great gates of the Basilica are thrown open; and oh, what a cry of joy bursts from the assembled crowd, as it is announced to them that Mary has been proclaimed to be, what every one with a Catholic heart knew that she was before, the Mother of God! . . . Men, women, and children, the noble and the low-born, the stately matron and the modest maiden, all crowd round the Bishops with acclamations. They will not leave them; they accompany them to their homes with long procession of lighted torches; they burn incense before them, after the eastern fashion, to do them honour. There was but little sleep in Ephesus that night; for very joy they remained awake: the whole town was one blaze of light, for each window was illuminated.

My own drift is somewhat different from that which has dictated this glowing description; but the substance of the argument of each of us is one and the same. I think certainly that the *Ecclesia docens* [teaching Church] is more happy when she has such enthusiastic partisans about her as are here represented, than when she cuts off the faithful from the study of her divine doctrines and the sympathy of her divine contemplations, and requires from them *fides implicita* [an assent of faith in a doctrine that is contained within a doctrine that is explicitly believed] in her word, which in the educated classes will terminate in indifference, and in the poorer in superstition.

—*The Rambler*, July 1859

14

Defender of Belief

14.1. "REFLECTIONS" ON KINGSLEY-NEWMAN CORRESPONDENCE

The gratuitous insult of Charles Kingsley is indicative of a political-social attitude in Victorian England that considered Roman Catholics "fair-game" for insults, even though they were untrue and unjust. Newman rose to the occasion first by an exchange of correspondence, which he published as a pamphlet: Mr. Kingsley and Dr. Newman: A Correspondence on the Question Whether Dr. Newman Teaches That Truth Is No Virtue? *The following "reflections" at the end of the pamphlet exemplify Newman's rhetorical skills in answering unsubstantiated charges:*

I shall attempt a brief analysis of the foregoing correspondence; and I trust that the wording which I shall adopt will not offend against the gravity due both to myself and to the occasion. It is impossible to do justice to the course of thought evolved in it without some familiarity of expression.

Mr. Kingsley begins then by exclaiming,—"O the chicanery, the wholesale fraud, the vile hypocrisy, the conscience-killing tyranny of Rome! We have not far to seek for an evidence of it. There's Father Newman to wit: one living specimen is worth a hundred dead ones. He, a Priest writing of Priests, tells us that lying is never any harm."

I interpose: "You are taking a most extraordinary liberty with my name. If I have said this, tell me when and where."

Mr. Kingsley replies: "You said it, Reverend Sir, in a Sermon which you preached, when a Protestant, as Vicar of St. Mary's, and published in 1844; and I could read you a very salutary lecture on the effects which that Sermon had at the time on my own opinion of you."

I make answer: "Oh . . . *Not*, it seems, as a Priest speaking of Priests;—but let us have the passage."

Mr. Kingsley relaxes: "Do you know, I like your *tone*. From your *tone* I rejoice, greatly rejoice, to be able to believe that you did not mean what you said."

I rejoin: "*Mean* it! I maintain I never *said* it, whether as a Protestant or as a Catholic."

Mr. Kingsley replies: "I waive that point."

I object: "Is it possible! What? waive the main question! I either said it or I didn't. You have made a monstrous charge against me; direct, distinct, public. You are bound to prove it as directly, as distinctly, as publicly;—or to own you can't."

"Well," says Mr. Kingsley, "if you are quite sure you did not say it, I'll take your word for it; I really will."

My *word*! I am dumb. Somehow I thought that it was my *word* that happened to be on trial. The *word* of a Professor of lying, that he does not lie!

But Mr. Kingsley re-assures me: "We are both gentlemen," he says: "I have done as much as one English gentleman can expect from another."

I begin to see: He thought me a gentleman at the very time that he said I taught lying on system. After all, it is not I, but it is Mr. Kingsley who did not mean what he said. . . .

While I feel then that Mr. Kingsley's February explanation is miserably insufficient in itself for his January enormity, still I feel also that the Correspondence, which lies between these two acts of his, constitutes a real satisfaction to those principles of historical and literary justice to which he has given so rude a shock.

Accordingly, I have put it into print, and make no further criticism on Mr. Kingsley.

J. H. N.

—Mr. Kingsley and Dr. Newman: A Correspondence
on the Question Whether Dr. Newman Teaches
That Truth Is No Virtue? 19–21

14.2. "COMING INTO PORT AFTER A ROUGH SEA"

At the time that Newman wrote his Apologia *(1864), rumors were circulating that he was on the verge of returning to the Church of England. At the beginning of the fifth chapter on "Position of my Mind since 1845," he emphatically denied these rumors:*

From the time that I became a Catholic, of course I have no further history of my religious opinions to narrate. In saying this, I do not mean to say that my mind has been idle, or that I have given up thinking on theological subjects; but that I have had no variations to record, and have had no anxiety of heart whatever. I have been in perfect peace and contentment; I never have had one doubt. I was not conscious to myself, on my conversion, of any change, intellectual or moral, wrought in my mind. I was not conscious of firmer faith in the fundamental truths of Revelation, or of more self-command; I had not more fervour; but it was like coming into port after a rough sea; and my happiness on that score remains to this day without interruption.

—Apologia pro Vita Sua, 238

14.3. "FAITH AND DOUBT"

The question of "faith and doubt" was an issue that Newman repeatedly addressed during his life. In this discourse, delivered soon after he became a Roman Catholic, he emphasized that faith and doubt are incompatible—a person "cannot believe by halves"—one either believes or does not. Newman then compared faith in God with trust in a friend: if a person is happy to be with a friend, similarly a Christian believer finds peace and joy in the Church. Nonetheless, arguments do not compel belief, since faith is a matter of grace; accordingly, Newman encouraged prospective converts not to experiment with faith, but to be certain of their decision before converting.

Those who are drawn by curiosity or a better motive to inquire into the Catholic Religion, sometimes put to us a strange question,—whether, if they took up the profession of it, they would be at liberty, when they felt inclined, to reconsider the question of its Divine authority; meaning, by "reconsideration," an inquiry springing from doubt of it, and possibly ending in a denial. The same question, in the form of an objection, is often asked by those who have no thoughts at all of becoming Catholics, and who enlarge upon it, as something terrible, that whoever once enters the pale of the Church, on him the door of egress is shut for ever; that, once a Catholic, he never, never can doubt again; that, whatever his misgivings may be, he must stifle them, nay must start from them as the suggestions of the evil spirit; in short, that he must give up altogether the search after truth, and do a violence to his mind, which is nothing short of immoral. This is what is said, my brethren, by certain objectors, and their own view is, or ought to be, if they are consistent, this,—that it is a fault ever to make up our mind once for all on any religious subject whatever; and that, however sacred a doctrine may be, and however evident to us,—let us say, for instance, the divinity of our Lord, or the existence of God,—we ought always to reserve to ourselves the liberty of doubting about it. . . .

It is, then, perfectly true, that the Church does not allow her children to entertain any doubt of her teaching; and that, first of all, simply for this reason, because they are Catholics only while they have faith, and faith is incompatible with doubt. No one can be a Catholic without a simple faith, that what the Church declares in God's name, is God's word, and therefore true. A man must simply believe that the Church is the oracle of God; he must be as certain of her mission, as he is of the mission of the Apostles. Now, would any one ever call him certain that the Apostles came from God, if after professing his certainty, he added, that perhaps he might have reason to doubt one day about their mission? Such an anticipation would be a real, though latent, doubt, betraying that he was not certain of it at present. A person who says, "I believe just at this moment, but perhaps I am excited without knowing it, and I cannot answer for myself, that I shall believe tomorrow," does not believe now. A man who says, "Perhaps I am in a kind of delusion, which will one day pass away from me, and leave me as I was before"; or "I believe as far as I can tell, but there may be arguments in the background which will change my view," such a man has not faith at all. When, then, Protestants quarrel with us for saying that those who join us must give up all ideas of ever doubting the Church in time to come, they do nothing else but quarrel with us for insisting on the necessity of faith in her. . . . I must insist upon this: faith implies a confidence in a man's mind, that the thing believed is really true; but, if it is once true, it never can be false. . . . And if I bargain to be allowed in time to come not to believe, or to doubt, that God became man, I am but asking to be allowed to doubt or disbelieve what I hold to be an eternal truth. I do not see the privilege of such a permission at all, or the meaning of wishing to secure it:—if at present I have no doubt whatever about it, then I am but asking leave to fall into error; if at present I have doubts about it, then I do not believe it at present, that is, I have not faith. But I cannot both really believe it now, and yet look forward to a time when perhaps I shall not believe it; to make provision for future doubt, is to doubt at present. It proves I am not in a fit state to become a Catholic now. I may love by halves, I may obey by halves; I cannot believe by halves: either I have faith, or I have it not.

And so again, when a man has become a Catholic, were he to set about following a doubt which has occurred to him, he has already disbelieved. I have not to warn him against losing his faith, he is not merely in danger of losing it, he has lost it; from the nature of the case he has already lost it; he fell from grace at the moment when he deliberately entertained and pursued his doubt. No one can determine to doubt what he is already sure of; but if he is not sure that the Church is from God, he does not believe it. It is not I who forbid him to doubt; he has taken the matter into his own hands when he determined on asking for leave; he has begun, not ended, in unbelief; his very wish, his purpose, is his sin. I do not make it so, it is such from the very state of the case. You sometimes hear, for example, of Catholics falling away, who will tell you it arose from reading the Scriptures, which opened their eyes to the "unscripturalness," so they speak, of the Church of the Living God. No; Scripture did not make them disbelieve (impossible!); they disbelieved *when* they opened the Bible; they opened it in an unbelieving spirit, and for an unbelieving purpose; they would not have opened it, had they not anticipated—I might say, hoped—that they should find things there inconsistent with Catholic teaching. They begin in self-will and disobedience, and they end in apostasy. This, then, is the direct and obvious reason why the Church cannot allow her children the liberty of doubting the truth of her word. He who really believes in it now, cannot imagine the future discovery of reasons to shake his faith; if he imagines it, he has not faith; and that so many Protestants think it a sort of tyranny in the Church to forbid any children of hers to doubt about her teaching, only shows they do not know what faith is—which is the case; it is a strange idea to them. Let a man cease to inquire, or cease to call himself her child.

This is my first remark, and now I go on to a second. You may easily conceive, my brethren, that they who are entering the Church, or at least those who have entered it, have more than faith; that they have some portion of Divine love also. They have heard in the Church of the charity of Him who died for them, and who has given them His Sacraments as the means of conveying the merits of His death to their souls, and they have felt more or less in those poor souls of theirs the beginnings of a responsive charity drawing them to Him. Now, does it stand with a loving trust, better than with faith, for a man to anticipate the possibility of doubting or denying the great mercies in which he is rejoicing? Take an instance; what would you think of a friend whom you loved, who could bargain that, in spite of his present trust in you, he might be allowed some day to doubt you? who, when a thought came into his mind, that you were playing a game with him, or that you were a knave, or a profligate, did not drive it from him with indignation, or laugh it away for its absurdity, but considered that he had an evident right to indulge it, nay, should be wanting in duty to himself, unless he did? Would you think that your friend trifled with truth, that he was unjust to his reason, that he was wanting in manliness, that he was hurting his mind if he shrank from the thought? or would you not call him cruel and miserable if he did not? For me, my brethren, if he took the latter course, may I never be intimate with so unpleasant a person; suspicious, jealous minds, minds that keep at a distance from me, that insist on their rights, fall back on their own centre, are ever fancying offences, and are cold, censorious, wayward, and uncertain, these are often to be borne as a cross; but give me for my friend one who will unite heart and hand with me, who will throw himself into my cause and interest, who will take my part when I am attacked, who will be sure beforehand that I am in the right, and, if he is critical, as he may have cause to be towards a being of sin and imperfection, will be so from very love and loyalty, from an anxiety that I should always show to advantage, and a wish that others should love me as heartily as he does. I should not say a friend trusted me, who listened to every idle story against me; and I should like his absence better than his company, if he gravely told me that it was a duty he owed to himself to encourage his misgivings of my honour.

Well, pass on to a higher subject;—could a man be said to trust in God, and to love God, who was familiar with doubts whether there was a God at all, or who bargained that, just as often as he pleased, he might be at liberty to doubt whether God was good, or just or mighty; and who maintained that, unless he did this, he was but a poor slave, that his mind was in bondage, and could render no free acceptable service to his Maker; that the very worship which God approved was one attended with a *caveat*, on the worshipper's part, that he did not promise to render it tomorrow; that he would not answer for himself that some argument might not come to light, which he had never heard before, which would make it a grave, moral duty in him to suspend his judgment and his devotion? Why, I should say, my brethren, that that man was worshipping his own mind, his own dear self and not God; that his idea of God was a mere accidental form which his thoughts took at this time or that,— for a long period or a short one, as the case might be,—not an image of the great Eternal Object, but a passing sentiment or imagination which meant nothing at all. I should say, and most men would agree with me, did they choose to give attention to the matter, that the person in question was a very self-conceited, self-wise man, and had neither love, nor faith, nor fear, nor anything supernatural about him; that his pride must be broken, and his heart new made, before he was capable of any religious act at all. The argument is the same, in its degree, when applied to the Church; she speaks to us as a messenger from God,—how can a man who feels this, who comes to her, who falls at her feet as such, make a reserve, that he may be allowed to doubt her at some future day? Let the world cry out, if it will, that his reason is in fetters; let it pronounce that he is a bigot, unless he reserves his right of doubting; but he knows full well himself that he would be an ingrate and a fool, if he did. Fetters, indeed! yes, "the cords of Adam," the fetters of love, these are what bind him to the Holy Church; he is, with the Apostle, the slave of Christ, the Church's Lord; united (never to part, as he trusts, while life lasts), to her Sacraments, to her Sacrifices, to her Saints, to the Blessed Mary her advocate, to Jesus, to God.

The truth is, that the world, knowing nothing of the blessings of the Catholic faith, and prophesying nothing but ill concerning it, fancies that a convert, after the first fervour is over, feels nothing but disappointment, weariness, and offence in his new religion, and is secretly desirous of retracing his steps. This is at the root of the alarm and irritation which it manifests at hearing that doubts are incompatible with a Catholic's profession, because it is sure that doubts will come upon him, and then how pitiable will be his state! That there can be peace, and joy, and knowledge, and freedom, and spiritual strength in the Church, is a thought far beyond the world's imagination; for it regards her simply as a frightful conspiracy against the happiness of man, seducing her victims by specious professions, and, when they are once hers, caring nothing for the misery which breaks upon them, so that by any means she may detain them in bondage. Accordingly, it conceives we are in perpetual warfare with our own reason, fierce objections ever rising within us, and we forcibly repressing them. It believes that, after the likeness of a vessel which has met with some accident at sea, we are ever baling out the water which rushes in upon us, and have hard work to keep afloat; we just manage to linger on, either by an unnatural strain on our minds, or by turning them away from the subject of religion. The world disbelieves our doctrines itself, and cannot understand our own believing them. It considers them so strange, that it is quite sure, though we will not confess it, that we are haunted day and night with doubts, and tormented with the apprehension of yielding to them. I really do think it is the world's judgment, that one principal part of a confessor's work is the putting down such misgivings in his penitents. It fancies that the reason is ever rebelling, like the flesh; that doubt, like concupiscence, is elicited by every sight and sound, and that temptation insinuates itself in every page of letter-press, and through the very voice of a Protestant polemic. When it sees a Catholic Priest, it looks hard at him, to make out how much there is of folly in his composition, and how much of hypocrisy.

But, my dear brethren, if these are your thoughts, you are simply in error. Trust me, rather than the world, when I tell you, that it is no difficult thing for a Catholic to believe; and that unless he grievously mismanages himself, the difficult thing is for him to doubt. He has received a gift which makes faith easy: it is not without an effort, a miserable effort, that any one who has received that gift, unlearns to believe. He does violence to his mind, not in exercising, but in withholding his faith. When objections occur to him, which they may easily do if he lives in the world, they are as odious and unwelcome to him as impure thoughts are to the virtuous. He does certainly shrink from them, he flings them away from him, but why? not in the first instance, because they are dangerous, but because they are cruel and base. His loving Lord has done everything for him, and has He deserved such a return? . . . He has poured on us His grace, He has been with us in our perplexities, He has led us on from one truth to another, He has forgiven us our sins, He has satisfied our reason, He has made faith easy, He has given us His Saints, He shows before us day by day His own Passion; why should I leave Him? What has He ever done to me but good? Why must I reexamine what I have examined once for all? Why must I listen to every idle word which flits past me against Him, on pain of being called a bigot and a slave, when, if I did, I should be behaving to the Most High, as you yourselves, who so call me, would not behave towards a human friend or benefactor? If I am convinced in my reason, and persuaded in my heart, why may I not be allowed to remain unmolested in my worship?

I have said enough on this subject; still there is a third point of view in which it may be useful to consider it. Personal prudence is not the first or second ground for refusing to hear objections to the Church, but a motive it is, and that from the peculiar nature of Divine faith, which cannot be treated as an ordinary conviction of belief. Faith is the gift of God, and not a mere act of our own, which we are free to exert when we will. It is quite distinct from an exercise of reason, though it follows upon it. I may feel the force of the argument for the Divine origin of the Church; I may see that I ought to believe; and yet I may be unable to believe. This is no imaginary case; there is many a man who has ground enough to believe, who wishes to believe, but who cannot believe. It is always indeed his own fault, for God gives grace to all who ask for it, and use it, but still such is the fact, that conviction is not faith. Take the parallel case of obedience; many a man knows he ought to obey God, and does not and cannot—through his own fault, indeed—but still he cannot; for through grace only can he obey. Now, faith is not a mere conviction in reason, it is a firm assent, it is a clear certainty greater than any other certainty; and this is wrought in the mind by the grace of God, and by it alone. As then men may be convinced, and not act according to their conviction, so may they be convinced, and not believe according to their conviction. They may confess that the argument is against them, that they have nothing to say for themselves, and that to believe is to be happy; and yet, after all, they avow they cannot believe, they do not know why, but they cannot; they acquiesce in unbelief, and they turn away from God and His Church. Their reason is convinced, and their doubts are moral ones, arising in their root from a fault of the will. In a word, the arguments for religion do not compel any one to believe, just as arguments for good conduct do not compel any one to obey. Obedience is the consequence of willing to obey, and faith is the consequence of willing to believe; we may see what is right, whether in matters of faith or obedience, of ourselves, but we cannot will what is right without the grace of God. Here is the difference between other exercises of reason, and arguments for the truth of religion. It requires no act of faith to assent to the truth that two and two make four; we cannot help assenting to it; and hence there is no merit in assenting to it; but there is merit in believing that the Church is from God; for though there are abundant reasons to prove it to us, yet we can, without an absurdity, quarrel with the conclusion; we may complain that it is not clearer, we may suspend our assent, we may doubt about it, if we will, and grace alone can turn a bad will into a good one.

And now you see why a Catholic dare not in prudence attend to such objections as are brought against his faith; he has no fear of their proving that the Church does not come from God, but he is afraid, if he listened to them without reason, lest God should punish him by the loss of his supernatural faith. This is one cause of that miserable state of mind, to which I have already alluded, in which men would fain be Catholics, and are not. They have trifled with conviction, they have listened to arguments against what they knew to be true, and a deadness of mind has fallen on them; faith has failed them, and, as time goes on, they betray in their words and their actions, the Divine judgment, with which they are visited. They become careless and unconcerned, or restless and unhappy, or impatient of contradiction; ever asking advice and quarrelling with it when given; not attempting to answer the arguments urged against them, but simply not believing. This is the whole of their case, they do not believe. And then it is quite an accident what becomes of them; perhaps they continue on in this perplexed and comfortless state, lingering about the Church, yet not of her; not knowing what they believe and what they do not, like blind men, or men deranged, who are deprived of the eye, whether of body or mind, and cannot guide themselves in consequence; ever exciting hopes of a return, and ever disappointing them;—or, if they are men of more vigorous minds, they launch forward in a course of infidelity, not really believing less, as they proceed, for from the first they believed nothing, but taking up, as time goes on, more and more consistent forms of error, till sometimes, if a free field is given them, they even develop into atheism. Such is the end of those who, under the pretence of inquiring after truth, trifle with conviction.

Here then are some of the reasons why the Catholic Church cannot consistently allow her children to doubt the divinity and the truth of her words. Mere investigation indeed into the grounds of our faith is not to doubt; nor is it doubting to consider the arguments urged against it, when there is good reason for doing so; but I am speaking of a real doubt, or a wanton entertainment of objections. Such a procedure the Church denounces, and not only for the reasons which I have assigned, but because it would be a plain abandonment of her office and character to act otherwise. How can she, who has the prerogative of infallibility, allow her children to doubt of her gift? It would be a simple inconsistency in her, who is the sure oracle of truth and messenger of heaven, to look with indifference on rebels to her authority. She simply does what the Apostles did before her, whom she has succeeded. . . . It is thus that the Church ever forbids inquiry in those who already acknowledge her authority; but if they will inquire, she cannot hinder it; but they are not justified in doing so.

And now I think you see, my brethren, why inquiry precedes faith, and does not follow it. You inquired before you joined the Church; you were satisfied, and God rewarded you with the grace of faith; were you now determined to inquire further, you would lead us to think you had lost it again, for inquiry and faith are in their very nature incompatible. I will add, what is very evident, that no other religious body has a right to demand such an exercise of faith in it, and a right to forbid you further inquiry, but the Catholic Church; and for this simple reason, that no other body even claims to be infallible, let alone the proof of such a claim. . . .

And now, my brethren, who are not Catholics, perhaps you will tell me, that, if all inquiry is to cease when you become Catholics, you ought to be very sure that the Church is from God before you join it. You speak truly; no one should enter the Church without a firm purpose of taking her word in all matters of doctrine and morals, and that, on the ground of her coming directly from the God of Truth. You must look the matter in the face, and count the cost. If you do not come in this spirit, you may as well not come at all; high and low, learned and ignorant, must come to learn. If you are right as far as this, you cannot go very wrong; you have the foundation; but, if you come in any other temper, you had better wait till you have got rid of it. You must come, I say, to the Church to learn; you must come, not to bring your own notions to her, but with the intention of ever being a learner; you must come with the intention of taking her for your portion, and of never leaving her. Do not come as an experiment; do not come as you would take sittings in a chapel, or tickets for a lecture-room; come to her as to your home, to the school of your souls, to the Mother of Saints, and to the vestibule of heaven. On the other hand, do not distress yourselves with thoughts whether, when you have joined her, your faith will last; this is a suggestion of your enemy to hold you back. He who has begun a good work in you, will perfect it; He who has chosen you, will be faithful to you; put your cause into His hand, wait upon Him, and you will surely persevere. What good work will you ever begin, if you bargain first to see the end of it? If you wish to do all at once, you will do nothing; he has done half the work, who has begun it well; you will not gain your Lord's praise at the final reckoning by hiding His talent. No; when He brings you from error to truth, He will have done the more difficult work (if aught is difficult to Him), and surely He will preserve you from returning from truth to error. Take the experience of those who have gone before you in the same course; they had many fears that their faith would fail them, before taking the great step, but those fears vanished on their taking it; they had fears, before they received the grace of faith, lest, after receiving it, they should lose it again, but no fears (except on the ground of their general frailness) after it was actually given them.

Be convinced in your reason that the Catholic Church is a teacher sent to you from God, and it is enough. I do not wish you to join her, till you are. If you are half convinced, pray for a full conviction, and wait till you have it. It is better indeed to come quickly, but better slowly than carelessly; and sometimes, as the proverb goes, the more haste, the worse speed. Only make yourselves sure that the delay is not from any fault of yours, which you can remedy. God deals with us very differently; conviction comes slowly to some men, quickly to others; in some it is the result of much thought and many reasonings, in others of a sudden illumination. . . . The case is the same now; some men are converted merely by entering a Catholic Church; others are converted by reading one book; others by one doctrine. They feel the weight of their sins, and they see that that religion must come from God which alone has the means of forgiving them. Or they are touched and overcome by the evident sanctity, beauty, and (as I may say) fragrance of the Catholic Religion. Or they long for a guide amid the strife of tongues; and the very doctrine of the Church about faith, which is so hard to many, is conviction to them. Others, again, hear many objections to the Church, and follow out the whole subject far and wide; conviction can scarcely come to them except as at the end of a long inquiry. As in a court of justice, one man's innocence may be proved at once, another's is the result of a careful investigation; one has nothing in his conduct or character to explain, against another there are many unfavourable presumptions at first sight; so Holy Church presents herself very differently to different minds who are contemplating her from without. God deals with them differently; but, if they are faithful to their light, at last, in their own time, though it may be a different time to each, He brings them to that one and the same state of mind, very definite and not to be mistaken, which we call *conviction*. They will have no doubt, whatever difficulties may still attach to the subject, that the Church is from God; they may not be able to answer this objection or that, but they will be certain in spite of it.

This is a point which should ever be kept in view: conviction is a state of mind, and it is something beyond and distinct from the mere arguments of which it is the result; it does not vary with their strength or their number. Arguments lead to a conclusion, and when the arguments are stronger, the conclusion is clearer; but conviction may be felt as strongly in consequence of a clear conclusion, as of one which is clearer. A man may be so sure upon six reasons, that he does not need a seventh, nor would feel surer if he had it. And so as regards the Catholic Church: men are convinced in very various ways,—what convinces one, does not convince another; but this is an accident; the time comes anyhow, sooner or later, when a man ought to be convinced, and is convinced, and then he is bound not to wait for any more arguments, though more arguments be producible. He will find himself in a condition when he may even refuse to hear more arguments in behalf of the Church; he does not wish to read or think more on the subject; his mind is quite made up. In such a case it is his duty to join the Church at once; he must not delay; let him be cautious in counsel, but prompt in execution. This it is that makes Catholics so anxious about him: it is not that they wish him to be precipitate; but, knowing the temptations which the evil one ever throws in our way, they are lovingly anxious for his soul, lest he has come to the point of conviction, and is passing it, and is losing his chance of conversion. If so, it may never return; God has not chosen every one to salvation: it is a rare gift to be a Catholic; it may be offered to us once in our lives and never again; and, if we have not seized on the "accepted time," nor know "in our day the things which are for our peace," oh, the misery for us!

What shall we be able to say when death comes, and we are not
converted, and it is directly and immediately our own doing that
we are not? . . .   —Discourse 11, *Discourses to
Mixed Congregations*, 214–237

14.4. THREE BROTHERS
WITH DIFFERENT CERTITUDES

In his Grammar of Assent, *Newman discussed an example of
three brothers, raised in the same family and presumably with
the same religious beliefs, who later in life diverge in their religious beliefs, with the result that one becomes an "unbeliever,"
another a "Humanitarian," and the third a Catholic—which
was respectively the situation of the three Newman brothers:
Charles, Francis, and John Henry.*

Thus, of three Protestants, one becomes a Catholic, a second
a Unitarian, and a third an unbeliever: how is this? The first
becomes a Catholic, because he assented, as a Protestant, to the
doctrine of our Lord's divinity, with a real assent and a genuine conviction, and because this certitude, taking possession of
his mind, led him on to welcome the Catholic doctrines of the
Real Presence and of the Theotocos [Mother of God], till his
Protestantism fell off from him, and he submitted himself to the
Church. The second became a Unitarian, because, proceeding on
the principle that Scripture was the rule of faith and that a man's
private judgment was its rule of interpretation, and finding that
the doctrine of the Nicene and Athanasian Creeds did not follow
by logical necessity from the text of Scripture, he said to himself,
"The word of God has been made of none effect by the traditions of men," and therefore nothing was left for him but to profess what he considered primitive Christianity, and to become
a Humanitarian. The third gradually subsided into infidelity,
because he started with the Protestant dogma, cherished in the
depths of his nature, that a priesthood was a corruption of the
simplicity of the Gospel. First, then, he would protest against the

sacrifice of the Mass; next he gave up baptismal regeneration, and the sacramental principle; then he asked himself whether dogmas were not a restraint on Christian liberty as well as sacraments; then came the question, what after all was the use of teachers of religion? why should any one stand between him and his Maker? After a time it struck him, that this obvious question had to be answered by the Apostles, as well as by the Anglican clergy; so he came to the conclusion that the true and only revelation of God to man is that which is written on the heart. This did for a time, and he remained a Deist. But then it occurred to him, that this inward moral law was there within the breast, whether there was a God or not, and that it was a roundabout way of enforcing that law, to say that it came from God, and simply unnecessary, considering it carried with it its own sacred and sovereign authority, as our feelings instinctively testified; and when he turned to look at the physical world around him, he really did not see what scientific proof there was there of the Being of God at all, and it seemed to him as if all things would go on quite as well as at present, without that hypothesis as with it; so he dropped it, and became a *purus, putus* Atheist.

Now the world will say, that in these three cases old certitudes were lost, and new were gained; but it is not so: each of the three men started with just one certitude, as he would have himself professed, had he examined himself narrowly; and he carried it out and carried it with him into a new system of belief. He was true to that one conviction from first to last; and on looking back on the past, would perhaps insist upon this, and say he had really been consistent all through, when others made much of his great changes in religious opinion. He has indeed made serious additions to his initial ruling principle, but he has lost no conviction of which he was originally possessed.

—*Grammar of Assent*, 245–247

15

Champion of Conscience

VATICAN I:
15.1. DESCRIPTION OF INFALLIBILITY

The First Vatican Council (1869–1870) described the conditions for the papal exercise of infallibility in its constitution Pastor Aeternus *(July 18, 1870); the key part of the description is as follows:*

Therefore, faithfully adhering to the tradition received from the beginning of the christian faith, to the glory of God our savior, for the exaltation of the Catholic religion and for the salvation of the christian people, with the approval of the Sacred Council, we teach and define as a divinely revealed dogma that when the Roman Pontiff speaks EX CATHEDRA, that is, when, in the exercise of his office as shepherd and teacher of all Christians, in virtue of his supreme apostolic authority, he defines a doctrine concerning faith or morals [*mores*] to be held [*tenenda*] by the whole Church, he possesses, by the divine assistance promised to him in blessed Peter, that infallibility which the divine Redeemer willed his Church to enjoy [*pollere*] in defining doctrine concerning faith or morals. Therefore, such definitions of the Roman Pontiff are of themselves, and not by the consent of the Church, irreformable.

—Vatican I, *Pastor Aeternus*, chapter 4

15.2. "CONSCIENCE AND
THE POPE"

Newman devoted an extensive section of his Letter Addressed
to the Duke of Norfolk on Occasion of Mr. Gladstone's Recent
Expostulation *to answering Gladstone's charge that the Pope's
"absolute authority" violated the conscience of Christians.*

. . . for what would become of the Pope's "absolute authority,"
as Mr. Gladstone calls it, if the private conscience had an absolute authority also?

I wish to answer this important objection distinctly.

1. First, I am using the word "conscience" in the high sense in
which I have already explained it,—not as a fancy or an opinion,
but as a dutiful obedience to what claims to be a divine voice,
speaking within us; and that this is the view properly to be taken
of it, I shall not attempt to prove here, but shall assume it as a
first principle.

2. Secondly, I observe that conscience is not a judgment
upon any speculative truth, any abstract doctrine, but bears
immediately on conduct, on something to be done or not
done. "Conscience," says St. Thomas, "is the practical judgment or dictate of reason, by which we judge what *hic et nunc*
[here and now] is to be done as being good, or to be avoided
as evil." Hence conscience cannot come into direct collision
with the Church's or the Pope's infallibility; which is engaged
in general propositions, and in the condemnation of particular and given errors.

3. Next, I observe that, conscience being a practical dictate,
a collision is possible between it and the Pope's authority only
when the Pope legislates, or gives particular orders, and the like.
But a Pope is not infallible in his laws, nor in his commands,
nor in his acts of state, nor in his administration, nor in his public policy. Let it be observed that the Vatican Council has left
him just as it found him here. Mr. Gladstone's language on this
point is to me quite unintelligible. Why, instead of using vague
terms, does he not point out precisely the very words by which

the Council has made the Pope in his acts infallible? Instead of so doing, he assumes a conclusion which is altogether false. He says, p. 34, "First comes the Pope's infallibility:" then in the next page he insinuates that, under his infallibility, come acts of excommunication, as if the Pope could not make mistakes in this field of action. He says, p. 35, "It may be sought to plead that the Pope does not propose to invade the country, to seize Woolwich, or burn Portsmouth. He will only, at the worst, excommunicate opponents . . . Is this a good answer? After all, even in the Middle Ages, it was not by the direct action of fleets and armies of their own that the Popes contended with kings who were refractory; it was mainly by interdicts," &c. What have excommunication and interdict to do with Infallibility? Was St. Peter infallible on that occasion at Antioch when St. Paul withstood him? was St. Victor infallible when he separated from his communion the Asiatic Churches? or Liberius when in like manner he excommunicated Athanasius? And, to come to later times, was Gregory XIII, when he had a medal struck in honour of the Bartholomew massacre? or Paul IV in his conduct towards Elizabeth? or Sextus V when he blessed the Armada? or Urban VIII when he persecuted Galileo? No Catholic ever pretends that these Popes were infallible in these acts. Since then infallibility alone could block the exercise of conscience, and the Pope is not infallible in that subject-matter in which conscience is of supreme authority, no deadlock, such as is implied in the objection which I am answering, can take place between conscience and the Pope.

4. But, of course, I have to say again, lest I should be misunderstood, that when I speak of Conscience, I mean conscience truly so called. When it has the right of opposing the supreme, though not infallible Authority of the Pope, it must be something more than that miserable counterfeit which, as I have said above, now goes by the name. If in a particular case it is to be taken as a sacred and sovereign monitor, its dictate, in order to prevail against the voice of the Pope, must follow upon serious thought, prayer, and all available means of arriving at a right judgment on the matter in question. And further, obedience to

the Pope is what is called "in possession"; that is, the *onus probandi* [burden of proof] of establishing a case against him lies, as in all cases of exception, on the side of conscience. Unless a man is able to say to himself, as in the Presence of God, that he must not, and dare not, act upon the Papal injunction, he is bound to obey it, and would commit a great sin in disobeying it. *Primâ facie* it is his bounden duty, even from a sentiment of loyalty, to believe the Pope right and to act accordingly. He must vanquish that mean, ungenerous, selfish, vulgar spirit of his nature, which, at the very first rumour of a command, places itself in opposition to the Superior who gives it, asks itself whether he is not exceeding his right, and rejoices, in a moral and practical matter to commence with scepticism. He must have no wilful determination to exercise a right of thinking, saying, doing just what he pleases, the question of truth and falsehood, right and wrong, the duty if possible of obedience, the love of speaking as his Head speaks, and of standing in all cases on his Head's side, being simply discarded. If this necessary rule were observed, collisions between the Pope's authority and the authority of conscience would be very rare. On the other hand, in the fact that, after all, in extraordinary cases, the conscience of each individual is free, we have a safeguard and security, were security necessary (which is a most gratuitous supposition), that no Pope ever will be able, as the objection supposes, to create a false conscience for his own ends.

—*A Letter Addressed to the Duke of Norfolk on Occasion of Mr. Gladstone's Recent Expostulation*, in *Certain Difficulties Felt by Anglicans in Catholic Teaching*, 2:255–258

15.3. "CONSCIENCE AND THE EXISTENCE OF GOD"

Many of the readers of Newman's Letter to the Duke of Norfolk *(1875) would have been familiar with Newman's* Grammar of Assent *(1870), where he described "conscience" as a moral sense and a sense of duty inherent in each individual and recognized*

by each person from childhood; conscience, as the voice of God
within each of us enables us to recognize the presence of God
in our lives.

I have already said I am not proposing here to prove the Being
of a God; yet I have found it impossible to avoid saying where
I look for the proof of it. For I am looking for that proof in the
same quarter as that from which I would commence a proof of
His attributes and character,—by the same means as those by
which I show how we apprehend Him, not merely as a notion,
but as a reality. The last indeed of these three investigations
alone concerns me here, but I cannot altogether exclude the two
former from my consideration. However, I repeat, what I am
directly aiming at, is to explain how we gain an image of God
and give a real assent to the proposition that He exists. And
next, in order to do this, of course I must start from some first
principle;—and that first principle, which I assume and shall not
attempt to prove, is that which I should also use as a foundation in those other two inquiries, viz. that we have by nature a
conscience.

I assume, then, that Conscience has a legitimate place among
our mental acts; as really so, as the action of memory, of reasoning, of imagination, or as the sense of the beautiful; that, as there
are objects which, when presented to the mind, cause it to feel
grief, regret, joy, or desire, so there are things which excite in us
approbation or blame, and which we in consequence call right
or wrong; and which, experienced in ourselves, kindle in us that
specific sense of pleasure or pain, which goes by the name of a
good or bad conscience. This being taken for granted, I shall
attempt to show that in this special feeling, which follows on the
commission of what we call right or wrong, lie the materials for
the real apprehension of a Divine Sovereign and Judge.

The feeling of conscience (being, I repeat, a certain keen
sensibility, pleasant or painful,—self-approval and hope, or
compunction and fear,—attendant on certain of our actions,
which in consequence we call right or wrong) is twofold:—it

is a moral sense, and a sense of duty; a judgment of the reason and a magisterial dictate. Of course its act is indivisible; still it has these two aspects, distinct from each other, and admitting of a separate consideration. Though I lost my sense of the obligation which I lie under to abstain from acts of dishonesty, I should not in consequence lose my sense that such actions were an outrage offered to my moral nature. Again; though I lost my sense of their moral deformity, I should not therefore lose my sense that they were forbidden to me. Thus conscience has both a critical and a judicial office, and though its promptings, in the breasts of the millions of human beings to whom it is given, are not in all cases correct, that does not necessarily interfere with the force of its testimony and of its sanction: its testimony that there is a right and a wrong, and its sanction to that testimony conveyed in the feelings which attend on right or wrong conduct. . . .

Let us then thus consider conscience, not as a rule of right conduct, but as a sanction of right conduct. This is its primary and most authoritative aspect; it is the ordinary sense of the word. Half the world would be puzzled to know what was meant by the moral sense; but every one knows what is meant by a good or bad conscience. Conscience is ever forcing on us by threats and by promises that we must follow the right and avoid the wrong; so far it is one and the same in the mind of every one, whatever be its particular errors in particular minds as to the acts which it orders to be done or to be avoided; and in this respect it corresponds to our perception of the beautiful and deformed. As we have naturally a sense of the beautiful and graceful in nature and art, though tastes proverbially differ, so we have a sense of duty and obligation, whether we all associate it with the same certain actions in particular or not. Here, however, Taste and Conscience part company: for the sense of beautifulness, as indeed the Moral Sense, has no special relations to persons, but contemplates objects in themselves; conscience, on the other hand, is concerned with persons primarily, and with actions mainly as viewed in their doers, or rather with self alone and one's own actions, and with others only indirectly and as if in association with self. And further, taste is its own evidence, appealing to nothing beyond its own sense of the beautiful or the ugly, and enjoying the specimens of the beautiful simply for their own sake; but conscience does not repose on itself, but vaguely reaches forward to something beyond self, and dimly discerns a sanction higher than self for its decisions, as is evidenced in that keen sense of obligation and responsibility which informs them. And hence it is that we are accustomed to speak of conscience as a voice, a term which we should never think of applying to the sense of the beautiful; and moreover a voice, or the echo of a voice, imperative and constraining, like no other dictate in the whole of our experience.

And again, in consequence of this prerogative of dictating and commanding, which is of its essence, Conscience has an intimate bearing on our affections and emotions, leading us to reverence and awe, hope and fear, especially fear, a feeling which is foreign for the most part, not only to Taste, but even to the Moral Sense, except in consequence of accidental associations. No fear is felt by any one who recognizes that his conduct has not been beautiful, though he may be mortified at himself, if perhaps he has thereby forfeited some advantage; but, if he has been betrayed into any kind of immorality, he has a lively sense of responsibility and guilt, though the act be no offence against society,—of distress and apprehension, even though it may be of present service to him,—of compunction and regret, though in itself it be most pleasurable,—of confusion of face, though it may have no witnesses. These various perturbations of mind which are characteristic of a bad conscience, and may be very considerable,— self-reproach, poignant shame, haunting remorse, chill dismay at the prospect of the future,—and their contraries, when the conscience is good, as real though less forcible, self-approval, inward peace, lightness of heart, and the like,—these emotions constitute a specific difference between conscience and our other intellectual senses,—common sense, good sense, sense of expedience, taste, sense of honour, and the like,—as indeed they would also constitute between conscience and the moral sense, supposing these two were not aspects of one and the same feeling, exercised upon one and the same subject-matter.

So much for the characteristic phenomena, which conscience presents, nor is it difficult to determine what they imply. I refer once more to our sense of the beautiful. This sense is attended by an intellectual enjoyment, and is free from whatever is of the nature of emotion, except in one case, viz. when it is excited by personal objects; then it is that the tranquil feeling of admiration is exchanged for the excitement of affection and passion. Conscience too, considered as a moral sense, an intellectual sentiment, is a sense of admiration and disgust, of approbation and blame: but it is something more than a moral sense; it is always, what the sense of the beautiful is only in certain cases; it is always emotional. No wonder then that it always implies what that sense only sometimes implies; that it always involves the recognition of a living object, towards which it is directed. Inanimate things cannot stir our affections; these are correlative with persons. If, as is the case, we feel responsibility, are ashamed, are frightened, at transgressing the voice of conscience, this implies that there is One to whom we are responsible, before whom we are ashamed, whose claims upon us we fear. If, on doing wrong, we feel the same tearful, broken-hearted sorrow which overwhelms us on hurting a mother; if, on doing right, we enjoy the same sunny serenity of mind, the same soothing, satisfactory delight which follows on our receiving praise from a father, we certainly have within us the image of some person, to whom our love and veneration look, in whose smile we find our happiness, for whom we yearn, towards whom we direct our pleadings, in whose anger we are troubled and waste away. These feelings in us are such as require for their exciting cause an intelligent being: we are not affectionate towards a stone, nor do we feel shame before a horse or a dog; we have no remorse or compunction on breaking mere human law: yet, so it is, conscience excites all these painful emotions, confusion, foreboding, self-condemnation; and on the other hand it sheds upon us a deep peace, a sense of security, a resignation, and a hope, which there is no sensible, no earthly object to elicit. "The wicked flees, when no one pursueth"; then why does he flee? whence his terror? Who is it that he sees in solitude, in darkness, in the hidden chambers of his heart? If the cause of these emotions does not belong to this visible world, the Object to which his perception is directed must be Supernatural and Divine; and thus the phenomena of Conscience, as a dictate, avail to impress the imagination with the picture of a Supreme Governor, a Judge, holy, just, powerful, all-seeing, retributive, and is the creative principle of religion, as the Moral Sense is the principle of ethics. . . .

How are we to explain this apprehension of things, which are one and individual, in the midst of a world of pluralities and transmutations, whether in the instance of brutes [animals] or again of children? But until we account for the knowledge which an infant has of his mother or his nurse, what reason have we to take exception at the doctrine, as strange and difficult, that in the dictate of conscience, without previous experiences or analogical reasoning, he is able gradually to perceive the voice, or the echoes of the voice, of a Master, living, personal, and sovereign?

I grant, of course, that we cannot assign a date, ever so early, before which he had learned nothing at all, and formed no mental associations, from the words and conduct of those who have the care of him. But still, if a child of five or six years old, when reason is at length fully awake, has already mastered and appropriated thoughts and beliefs, in consequence of their teaching, in such sort as to be able to handle and apply them familiarly, according to the occasion, as principles of intellectual action, those beliefs at the very least must be singularly congenial to his mind, if not connatural with its initial action. And that such a spontaneous reception of religious truths is common with children, I shall take for granted, till I am convinced that I am wrong in so doing. The child keenly understands that there is a difference between right and wrong; and when he has done what he believes to be wrong, he is conscious that he is offending One to whom he is amenable, whom he does not see, who sees him. His mind reaches forward with a strong presentiment to the thought of a Moral Governor, sovereign over him, mindful, and just. It comes to him like an impulse of nature to entertain it.

It is my wish to take an ordinary child, but still one who is safe from influences destructive of his religious instincts. Supposing he has offended his parents, he will all alone and without effort, as if it were the most natural of acts, place himself in the presence of God, and beg of Him to set him right with them. Let us consider how much is contained in this simple act. First, it involves the impression on his mind of an unseen Being with whom he is in immediate relation, and that relation so familiar that he can address Him whenever he himself chooses; next, of One whose goodwill towards him he is assured of, and can take for granted—nay, who loves him better, and is nearer to him, than his parents; further, of One who can hear him, wherever he happens to be, and who can read his thoughts, for his prayer need not be vocal; lastly, of One who can effect a critical change in the state of feeling of others towards him. That is, we shall not be wrong in holding that this child has in his mind the image of an Invisible Being, who exercises a particular providence among us, who is present every where, who is heart-reading, heart-changing, ever-accessible, open to impetration. What a strong and intimate vision of God must he have already attained, if, as I have supposed, an ordinary trouble of mind has the spontaneous effect of leading him for consolation and aid to an Invisible Personal Power!

Moreover, this image brought before his mental vision is the image of One who by implicit threat and promise commands certain things which he, the same child coincidently, by the same act of his mind, approves; which receive the adhesion of his moral sense and judgment, as right and good. It is the image of One who is good, inasmuch as enjoining and enforcing what is right and good, and who, in consequence, not only excites in the child hope and fear,—nay (it may be added), gratitude towards Him, as giving a law and maintaining it by reward and punishment,—but kindles in him love towards Him, as giving him a good law, and, therefore as being good Himself, for it is the property of goodness to kindle love, or rather the very object of love is goodness; and all those distinct elements of the moral law, which the typical child, whom I am supposing, more or less consciously loves and approves,—truth, purity, justice, kindness, and the like,—are but shapes and aspects of goodness. And having in his degree a sensibility towards them all, for the sake of them all he is moved to love the Lawgiver, who enjoins them upon him. And, as he can contemplate these qualities and their manifestations under the common name of goodness, he is prepared to think of them as indivisible, correlative, supplementary of each other in one and the same Personality, so that there is no aspect of goodness which God is not; and that the more, because the notion of a perfection embracing all possible excellences, both moral and intellectual, is especially congenial to the mind, and there are in fact intellectual attributes, as well as moral, included in the child's image of God, as above represented.

Such is the apprehension which even a child may have of his Sovereign Lawgiver and Judge; which is possible in the case of children, because, at least, some children possess it, whether others possess it or no; and which, when it is found in children, is found to act promptly and keenly, by reason of the paucity of their ideas. It is an image of the good God, good in Himself, good relatively to the child, with whatever incompleteness; an image, before it has been reflected on, and before it is recognized by him as a notion. Though he cannot explain or define the word "God," when told to use it, his acts show that to him it is far more than a word. He listens, indeed, with wonder and interest to fables or tales; he has a dim, shadowy sense of what he hears about persons and matters of this world; but he has that within him which actually vibrates, responds, and gives a deep meaning to the lessons of his first teachers about the will and the providence of God.

How far this initial religious knowledge comes from without, and how far from within, how much is natural, how much implies a special divine aid which is above nature, we have no means of determining, nor is it necessary for my present purpose to determine. I am not engaged in tracing the image of God in the mind of a child or a man to its first origins, but showing that he can become possessed of such an image, over and above all mere notions of God, and in what that image consists. Whether its elements, latent in the mind, would ever be elicited without extrinsic help is very doubtful; but whatever be the actual history of the first formation of the divine image within us, so far at least is certain, that, by informations external to ourselves, as time goes on, it admits of being strengthened and improved. It is certain too, that, whether it grows brighter and stronger, or, on the other hand, is dimmed, distorted, or obliterated, depends on each of us individually, and on his circumstances. It is more than probable that, in the event, from neglect, from the temptations of life, from bad companions, or from the urgency of secular occupations, the light of the soul will fade away and die out. Men transgress their sense of duty, and gradually lose those sentiments of shame and fear, the natural supplements of transgression, which, as I have said, are the witnesses of the Unseen Judge. And, even were it deemed impossible that those who had in their first youth a genuine apprehension of Him, could ever utterly lose it, yet that apprehension may become almost undistinguishable from an inferential acceptance of the great truth, or may dwindle into a mere notion of their intellect. On the contrary, the image of God, if duly cherished, may expand, deepen, and be completed, with the growth of their powers and in the course of life, under the varied lessons, within and without them, which are brought home to them concerning that same God, One and Personal, by means of education, social intercourse, experience, and literature.

To a mind thus carefully formed upon the basis of its natural conscience, the world, both of nature and of man, does but give back a reflection of those truths about the One Living God, which have been familiar to it from childhood. Good and evil meet us daily as we pass through life, and there are those who think it philosophical to act towards the manifestations of each with some sort of impartiality, as if evil had as much right to be there as good, or even a better, as having more striking triumphs and a broader jurisdiction. And because the course of things is determined by fixed laws, they consider that those laws preclude the present agency of the Creator in the carrying out of particular issues. It is otherwise with the theology of a religious imagination. It has a living hold on truths which are really to be found in the world, though they are not upon the surface. It is able to pronounce by anticipation, what it takes a long argument to prove—that good is the rule, and evil the exception. It is able to assume that, uniform as are the laws of nature, they are consistent with a particular Providence. It interprets what it sees around it by this previous inward teaching, as the true key of that maze of vast complicated disorder; and thus it gains a more and more consistent and luminous vision of God from the most unpromising materials. Thus conscience is a connecting principle between the creature and his Creator; and the firmest hold of theological truths is gained by habits of personal religion. When men begin all their works with the thought of God, acting for His sake, and to fulfil His will, when they ask His blessing on themselves and their life, pray to Him for the objects they desire, and see Him in the event, whether it be according to their prayers or not, they will find everything that happens tends to confirm them in the truths about Him which live in their imagination, varied and unearthly as those truths may be. Then they are brought into His presence as that of a Living Person, and are able to hold converse with Him, and that with a directness and simplicity, with a confidence and intimacy, . . . which we use towards an earthly superior; so that it is doubtful whether we realize the company of our fellow-men with greater keenness than these favoured minds are able to contemplate and adore the Unseen, Incomprehensible Creator.

—An Essay in Aid of a Grammar of Assent, 104–118

15.4. INTERPRETATION OF
THE "VATICAN DEFINITION"

In contrast to those, on the one hand, who simply rejected the First Vatican Council's definition and those, on the other hand, who considered every papal statement an exercise of infallibility, Newman adopted "a wise and gentle minimism" that considered such definitions "of rare occurrence":

From these various considerations it follows, that Papal and Synodal definitions, obligatory on our faith, are of rare occurrence; and this is confessed by all sober theologians. Father [Edmund] O'Reilly, for instance, of Dublin, one of the first theologians of the day, says:—

"The Papal Infallibility is comparatively seldom brought into action. I am very far from denying that the Vicar of Christ is largely assisted by God in the fulfilment of his sublime office, that he receives great light and strength to do well the great work entrusted to him and imposed on him, that he is continually guided from above in the government of the Catholic Church. But this is not the meaning of Infallibility. . . . What is the use of dragging in the Infallibility in connexion with Papal acts with which it has nothing to do,—papal acts, which are very good and very holy, and entitled to all respect and obedience, acts in which the Pontiff is commonly not mistaken, but in which he could be mistaken and still remain infallible in the only sense in which he has been declared to be so?" (*Irish Monthly*, 2, no. 10 [1874]).

This great authority goes on to disclaim any desire to minimize, but there is, I hope, no real difference between us here. He, I am sure, would sanction me in my repugnance to impose upon the faith of others more than what the Church distinctly claims of them: and I should follow him in thinking it a more scriptural, Christian, dutiful, happy frame of mind, to be easy, than to be difficult, of belief. I have already spoken of that uncatholic spirit, which starts with a grudging faith in the word of the Church, and determines to hold nothing but what it is, as if by demonstration, compelled to believe. To be a true Catholic a man must have a generous loyalty towards ecclesiastical authority, and accept what is taught him with what is called the *pietas fidei* [piety of faith], and only such a tone of mind has a claim, and it certainly has a claim, to be met and to be handled with a wise and gentle *minimism*. Still the fact remains, that there has been of late years a fierce and intolerant temper abroad, which scorns and virtually tramples on the little ones of Christ.

—*A Letter Addressed to the Duke of Norfolk on Occasion of Mr. Gladstone's Recent Expostulation*, in *Certain Difficulties Felt by Anglicans in Catholic Teaching*, 2:33–39

15.5. HONORARY FELLOW OF TRINITY COLLEGE

In 1877, Newman received an unexpected invitation to become the first Honorary Fellow of Trinity College, Oxford, his undergraduate alma mater. Newman's appreciation of this honor is evident in the following letter, which he wrote to Bishop Ullathorne about accepting the honor.

The Oratory: Dec. 18, 1877.

My dear Lord,—I have just received a great compliment, perhaps the greatest I have ever received, and I don't like not to tell you of it one of the first.

My old College, Trinity College, where I was an undergraduate from the age of 16 to 21, till I gained a fellowship at Oriel, has made me an Honorary Fellow of their Society. Of course it involves no duties, rights or conditions, not even that of belonging to the University, certainly not that of having a vote as Master of Arts, but it is a mark of extreme kindness to me from men I have never seen, and it is the only instance of their exercising their power since it was given them.

Trinity College has been the one and only seat of my affections at Oxford, and to see once more, before I am taken away, what I never thought I should see again, the place where I began the battle of life, with my good angel by my side, is a prospect almost too much for me to bear.

I have been considering for these two days, since the offer came to me, whether there would be any inconsistency in my accepting it, but it is so pure a compliment in its very title that I do not see that I need fear its being interpreted by the world as anything else.

Begging your Lordship's blessing,
I am your obedient and affectionate servant in Christ,
JOHN H. NEWMAN.

P.S.—The Pope made me a D.D., but I don't call an act of the Pope's a "*compliment.*"

—Wilfrid Ward, *Life of Cardinal Newman,* 2:426

16

Cardinal

16.1. CONGRATULATORY MESSAGES

Once the news broke of Newman's elevation to the cardinalate, numerous people sent their congratulations. Among these was a letter from the new president of Trinity College, Oxford, which had named Newman an honorary fellow the year before:

TRINITY COLLEGE, OXFORD, Mar. 28, 1879

DEAR SIR,

I have been requested to make known to you that it has been unanimously resolved that "The President and Fellows of Trinity desire to offer their most sincere congratulations to the Very Rev. J. H. Newman on his nomination to the rank of Cardinal; and to assure him of the deep sympathy of the College, which is at once his earliest and latest in Oxford, on an occasion of such great and general interest and such personal moment to himself; and to record their hope that he may long be spared to fill the high position to which he has been called."

Whilst conveying this imperfect expression of our feeling I trust that, although I am at present personally a stranger to you, I may be permitted to look forward to the pleasure of offering you hospitality at my lodgings on some early occasion.

I have the honour to remain, Dear Sir,
Yours very faithfully,
J. PERCIVAL, President

Newman promptly replied to the president of Trinity College:

THE ORATORY, BIRMINGHAM, Mar. 30, 1879.

DEAR MR. PRESIDENT, I had been looking out, ever since I heard of your election, for the time when you would come into residence, and when I might be allowed to pay my respects to you—and now you anticipate me with so kind an invitation, and such warm congratulations on my recent promotion, from yourself and your Fellows.

I hope you and they will understand how very pleasant it is to me to find the events which happen to me a subject of such friendly interest to my friends at Trinity, and with what pride I reflect that, if a historical title and high ecclesiastical distinction goes for anything in college estimation, I shall be thought, when the name of a Cardinal appears on of your list of members, not to have done discredit to your generous act of last year, when you singled me out for your honorary Fellowship.

I am, dear Mr. President,

With much respect,

Sincerely yours,

JOHN H. NEWMAN

P.S.—As to my movements, at present I am quite uncertain where I shall be in the weeks before us; but I certainly shall not forget your kind proposal.

—*Addresses to Cardinal Newman with His Replies*, 43–45

16.2. BIGLIETTO SPEECH

On Monday morning, May 12, 1879, Newman went to the Palazzo della Pigna, the residence of Cardinal Edward Henry Howard (1829–1892) to receive the messenger from the Vatican bearing the official letter (biglietto) from the Cardinal-Secretary of State, informing him that in a secret Consistory that morning Pope Leo XIII had named him a Cardinal. Soon after midday the consistorial messenger arrived and, in the presence of a large number of people assembled for the ceremony, handed the biglietto to Newman, who broke the seal and gave the letter to Bishop William Clifford (1823–1893) of Clifton, who read the announcement. Following a few words of appreciation in Italian to both the Pope and the papal representative who had delivered the biglietto, Newman spoke in English, first, pointing out that the honor was not only personal, but a "pleasure" for English Catholics and even Protestants. Newman then reminisced about his lifelong "desire to serve the Church"—a service that had been characterized by his opposition to "Liberalism in Religion," which he characterized as "the doctrine that there is no positive truth in religion, but that one creed is as good as another."

First of all then, I am led to speak of the wonder and profound gratitude which came upon me, and which is upon me still, at the condescension and love towards me of the Holy Father in singling me out for so immense an honour. It was a great surprise. Such an elevation had never come into my thoughts, and seemed to be out of keeping with all my antecedents. I had passed through many trials, but they were over; and now the end of all things had almost come to me, and I was at peace. And was it possible that after all I had lived through so many years for this?

Nor is it easy to see how I could have borne so great a shock, had not the Holy Father resolved on a second act of condescension towards me, which tempered it, and was to all who heard of it a touching evidence of his kindly and generous nature. He felt for me, and he told me the reasons why he raised me to this high position. Besides other words of encouragement, he said his act was a recognition of my zeal and good service for so many years in the Catholic cause; moreover, he judged it would give pleasure to English Catholics, and even to Protestant England, if I received some mark of his favour. After such gracious words from his Holiness, I should have been insensible and heartless if I had had scruples any longer.

This is what he had the kindness to say to me, and what could I want more? In a long course of years I have made many mistakes. I have nothing of that high perfection which belongs to the writings of Saints, viz., that error cannot be found in them; but what I trust that I may claim all through what I have written, is this,—an honest intention, an absence of private ends, a temper of obedience, a willingness to be corrected, a dread of error, a desire to serve Holy Church, and, through Divine mercy, a fair measure of success. And, I rejoice to say, to one great mischief I have from the first opposed myself. For thirty, forty, fifty years I have resisted to the best of my powers the spirit of liberalism in religion. Never did Holy Church need champions against it more sorely than now, when, alas! it is an error overspreading, as a snare, the whole earth; and on this great occasion, when it is natural for one who is in my place to look out upon the world, and upon Holy Church as in it, and upon her future, it will not, I hope, be considered out of place, if I renew the protest against it which I have made so often.

Liberalism in religion is the doctrine that there is no positive truth in religion, but that one creed is as good as another, and this is the teaching which is gaining substance and force daily. It is inconsistent with any recognition of any religion, as true. It teaches that all are to be tolerated, for all are matters of opinion. Revealed religion is not a truth, but a sentiment and a taste; not an objective fact, not miraculous; and it is the right of each individual to make it say just what strikes his fancy. Devotion is not necessarily founded on faith. Men may go to Protestant Churches and to Catholic, may get good from both and belong to neither. They may fraternise together in spiritual thoughts and feelings, without having any views at all of doctrine in common, or seeing the need of them. Since, then, religion is so personal a peculiarity and so private a possession, we must of necessity ignore it in the intercourse of man with man. If a man puts on a new religion every morning, what is that to you? It is as impertinent to think about a man's religion as about his sources of income or his management of his family. Religion is in no sense the bond of society.

Hitherto the civil Power has been Christian. Even in countries separated from the Church, as in my own, the dictum was in force, when I was young, that: "Christianity was the law of the land." Now, everywhere that goodly framework of society, which is the creation of Christianity, is throwing off Christianity. The dictum to which I have referred, with a hundred others which followed upon it, is gone, or is going everywhere; and, by the end of the century, unless the Almighty interferes, it will be forgotten. Hitherto, it has been considered that religion alone, with its supernatural sanctions, was strong enough to secure submission of the masses of our population to law and order; now the Philosophers and Politicians are bent on satisfying this problem without the aid of Christianity. Instead of the Church's authority and teaching, they would substitute first of all a universal and a thoroughly secular education, calculated to bring home to every individual that to be orderly, industrious, and sober, is his personal interest. Then, for great working principles to take the place of religion, for the use of the masses thus carefully educated, it provides—the broad fundamental ethical truths, of justice, benevolence, veracity, and the like; proved experience; and those natural laws which exist and act spontaneously in society, and in social matters, whether physical or psychological; for instance, in government, trade, finance, sanitary experiments, and the intercourse of nations. As to Religion, it is a private luxury, which a man may have if he will; but which of course he must pay for, and which he must not obtrude upon others, or indulge in to their annoyance.

The general character of this great apostasia is one and the same everywhere; but in detail, and in character, it varies in different countries. For myself, I would rather speak of it in my own country, which I know. There, I think it threatens to have a formidable success; though it is not easy to see what will be its ultimate issue. At first sight it might be thought that Englishmen are too religious for a movement which, on the Continent, seems to be founded on infidelity; but the misfortune with us is, that, though it ends in infidelity as in other places, it does not necessarily arise out of infidelity. It must be recollected that the religious sects, which sprang up in England three centuries ago, and which are so powerful now, have ever been fiercely opposed to the Union of Church and State, and would advocate the un-Christianising of the monarchy and all that belongs to it, under the notion that such a catastrophe would make Christianity much more pure and much more powerful. Next the liberal principle is forced on us from the necessity of the case. Consider what follows from the very fact of these many sects. They constitute the religion, it is supposed, of half the population; and, recollect, our mode of government is popular. Every dozen men taken at random whom you meet in the streets has a share in political power,—when you inquire into their forms of belief, perhaps they represent one or other of as many as seven religions; how can they possibly act together in municipal or in national matters, if each insists on the recognition of his own religious denomination? All action would be at a deadlock unless the subject of religion was ignored. We cannot help ourselves. And, thirdly, it must be borne in mind, that there is much in the liberalistic theory which is good and true; for example, not to say more, the precepts of justice, truthfulness, sobriety, self-command, benevolence, which, as I have already noted, are among its avowed principles, and the natural laws of society. It is not till we find that this array of principles is intended to supersede, to block out, religion, that we pronounce it to be evil. There never was a device of the Enemy so cleverly framed and with such promise of success. And already it has answered to the expectations which have been formed of it. It is sweeping into its own ranks great numbers of able, earnest, virtuous men, elderly men of approved antecedents, young men with a career before them.

Such is the state of things in England, and it is well that it should be realised by all of us; but it must not be supposed for a moment that I am afraid of it. I lament it deeply, because I foresee that it may be the ruin of many souls; but I have no fear at all that it really can do aught of serious harm to the Word of God, to Holy Church, to our Almighty King, the Lion of the tribe of Judah, Faithful and True, or to His Vicar on earth. Christianity has been too often in what seemed deadly peril, that we should fear for it any new trial now. So far is certain; on the other hand, what is uncertain, and in these great contests commonly is uncertain, and what is commonly a great surprise, when it is witnessed, is the particular mode by which, in the event, Providence rescues and saves His elect inheritance. Sometimes our enemy is turned into a friend; sometimes he is despoiled of that special virulence of evil which was so threatening; sometimes he falls to pieces of himself; sometimes he does just so much as is beneficial, and then is removed. Commonly the Church has nothing more to do than to go on in her own proper duties, in confidence and peace; to stand still and to see the salvation of God.

—*Addresses to Cardinal Newman with His Replies*, 62–70

16.3. ROMAN ADDRESS
TO CARDINAL NEWMAN

On Wednesday, May 14, 1879, the newly created Cardinal Newman went to the English College to receive an address and gifts of vestments from the English, Irish, Scotch, and American residents in Rome. On each vestment was embroidered the cardinal's coat-of-arms with his motto Cor ad cor loquitur ("Heart speaks to Heart"). After the Cardinal was seated, Lady Herbert of Lea (1822–1911) read the following address, which expressed not only admiration for Newman's writings, but also appreciation for his role as "their spiritual father and their guide in the paths of holiness":

MY LORD CARDINAL,

We, your devoted English, Scotch, Irish, and American children at present residing in Rome, earnestly wishing to testify our deep and affectionate veneration for your Eminence's person and character, together with our hearty joy at your elevation to the Sacred Purple, venture to lay this humble offering at your feet. We feel that in making you a Cardinal the Holy Father has not only given public testimony of his appreciation of your great merits and of the value of your admirable writings in defence of

God and His Church, but has also conferred the greatest possible honour on all English-speaking Catholics, who have long looked up to you as their spiritual father and their guide in the paths of holiness. We hope your Eminence will excuse the shortness and simplicity of this Address, which is but the expression of the feeling contained in your Eminence's motto, "Heart speaking to Heart," for your Eminence has long won the first place in the hearts of all. That God may greatly prolong the years which have been so devoted to His service in the cause of truth is the earnest prayer of your Eminence's faithful and loving children.

—*Addresses to Cardinal Newman with His Replies*, 72–73

16.4. NEWMAN'S HOMECOMING ADDRESS

After an exhausting round of ceremonies in Rome and a strenuous return trip, which was plagued with illness, Cardinal Newman arrived back at the Birmingham Oratory to welcoming crowds. His address on this occasion was recorded by William Paine Neville (1824–1905), an Oratorian, who had been received in the Roman Catholic Church by Newman in 1851 and became his aide and literary executor:

My dear Children,—I am desirous of thanking you for the great sympathy you have shown towards me, for your congratulations, for your welcome, and for your good prayers; but I feel so very weak—for I have not recovered yet from a long illness—that I hardly know how I can be able to say ever so few words, or to express in any degree the great pleasure and gratitude to you which I feel.

To come home again! In that word "home" how much is included. I know well that there is a more heroic life than a home life. We know the blessed Apostles—how they went about, and we listen to St. Paul's words—those touching words—in which he speaks of himself and says he was an outcast. Then we know, too, our Blessed Lord—that He "had not where to lay His head." Therefore, of course, there is a higher life, a more heroic life, than that of home. But still, that is given to few. The home life—the idea of home—is consecrated to us by our patron and founder St. Philip, for he made the idea of home the very essence of his religion and institute. We have even a great example in Our Lord Himself; for though in His public ministry He had not where to lay His head, yet we know that for the first thirty years of His life He had a home, and He therefore consecrated, in a special way, the life of home. And as, indeed, Almighty God has been pleased to continue the world, not, as angels, by a separate creation of each, but by means of the Family, so it was fitting that the congregation of St. Philip should be the ideal, the realisation of the Family in its perfection, and a pattern to every family in the parish, in the town, and throughout the whole of Christendom. Therefore, I do indeed feel pleasure to come home again. Although I am not insensible of the great grace of being in the Holy City, which is the centre of grace, nor of the immense honour which has been conferred upon me, nor of the exceeding kindness and affection to me personally of the Holy Father—I may say more than affection, for he was to me as though he had been all my life my father—to see the grace which shone from his face and spoke in his voice; yet I feel I may rejoice in coming home again—as if it were to my long home—to that home which extends to heaven, "the home of our eternity." And although there has been much of sickness, and much sadness in being prevented from enjoying the privileges of being in the Holy City, yet Almighty God has brought me home again in spite of all difficulties, fears, obstacles, troubles, and trials. I almost feared I should never come back, but God in His mercy has ordered it otherwise. And now I will ask you, my dear friends, to pray for me, that I may be as the presence of the Holy Father amongst you, and that the Holy Spirit of God may be upon this Church, upon this great city, upon its Bishop, upon all its priests, upon all its inhabitants, men, women and children, and as a pledge and beginning of it, I give you my benediction.

—Wilfrid Ward, *Life of Cardinal Newman*, 2:470–471

17

Blessed John Henry Newman

17.1. BICENTENNIAL OF NEWMAN'S BIRTH: JOHN PAUL II

Pope John Paul II paid tribute to Newman on a number of occasions. In addition to declaring Newman "Venerable" on January 22, 1991, the pope issued statements on the centennial of Newman's cardinalate (1979) and the centennial of his death (1990); the following is an excerpt from the letter that the pope sent to Archbishop Vincent Nichols of Birmingham on January 22, 2001, in commemoration of the bicentennial of Newman's birth:

On the occasion of the second centenary of the birth of the Venerable Servant of God John Henry Newman, I gladly join you, your Brother Bishops of England and Wales, the priests of the Birmingham Oratory and a host of voices throughout the world in praising God for the gift of the great English Cardinal and for his enduring witness.

As Newman pondered the mysterious divine plan unfolding in his own life, he came to a deep and abiding sense that "God has created me to do Him some definite service. He has committed some work to me which He has not committed to another. I have my mission" (*Meditations and Devotions*). How true that thought now appears as we consider his long life and the influence which he has had beyond death. He was born at a particular time—February 21,1801; in a particular place—London;

and to a particular family—the first-born of John Newman and Jemima Fourdrinier. But the particular mission entrusted to him by God ensures that *John Henry Newman belongs to every time and place and people.*

Newman was born in troubled times which knew not only political and military upheaval but also turbulence of soul. Old certitudes were shaken, and believers were faced with the threat of rationalism on the one hand and fideism on the other. Rationalism brought with it a rejection of both authority and transcendence, while fideism turned from the challenges of history and the tasks of this world to a distorted dependence upon authority and the supernatural. In such a world, Newman came eventually to *a remarkable synthesis of faith and reason* which were for him "like two wings on which the human spirit rises to the contemplation of truth" (John Paul II, *Fides et ratio*, Introduction; §74). It was the passionate contemplation of truth which also led him to a liberating acceptance of the authority which has its roots in Christ, and to the sense of the supernatural which opens the human mind and heart to the full range of possibilities revealed in Christ. "Lead kindly light amid the encircling gloom, lead Thou me on," Newman wrote in *The Pillar of the Cloud*; and for him Christ was the light at the heart of every kind of darkness. For his tomb he chose the inscription: *Ex umbris et imaginibus in veritatem* [From shadows and images into the truth]; and it was clear at the end of his life's journey that Christ was the truth he had found.

But Newman's search was shot through with pain. Once he had come to that unshakeable sense of the mission entrusted to him by God, he declared: "Therefore, I will trust Him . . . If I am in sickness, my sickness may serve Him, in perplexity, my perplexity may serve Him . . . He does nothing in vain . . . He may take away my friends. He may throw me among strangers. He may make me feel desolate, make my spirits sink, hide the future from me. Still, He knows what He is about" (*Meditations and Devotions*). All these trials he knew in his life; but rather than diminish or destroy him they paradoxically strengthened his faith in the God who had called him, and confirmed him in the conviction that God "does nothing in vain." In the end, therefore, what shines forth in Newman is *the mystery of the Lord's Cross*: this was the heart of his mission, the absolute truth which he contemplated, the "kindly light" which led him on.

As we thank God for the gift of the Venerable John Henry Newman on the 200th anniversary of his birth, we pray that this sure and eloquent guide in our perplexity will also become for us in all our needs a powerful intercessor before the throne of grace. Let us pray that the time will soon come when the Church can officially and publicly proclaim the exemplary holiness of Cardinal John Henry Newman, one of the most distinguished and versatile champions of English spirituality.

—Letter of Pope John Paul II to
Archbishop Vincent Nichols
of Birmingham, January 22, 2001

17.2. BEATIFICATION HOMILY: BENEDICT XVI

On September 19, 2010, Pope Benedict XVI beatified Cardinal John Henry Newman at Cofton Park, Rednal, Birmingham, which is near the house where Newman and his fellow Oratorians went for relaxation, reading, and writing. The Birmingham Oratory Cemetery, which is adjacent to this house, was the place where Newman was originally buried; however, when his grave was opened on October 2, 2008, as part of the process of beatification, no human remains were found; his body had apparently disintegrated in the damp soil of the area. Some soil, as well as a few objects from the grave, were later placed in a reliquary in the chapel dedicated to his memory at the Birmingham Oratory, which is located some eight miles away. The following reading is an excerpt from the homily of Pope Benedict XVI at the mass of Beatification:

England has a long tradition of martyr saints, whose courageous witness has sustained and inspired the Catholic community here for centuries. Yet it is right and fitting that we should recognize today the holiness of a confessor, a son of this nation who, while not called to shed his blood for the Lord, nevertheless bore eloquent witness to him in the course of a long life devoted to the priestly ministry, and especially to preaching, teaching, and writing. He is worthy to take his place in a long line of saints and scholars from these islands, Saint Bede, Saint Hilda, Saint Aelred, Blessed Duns Scotus, to name but a few. In Blessed John Henry, that tradition of gentle scholarship, deep human wisdom and profound love for the Lord has borne rich fruit, as a sign of the abiding presence of the Holy Spirit deep within the heart of God's people, bringing forth abundant gifts of holiness.

Cardinal Newman's motto, *Cor ad cor loquitur*, or "Heart speaks unto heart," gives us an insight into his understanding of the Christian life as a call to holiness, experienced as the profound desire of the human heart to enter into intimate communion with the Heart of God. He reminds us that faithfulness to prayer gradually transforms us into the divine likeness. As he wrote in one of his many fine sermons, "a habit of prayer, the practice of turning to God and the unseen world in every season, in every place, in every emergency—prayer, I say, has what may be called a natural effect in spiritualizing and elevating the soul. A man is no longer what he was before; gradually . . . he has imbibed a new set of ideas, and become imbued with fresh principles" (*Parochial and Plain Sermons*, iv, 230–231). Today's Gospel tells us that no one can be the servant of two masters (cf. Lk 16:13), and Blessed John Henry's teaching on prayer explains how the faithful Christian is definitively taken into the service of the one true Master, who alone has a claim to our unconditional devotion (cf. Mt 23:10). Newman helps us to understand what this means for our daily lives: he tells us that our divine Master has assigned a specific task to each one of us, a "definite service," committed uniquely to every single person: "I have my mission," he wrote, "I am a link in a chain, a bond of connexion between persons. He has not created me for naught. I shall do good, I shall do his work; I shall be an angel of peace, a preacher of truth in my own place . . . if I do but keep his commandments and serve him in my calling" (*Meditations and Devotions*, 301–302).

The definite service to which Blessed John Henry was called involved applying his keen intellect and his prolific pen to many of the most pressing "subjects of the day." His insights into the relationship between faith and reason, into the vital place of revealed religion in civilized society, and into the need for a broadly-based and wide-ranging approach to education were not only of profound importance for Victorian England, but continue today to inspire and enlighten many all over the world. I would like to pay particular tribute to his vision for education, which has done so much to shape the ethos that is the driving force behind Catholic schools and colleges today. Firmly opposed to any reductive or utilitarian approach, he sought to achieve an educational environment in which intellectual training, moral discipline and religious commitment would come together. The project to found a Catholic University in Ireland provided him with an opportunity to develop his ideas on the subject, and the collection of discourses that he published as *The Idea of a University* holds up an ideal from which all those engaged in academic formation can continue to learn. And indeed, what better goal could teachers of religion set themselves than Blessed John Henry's famous appeal for an intelligent, well-instructed laity: "I want a laity, not arrogant, not rash in speech, not disputatious, but men who know their religion, who enter into it, who know just where they stand, who know what they hold and what they do not, who know their creed so well that they can give an account of it, who know so much of history that they can defend it" (*The Present Position of Catholics in England*, ix, 390). On this day when the author of those words is raised to the altars, I pray that, through his intercession and example, all who are engaged in the task of teaching and catechesis will be inspired to greater effort by the vision he so clearly sets before us.

While it is John Henry Newman's intellectual legacy that has understandably received most attention in the vast literature devoted to his life and work, I prefer on this occasion to conclude with a brief reflection on his life as a priest, a pastor of souls. The warmth and humanity underlying his appreciation of the pastoral ministry is beautifully expressed in another of his famous sermons: "Had Angels been your priests, my brethren, they could not have condoled with you, sympathized with you, have had compassion on you, felt tenderly for you, and made allowances for you, as we can; they could not have been your patterns and guides, and have led you on from your old selves into a new life, as they can who come from the midst of you" ("Men, not Angels: the Priests of the Gospel," *Discourses to Mixed Congregations*, 3). He lived out that profoundly human vision of priestly ministry in his devoted care for the people of Birmingham during the years that he spent at the Oratory he founded, visiting the sick and the poor, comforting the bereaved, caring for those in prison. No wonder that on his death so many thousands of people lined the local streets as his body was taken to its place of burial not half a mile from here. One hundred and twenty years later, great crowds have assembled once again to rejoice in the Church's solemn recognition of the outstanding holiness of this much-loved father of souls. What better way to express the joy of this moment than by turning to our heavenly Father in heartfelt thanksgiving, praying in the words that Blessed John Henry Newman placed on the lips of the choirs of angels in heaven:

> Praise to the Holiest in the height
> And in the depth be praise;
> In all his words most wonderful,
> Most sure in all his ways!
> ("The Dream of Gerontius")

—Homily of Pope Benedict XVI

Appendix 1

John Henry Newman:
A Brief Chronology

1801   February 21. Born, Old Broad Street, London;
          Baptized: April 9

1808   May 1. Enrolled at Ealing School

1816   August–December. "First conversion"
          December 14. Enrolled at Trinity College, Oxford

1820   December 5. Took B.A. degree "under the line"

1822   April 12. Elected Fellow of Oriel College

1824   June 13. Ordained deacon of the Church of England

1825   May 29. Ordained priest of the Church of England

1826   July 2. Preached his first University sermon

1828   January 5. "We lost my sister Mary suddenly"

          March 14. "Instituted by the Bishop of Oxford
          to St. Mary's"

1832   December 8. Beginning of Mediterranean voyage
          with Froudes

1833   June 16. Wrote "Lead, Kindly Light" ("The Pillar
          of the Cloud")

          July 14. Keble's Assize sermon on "National
          Apostasy"

1834   March. Published first volume of *Parochial Sermons*

1841   January 25. Published *Tract XC*

June 1. Preached his fourteenth University Sermon

1843   February 2. Preached his fifteenth University Sermon

September 25. Preached "The Parting of Friends" at Littlemore

1845   October 9. Received as Roman Catholic by Dominic Barberi

1847   May 30. Ordained a Roman Catholic priest in Rome

1848   February 1. Established the English Oratory

1851   November 5. Beginning of Achilli trial

1852   May 10. Delivered first university lecture in Dublin

July 13. Preached sermon: "The Second Spring"

1853   January 31. Fined £100 at conclusion of Achilli trial

1854   March 22. Opening of the London Oratory at Brompton

June 4. Installed as rector of the Catholic University in Dublin

1855   Autumn. Separation of London and Birmingham Oratories

1856   May 1. Dedication of Catholic University Church of Saints Peter and Paul

1857   March. Informed Irish bishops of his proposed resignation as rector

August. Invited by Wiseman to supervise new translation of the Bible

1859   March 21. Assumed editorship of *Rambler*

May 2. Foundation of Oratory School

1864   April–June. *Apologia pro Vita Sua* published
        in fascicles

1865   May–June "The Dream of Gerontius" published in
        The Month

1870   March 15. *An Essay in Aid of a Grammar of Assent*
        published

1875   January 14. *A Letter to the Duke of Norfolk*
        published

1878   February 26–28. Visit to Oxford: Honorary Fellow
        of Trinity College

1879   May 15. Received the "red hat" from Pope Leo XIII
        in public consistory

1890   August 11. Newman's death; burial at Rednal on
        August 19

1900   October 3. Premiere of Sir Edward Elgar's
        The Dream of Gerontius

1991   January 22. Declared "Venerable" by Pope John Paul II

2010   September 19. Beatified by Pope Benedict XVI

Appendix 2

Persons

Giacomo Achilli (b. 1802?), a Dominican priest ordained in 1825, was suspended for immorality; after delivering a series of anti-Catholic lectures in England, he sued Newman for libel after Newman accused Achilli of misconduct in *The Present Position of Catholics in England*; after a trial extending nearly two years (1852–1853), Newman was found guilty and fined £100 and had to pay £14,000 in legal fees, which wase raised by worldwide subscription.

Ambrose, St. (337/340–397), Roman governor of Liguria and Emilia, was chosen to be Bishop of Milan; a doctor of the Church, he opposed Arianism.

Arius (250/256–336), the father of "Arianism," was a priest of Alexandria who taught that Christ was a creature who was raised by God the Father to the dignity of the Son of God; Arianism was condemned by the Council of Nicaea (325), which taught that God the Father and God the Son are "consubstantial" (of one substance).

Matthew Arnold (1822–1888), son of Thomas Arnold, was a graduate of Balliol and fellow of Oriel and later professor of poetry at Oxford.

Thomas Arnold (1795–1842), a fellow of Oriel but an opponent of the Tractarian Movement, was headmaster of Rugby.

Athanasius, St. (296/298–373), patriarch of Alexandria; played a leading role in the Church's opposition to Arius and Arianism.

Augustine, St. (354–430), bishop of Hippo Regius (present-day Annaba, Algeria), theologian, doctor of the Church and author of *City of God*, *Christian Doctrine*, *Confessions*; was an opponent of Arianism.

Dominic Barberi, Bl., (1792–1849), an Italian Passionist who founded a monastery at Aston Hall in 1842, "admitted" Newman into the Roman Catholic Church on October 9, 1845.

Alessandro Barnabò (1801–1874), an official in the Vatican Congregation of Propaganda Fide: vice-secretary (1847–1848); secretary (1848–1856); prefect (1856–1874).

Herbert Rose Barraud (1845–1896?), a well-known Victorian photographer; photographed Newman.

Edward Bellasis (1800–1873), a lawyer who became a Roman Catholic in 1850, aided Newman during the Achilli trial; two of his sons joined the Birmingham Oratory.

John William Bowden (1798–1844), Newman's closest friend among the students at Trinity College.

Adam de Brome (d. 1332), almoner to Edward II and founder of the "Hall of the Blessed Mary" (Oriel College); is buried in a side chapel of St. Mary's Church, where Newman often gave lectures.

Thomas Joseph Brown, O.S.B. (1796–1880), ordained a priest in 1823; appointed vicar apostolic of the Wales District in 1840 and then bishop of Newport and Menevia in 1850; Brown denounced Newman's "On Consulting the Faithful" to Rome.

Bishop Joseph Butler (1692–1752), Anglican bishop of Bristol (1738–1750) and Durham (1750–1752); influenced Newman through his *Analogy of Religion, Natural and Revealed* (1736).

John Moore Capes (1812–1889) became a Roman Catholic on June 27, 1845, founded the *Rambler* in 1848, but rejoined the Church of England in 1870 and criticized Newman for accepting the definition of infallibility; Capes returned to the Roman Catholic Church a dozen years later.

Richard William Church (1815–1890), fellow of Oriel, junior proctor who vetoed the condemnation of *Tract XC;* later dean of St. Paul's (London) and good friend of Newman.

William Hugh Joseph Clifford (1823–1893), bishop of Clifton (1857–1893) and a participant at the First Vatican Council (1869–1870); preached at Newman's funeral.

William John Copeland (1804–1885), a scholar and fellow of Trinity College, Oxford; was Newman's curate at Littlemore in 1840 and later Anglican vicar of Farnham, Essex; he edited Newman's *Parochial and Plain Sermons* in 1868.

Edward Copleston (1776–1849), professor of poetry (1802–1812) and provost of Oriel (1814–1828) before being named bishop of Llandaff (Wales).

Paul Cardinal Cullen (1803–1878), rector of the Irish College in Rome (1832–1850) before being named archbishop of Armagh in 1850 and archbishop of Dublin in 1852; in 1866 was the first Irish bishop to be named a cardinal.

John Dobrée Dalgairns (1818–1876), a scholar of Exeter College (Oxford) and a resident at Littlemore (1842–1845); received as a Roman Catholic by Fr. Dominic Barberi in September 1845; subsequently, joined Newman in Rome for his Oratorian novitiate in 1847 and was stationed at the Birmingham Oratory 1847–1849 and 1855–1856, but then went to the London Oratory, where he succeeded Faber as superior.

Charles Darwin (1809–1882), a geologist and naturalist, whose *On the Origins of Species* (1859) explained the diversity in nature by the evolution of species through natural selection.

Charles Dickens (1812–1870), Victorian novelist whose writings displayed a mastery of style and an advocacy of social concerns.

Philip Doddridge (1702–1751), a non-conformist minister and hymn writer; his *Rise and Progress of Religion in the Soul* was used by Newman in his Anglican pastoral ministry; *The Rise and Progress of Religion* is available at *www.ccel.org/d/doddridge/rise/rise.htm*).

Johann Joseph Ignaz von Döllinger (1799–1890), a German priest and professor who taught theology and church history at the University of Munich; he was excommunicated in 1871 for not accepting the teaching of Vatican I on infallibility.

Donatus Magnus (died c. 355); gave his name to "Donatism," the doctrine that sacraments administered by unworthy clerics are invalid; was bishop of Carthage (313–347), until deposed by the Council of Arles (347); he lived the rest of his life in exile in Gaul.

Frederick William Faber (1814–1863), a scholar and fellow of University College, who became a Roman Catholic in November 1845; he founded a religious community known as the Brothers of the Will of God, which eventually merged with the English Oratory; an indefatigable preacher, prolific author, and hymn writer, Faber became superior of the London Oratory (1849).

James Anthony Froude (1818–1894), son of Robert Hurrell Froude and a brother of Richard Hurrell Froude; educated at Oriel College, Oxford; he became editor of *Fraser's Magazine*, rector of St. Andrew's University, and Regius Professor of Modern History at Oxford.

Richard Hurrell Froude (1803–1836) was like Newman a fellow of Oriel and one of the leaders of the Oxford Movement until his early death in the midst of the Tractarian Movement.

Robert Hurrell Froude (1770–1859), archdeacon of Totnes and rector of Dartington, was the father of Richard Hurrell Froude, William Froude, and James Anthony Fourde.

William Froude (1810–1879), son of Robert Hurrell Froude, graduated from Oxford with a first in mathematics and then worked for the South Eastern Railway before becoming a naval architect; his correspondence with Newman is reflected in the *Grammar of Assent*.

Maria Rosina Giberne (1802–1885), sister-in-law of Walter Mayers, met Newman in 1827 and continued contact all her life; she became a Roman Catholic in 1845 and entered the Visitation convent in Autun in 1863.

William Ewart Gladstone (1809–1898) was chancellor of the exchequer (1852–1855, 1859–1866, 1873–1874, 1880–1882) and prime minister (December 1868–February 1874; April 1880–June 1885; February–July 1886; August 1892–March 1894).

Francis Joseph Grimshaw (1901–1965), bishop of Plymouth (1947–1954), archbishop of Birmingham (1954–1965).

John Gutch (1746–1831) was rector of St. Clement's Church, Oxford, where Newman served as his curate (1824–1826).

Renn Dickson Hampden (1793–1868), a student and later fellow of Oriel, graduated with a double first in 1813 and was Bampton lecturer in 1832; he was appointed professor of moral theology in 1834 and Regius Professor of Divinity in 1836; he was consecrated bishop of Hereford in 1848.

Edward Hawkins (1789–1882), a student at St. John's, who graduated with a double first in 1811; provost of Oriel College (1828–1882); Newman's predecessor as vicar of St. Mary's (1823–1828).

Mary Elizabeth Ashe à Court-Repington Herbert (1822–1911), an author, translator and philanthropist; the wife of Sidney Herbert and mother-in-law of Baron Friedrich von Hügel.

Sidney Herbert (1810–1861), a graduate of Oriel College, Oxford; named First Baron Herbert of Lea in 1861; Herbert served as secretary of state for the colonies and secretary of state for war and became a friend of Florence Nightingale.

Gerard Manley Hopkins (1844), received into the Catholic Church by Newman in 1866; entered the Jesuits in 1868; after ordination in 1877, he taught in various schools, including University College Dublin.

Edward Henry Cardinal Howard (1829–1892), after receiving his primary education at Oscott and serving as an officer with the Life Guards (British Army), entered the English College at Rome; after ordination served as a missionary in Goa, India; returning to Rome, he worked with English people who wished to convert from Anglicanism to the Catholic Church; named titular archbishop of Neocaesaria in 1872 and a cardinal in 1877; Newman received the *biglietto* announcing his appointment as cardinal at Cardinal Howard's residence in Rome.

Baron Friedrich von Hügel (1852–1925), an influential Roman Catholic layman, religious writer and multilingual intellectual of Austrian-Scottish background, arrived in England in 1867; awarded honorary doctorates by both St. Andrews (1914) and Oxford (1920).

Richard Holt Hutton (1826–1897), journalist, joint editor of *The Spectator* and biographer of Cardinal Newman.

Thomas Henry Huxley (1825–1895) identified himself as "Darwin's Bulldog"; debated evolution with Samuel Wilberforce on June 30, 1860, at the Oxford University Museum.

Manuel Johnson (1805–1859), keeper of the Radcliffe Observatory at Oxford; aka "Observer Johnson"; Newman's host on his last night in Oxford in 1846.

John Keble (1792–1866), professor of poetry at Oxford (1831–1841) and like Newman a fellow of Oriel College; gave the Assize Sermon on July 14, 1833, which Newman considered the beginning of the Oxford Movement; in 1836, Keble became vicar of Hursley, a post that he held for the rest of his life.

Thomas Keble (1793–1875), John's younger brother, who wrote four *Tracts for the Times* (12, 22, 43, 84), three of them under the pseudonym "Richard Nelson."

Charles Kingsley (1819–1875), Anglican clergyman, educated at Magdalene College, Cambridge; author of *Westward Ho!* (1855) and Regius Professor of Modern History at Cambridge (1860–1869).

Jean-Baptiste Henri-Dominique Lacordaire (1802–1861), member of the Académie Française (1860), restorer of the Dominican order in France, whose preaching at Notre Dame attracted thousands and whose political liberalism and ultramontane theology excited Newman.

Felicité Robert de Lamennais (1782–1854), a Roman Catholic priest who felt that the Church in France could have no real liberty under a royal government; a co-founder of *L'Avenir*; after his views were rejected by Pope Gregory XVI (born 1765; pope 1831–1846), he left the Church and died excommunicated.

John Locke (1632–1704), a philosopher considered the first of the British Empiricists; Newman disagreed with Locke's idea that assent depends on the degree of evidence that a person has.

Henry Edward Manning (1808–1892), graduate of Balliol, fellow of Merton, rector of Wool Lavington and then of Graffham, Sussex; became a Roman Catholic and later archbishop of Westminster (1865) and a cardinal (1875).

Walter Mayers (1790–1828), an Evangelical Anglican clergyman; senior classical master at Ealing School (1814–1822), while Newman was a student there; in his *Apologia* (4), Newman described Mayers as "the human means of the beginning of divine faith"; Mayers later became curate of Over Worton, where Newman preached his first sermon on June 23, 1824; four years later, Newman preached the sermon at Mayers's funeral.

James Charles McGuigin (1894–1974), ordained a priest of Edmonton (1918), archbishop of Regina (1930–1934) and Toronto (1934–1971), named cardinal in 1946, approved prayer for Newman's beatification.

John McIntyre (1855–1935), auxiliary bishop of Birmingham (1912–1917), member of Roman Curia (1917–1921), archbishop of Birmingham (1921–1928).

Sir John Everett Millais (1829–1896), "one of the most successful British painters of his time," who "received many British and foreign honours and was created a baronet in 1885"; painted Newman in his cardinal's robes in 1881.

David Moriarity (1814–1877), vice rector of the Irish College at Paris, then president of All Hallows College; named coadjutor bishop of Kerry in 1854; became bishop in 1856; a friend whom Newman consulted about Irish matters and an inopportunist at Vatican I.

Anne Mozley (1809–1891), sister-in-law of Newman's sisters, was asked by Newman to edit the letters of his Anglican years—a project which she was able to complete within a few weeks of his death: *Letters and Correspondence of John Henry Newman during His Life in the English Church with a Brief Autobiography.*

James Bowling Mozley (1813–1878), educated at Oriel and later a fellow of Magdalen College; ordained an Anglican deacon in 1838 and priest in 1844; co-editor of the *Christian Remembrancer*; became Regius Professor of Divinity in 1871; he married Newman's sister Jemima.

Thomas Mozley (1806–1893), a pupil of Newman and later fellow of Oriel, married Newman's sister Harriet in 1836 and became a writer for *The Times* in 1844; his *Reminiscences,*

Chiefly of Oriel College and the Oxford Movement (1882) was severely criticized by Newman.

Philip Neri / Filippo de Neri, St. (1515–1595) was the founder of the society of priests known as the "Congregation of the Oratory"; its mother church, Santa Maria in Vallicella, in Rome, is popularly known as "Chiesa Nuova" (New Church).

Nestorius (c. 386–c. 451), patriarch of Constantinople (428–431), whose teaching that Mary was Mother of Christ (*Christotokos*) but not Mother of God (*Theotokos*) was condemned by the Council of Ephesus (432); retired to a monastery, where he died.

William Paine Neville (1824–1905), received into the Roman Catholic Church by Newman in 1851; became a novice at the Birmingham Oratory in 1852 and was ordained in 1861; after Ambrose St. John's death in 1875, Neville became Newman's aide; Newman's last recorded whispered words were: "William, William"; Neville was Newman's literary executor.

Charles Robert Newman (1802–1884), Newman's younger brother; after working for the Bank of England (1825–1832) was supported by his family and lived in seclusion the last decades of his life in Tenby.

Elizabeth Good Newman (1765–1852), Newman's aunt, whom he and his brother Francis supported; she later lived with his sister Jemima.

Francis William Newman (1805–1897), Newman's youngest brother, attended Worcester College and obtained a double first; elected fellow of Balliol; from 1830 to 1833 he was a missionary in Persia; later professor of classical literature at Manchester (1840–1846) and professor of Latin at London (1846–1869); his *Early History of Cardinal Newman* (1891) was an example of sibling rivalry.

Harriet Newman (1803–1852), Newman's oldest sister, who-married Thomas Mozley in 1836 and broke off relations with her brother before his entrance into the Roman Catholic Church.

Jemima Newman (1808–1879), Newman's second sister, married John Mozley, a printer and publisher at Derby; while disapproving of Newman's entrance into the Roman Catholic Church, she remained on relatively friendly terms with him.

Jemima Fourdrinier Newman (1772–1836), Newman's mother; married John Newman in 1799.

John Newman (1767–1824), Newman's father, a banker, married Jemima Fourdrinier in 1799.

Mary Newman (1809–1828), Newman's youngest sister, whose early death he mourned in a poem, "Consolations in Bereavement."

George Nicholas (d. 1829), headmaster of Ealing School when Newman was a student.

Duke of Norfolk, Henry Fitzalan-Howard (1847–1917), premier duke and premier earl (of Arundel) in the English peerage; also earl marshal and chief butler, attended the Birmingham Oratory School; a generous benefactor of the Roman Catholic Church, to whom Newman dedicated his *Letter to the Duke of Norfolk.*

Vincent Gerard Nichols (1945–), auxiliary bishop of Westminster (1991–2000), archbishop of Birmingham (2000–2009), archbishop of Westminster (2009).

Edmund O'Reilly (1811–1878), ordained and appointed to the chair of theology at Maynooth after a competitive exam; became a Jesuit in 1851 and Jesuit provincial of Ireland (1863–1870); his interpretation of infallibility is cited by Newman in his *Letter to the Duke of Norfolk.*

Sir Robert Peel (1788–1850), member of parliament for Oxford and later for Tamworth; prime minister (1834–1835, 1841–1846); as home secretary he was the creator of the police force, nicknamed "Bobbies" after him.

Giovanni Perrone (1794–1876), professor of dogmatic theology at the Roman College for most of his life, except for three years of exile in England during the Roman Republic and his tenure as rector at Ferrara.

Pope Pius IX (1792–1878), Giovanni Maria Mastai-Ferretti, archbishop of Spoleto (1827), bishop of Imola (1832), pope (1846).

Edward Bouverie Pusey (1800–1882), like Newman a fellow of Oriel College and a leader of the Oxford Movement; appointed Regius Professor of Hebrew and a canon of Christ Church in 1828.

Henry Dudley "Ignatius" Ryder (1837–1907), a nephew of Cardinal Manning; Newman's successor as provost of the Birmingham Oratory. Ryder wrote three pamphlets against W. G. Ward's views of infallibility.

Ambrose Saint John (1815–1875), a student at Christ Church (Oxford); became a Roman Catholic in 1845; a student with Newman in Rome, he became member of the Birmingham Oratory.

Francis de Sales, St. (1567–1622), author of *An Introduction to the Devout Life;* became bishop of Geneva in 1602; Newman adapted his cardinalatial motto—*Cor ad cor loquitur*—from the writings of Francis de Sales.

Caroline Sargent (1833–1837), the wife of Henry Edward Manning.

Thomas Scott (1747–1821), rector of Aston Sandford and a founder of the Church Missionary Society; the author of a

Commentary on the Whole Bible (1788–1792); in his *Apologia,* Newman described Scott as the person "to whom (humanly speaking), I almost owe my soul."

Thomas Short (1789–1879), formerly a tutor at Rugby, became a fellow of Trinity College, Oxford, in 1816, where he served as tutor for four decades (1816–1856) and lived to see Newman named Trinity's first honorary fellow (1878).

Richard Simpson (1820–1876), a student at Oriel (1839–1843), who served briefly as vicar of Mitcham (1844–1845) before becoming a Roman Catholic (1846); associated with the *Rambler.*

John Bird Sumner (1780–1862), author of *Apostolical Preaching* (1815); appointed bishop of Chester in 1828 and archbishop of Canterbury in 1848.

George Talbot (1816–1886), a monsignor who described Newman as "the most dangerous man in England"; representative of the English bishops in Rome during the pontificate of Pope Pius IX.

Bernard Ullathorne (1806–1889), vicar apostolic of the Central District (1848–1850); became bishop of Birmingham in 1850, when the British hierarchy was restored; named titular archbishop of Cabasa on his retirement in 1888.

William George Ward (1812–1882), scholar of Lincoln College and author of *Ideal of a Christian Church* (1844); condemned by convocation and deprived of his degrees, he taught at St. Edmund's, Ware (1851–1858), and was editor of the *Dublin Review* (1863–1878).

Wilfrid Philip Ward (1856–1916), son of William George Ward and father of Maisie Ward (1889–1975); editor of the *Dublin Review* and author of a two-volume *Life of Cardinal Newman* (1912).

John Wesley (1703–1791), an Anglican clergyman, one of the founders of the "Methodist Movement," which emphasized personal holiness and concern for others, especially the poor and disadvantaged.

Richard Whately (1787–1863), fellow of Oriel and principal of St. Alban Hall, where Newman was vice principal; appointed Anglican archbishop of Dublin in 1831.

Robert Isaac Wilberforce (1802–1857), obtained a double first at Oriel in 1823; was elected a fellow and was a tutor along with Newman and Froude; became a Roman Catholic in 1854.

Samuel Wilberforce (1805–1873), third son of William Wilberforce; went up to Oriel in 1823; married to the oldest daughter of John Sargent, he was appointed bishop of Oxford in 1845 and bishop of Winchester in 1869.

Nicholas Wiseman (1802–1865), rector of the English College in Rome (1828–1840), president of Oscott College and coadjutor bishop of the Midland district (1840–1847), then bishop of the London district (1847–1850); named cardinal and archbishop of Westminster in 1850.

Select Bibliography

NEWMAN'S WRITINGS

Most of the works that Newman published during his lifetime were republished in a "uniform edition" by Longmans, Green and Company and are available at *www.newmanreader.org*, which also provides biographical resources and pictures of Newman. All of the citations of Newman's writings in this book are from *www.newmanreader.org*. Many of Newman's writings have been scanned into the electronic Newman Research Library and may be conveniently searched at: *www.newmanreader.org/ newmanresearch/*. Specific terms or phrases from Newman's writings can also be found by accessing *www.Google.com* and entering: «phrase» site: *newmanreader.org*. For recent literature on Newman, the website of the International Centre of Newman Friends provides a multi-lingual bibliography on Newman from 1990 to the present: *www.newmanfriendsinternational. org*. *The Letters and Diaries of John Henry Newman*, edited by Charles Stephen Dessain et al., 32 vols. (Oxford and London, 1961–2008) is available by subscription at *www.nlx.com/ collections/88*.

BIOGRAPHIES OF NEWMAN

There are numerous biographies of Newman; two of the most helpful introductions to Newman's life are Keith Beaumont, *Blessed John Henry Newman: Theologian and Spiritual Guide for Our Times* (London: CTS; Fort Collins, Colo.: Ignatius, 2010) and Brian Martin, *John Henry Newman: His Life and Work* (London: Chatto & Windus, 1982; New York: Continuum, 2000); in addition, *Blessed John Henry Newman: A Richly Illustrated Portrait* by Kathleen Dietz and Mary-Birgit Dechant (Leominster, Herefordshire, U.K.: Gracewing, 2010) provides numerous illustrations of Newman's life.

The definitive biography of Newman has been written by Ian Ker, *John Henry Newman: A Biography* (Oxford: Clarendon Press, 1988). Other lengthy biographies include: Meriol Trevor's two-volume work: *Newman: The Pillar of the Cloud* (Garden City, N.Y.: Doubleday, 1962) and *Newman: Life in Winter* (Garden City, N.Y.: Doubleday, 1963); these two volumes are available in an abridgement: *Newman's Journey* (Glasgow: William Collins Sons & Company, 1974). Other valuable biographies include Maisie Ward, *Young Mr. Newman* (New York: Sheed & Ward, 1948) and Wilfrid Ward, *The Life of John Henry Cardinal Newman: Based on His Private Journals and Correspondence*, 2 vols. (London: Longmans, Green, 1912); Ward's biography and his *The Genius of Newman* (1914) are available at *www.newmanreader.org*, which also provides Richard Hutton's *Cardinal Newman* (1891) and Wilfrid Meynell's *Cardinal Newman* (1907).

INTRODUCTIONS TO
NEWMAN'S THOUGHT:

Two very useful introductions to Newman's thought are Charles Frederick Harrold, *John Henry Newman: An Exposition and Critical Study of His Mind, Thought and Art* (New York: Longmans, Green, 1945) and Thomas J. Norris, *Newman and His Theological Method* (Leiden: E. J. Brill, 1977).

NEWMAN'S SPIRITUALITY

Newman's spirituality has been the topic of a number of books, including Vincent Ferrer Blehl, *The White Stone: The Spiritual Theology of John Henry Newman* (Petersham, Mass.: St. Bede's Publications, 1993) and *Pilgrim Journey: John Henry Newman 1801–1845* (London: Burns & Oates; New York: Paulist Press, 2001); Louis Bouyer, *Cardinal Newman: His Life and Spirituality* (New York: P. J. Kenedy, 1958); C. S. Dessain, *Newman's Spiritual Themes* (Dublin: Veritas, 1977); Hilda Graef, *God and Myself: The Spirituality of John Henry Newman* (London: Peter Davies, 1967); Jean Honoré, *The Spiritual Journey of Newman* (New York: Alba House, 1992).

MODERN SPIRITUAL MASTERS
Robert Ellsberg, Series Editor

This series introduces the essential writing and vision of some of the great spiritual teachers of our time. While many of these figures are rooted in long-established traditions of spirituality, others have charted new, untested paths. In each case, however, they have engaged in a spiritual journey shaped by the challenges and concerns of our age. Together with the saints and witnesses of previous centuries, these modern spiritual masters may serve as guides and companions to a new generation of seekers.

Already published:

Simone Weil (edited by Eric O. Springsted)

Dietrich Bonhoeffer (edited by Robert Coles)

Henri Nouwen (edited by Robert A. Jonas)

Charles de Foucauld (edited by Robert Ellsberg)

Pierre Teilhard de Chardin (edited by Ursula King)

Anthony de Mello (edited by William Dych, S.J.)

Oscar Romero (by Marie Dennis, Rennie Golden, and Scott Wright)

Eberhard Arnold (edited by Johann Christoph Arnold)

Thomas Merton (edited by Christine M. Bochen)

Thich Nhat Hanh (edited by Robert Ellsberg)

Mother Teresa (edited by Jean Maalouf)

Rufus Jones (edited by Kerry Walters)

Edith Stein (edited by John Sullivan, O.C.D.)

John Main (edited by Laurence Freeman)

Mohandas Gandhi (edited by John Dear)

Mother Maria Skobtsova (introduction by Jim Forest)

Evelyn Underhill (edited by Emilie Griffin)

St. Thérèse of Lisieux (edited by Mary Frohlich)

Flannery O'Connor (edited by Robert Ellsberg)

Clarence Jordan (edited by Joyce Hollyday)

G. K. Chesterton (edited by William Griffin)

Alfred Delp, S.J. (introduction by Thomas Merton)

Bede Griffiths (edited by Thomas Matus)

Karl Rahner (edited by Philip Endean)

Pedro Arrupe (edited by Kevin F. Burke, S.J.)

Sadhu Sundar Singh (edited by Charles E. Moore)

Romano Guardini (edited by Robert A. Krieg)

Albert Schweitzer (edited by James Brabazon)

Caryll Houselander (edited by Wendy M. Wright)

Brother Roger of Taizé (edited by Marcello Fidanzio)

Dorothee Soelle (edited by Dianne L. Oliver)

Leo Tolstoy (edited by Charles E. Moore)

Howard Thurman (edited by Luther E. Smith, Jr.)

Swami Abhishiktananda (edited by Shirley du Boulay)

Carlo Carretto (edited by Robert Ellsberg)

Pope John XXIII (edited by Jean Maalouf)

Modern Spiritual Masters (edited by Robert Ellsberg)

Jean Vanier (edited by Carolyn Whitney-Brown)

The Dalai Lama (edited by Thomas A. Forsthoefel)

Catherine de Hueck Doherty (edited by
David Meconi, S.J.)